SO-BJL-492

2.08 - Nicholas - 7/66 (Griffin)

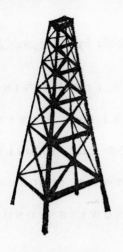

THE
GREAT
OILDORADO

Other Books by Hildegarde Dolson

THE FORM DIVINE

THE HUSBAND WHO RAN AWAY

WE SHOOK THE FAMILY TREE

SORRY TO BE SO CHEERFUL

A GROWING WONDER

THE
GREAT
OILDORADO

*The gaudy and turbulent years
of the first oil rush:*

Pennsylvania 1859-1880

by Hildegarde Dolson

RANDOM HOUSE
NEW YORK

for Charles Norman

ACKNOWLEDGMENTS

James Stevenson, publisher of the Titusville, Pennsylvania, *Herald* and current owner of Pithole, the ghost town with the enchanted past, has given me such a rich lot of material and expert advice that my gratitude rises to gusher heights. The old letters, documents and producers' secret code from his collection (now given to the Drake Museum) first brought oil history alive for me. And the early issues of the *Herald* furnished accounts of everything from sporting-houses to the splurges of the first oil kings. I'm especially thankful for the visits to Pithole, when the owner re-created for me the people and places that made that boomtown unique. The oil-rush days came roaring back from the dead so lustily, during those tours, that I felt scorn for the thin-aired antics of the Forty-niners. (By the way, Pithole is now open to the public.) I am also indebted to Mr. Stevenson for reading my book in manuscript and catching a barrelful of errors. If any slipped through, the blame is squarely on the head of the writer, a happy novice who needed all the help she could get, and is deeply grateful for all she got.

John Budke of Franklin supplied me with the kind of anecdotes and local lore any writer would sell his grandmother to get hold of. If readers enjoy the stories as much as I did, they'll join me in blessing Mr. Budke.

Ernest Miller of the West Penn Oil Company, Warren, is an early-oil-days aficionado and fellow writer I've borrowed from gratefully. His book on John Wilkes Booth as oil man has been a fine source of fresh material on that charming monster. And his account of the infamous South Improvement Company is the best short version I've read anywhere.

Carolee Kinnear Michener of the Franklin *News Herald* has dug up characters I never even knew our mutual hometown could claim, such as Johnny Appleseed. Her articles on early history have been a bonanza, and her tips on where to look for what saved me from dusty frustration, during research. I'm also grateful to the *News Herald's* managing editor, Taylor Foster, and Wayne Bleakley, the publisher, for their helpful co-operation.

William Copithorne of Standard Oil of New Jersey arranged to let me use that firm's excellent research library, and gave me much-valued encouragement as he read my chapters piecemeal. And the librarian, Paul Allen, has been a staunch help, generous with good advice and the long-term loan of books. My thanks also to Ed Esmay and Dick Wilcox of Standard Oil for their kindness.

Isabelle Beers of the Franklin Library was constantly thoughtful and generous with research material, and placed endless rolls of microfilm on the machine there, so that I might read the Venango *Spectator* at its vituperative best during the Civil War. Phyllis Geisler typed up all the articles I couldn't copy in feverish longhand, and Virginia Dillman of the library staff was very helpful too.

Mina Bryan's enthusiasm for this project, and her suggestions on the manuscript, have been eagerly and gratefully received. Thanks to her, I spent a delightful, informative evening with Tom Roberts, great-nephew of the inventor of the torpedo used on wells.

James Boudreau of the Ethyl Corporation spread out a wonderful lot of collectors' items for my use and enjoyment: old stock prospectuses, account books, and boom-day songs.

Old friends in Franklin have done so much for this book I can only issue a massive affectionate thank-you to Katherine Officer, Mary and George Southard, Mabel Egbert, Mary Hancock and Mahala Sibley. Henry Smith loaned valuable books. Mrs. Kenneth Marwood and Delia Raymond contributed lively leads to new material. Martha Bring Curtis set me on the track of a dozen rewarding sources and alerted allies all down the line.

Mrs. R. L. Browne of Oil City gave me a wealth of material about her grandmother, Mrs. Milton Egbert, who brought back the first Worth gown to the mud of Petroleum Centre. Among the other Oil City people who helped, my special thanks to Ed Boyle, publisher of the *Derrick*, Ed Wallace, Mrs. Grant McElhatten of the library, Percy Beers, and Charles Suhr of Pennzoil, who is the owner of the prized Culver scrapbook.

I am indebted to the Pennsylvania State Historical and Museum Commission for maps, advice and reprint permissions. My fervent thanks to Dr. Stevens, the director, and to Don Kent.

The Drake Museum in Titusville was a valuable research source, with its Townsend and Drake letters, several thousand Mather photographs, and bound files of the racy Pithole *Record*. I'm grateful to the new curator, A. C. Thompson, for turning up long-buried prize items, including Pithole playbills that make me wish I'd been there when the curtain went up.

Affectionate thanks to my cousin Priscilla Gill Flint for her help with Meadville lore.

Any writer on early oil days is enormously indebted to the scholarly works of Dr. Paul Giddens. He has laid a solid groundwork the rest of us tread on thankfully.

The Yale University Library kindly let me study the Roger Sherman papers, and quote from them.

The American Petroleum Institute has checked figures and furnished tabulations with efficient speed. My thanks to Regina Weiler and to Carol Culbertson. I am grateful to Rodney Huber, in charge of Oil Centennial plans, for his co-operation.

J. P. Jones of the Pennsylvania Grade Crude Oil Association and William Lytle of the Pennsylvania Topographic and Geologic Survey have kindly checked over current production figures, and provided the latest statistics on crude and refined oil in our state.

Shirley Worth has typed the manuscript from its early pencil-smudged drafts to the final, almost frighteningly neat version. My thanks for all the late hours she kept, to meet deadlines.

Dr. Stanley Swartley and Dr. Julian Ross of Allegheny College, Meadville, have encouraged and advised me on this book, but my gratitude to these two cherished friends stretches over a thirty-year span, from my student days. Never has a young would-be writer been luckier, in having such teachers and counselors. And my thanks to Phil Benjamin, head of Allegheny's library, for his many kindnesses.

My sister-in-law Jan Dolson and her son Bob were a constant help in Venango County, as guides and delightful companions. My entire family is the most loyal claque ever, and the nicest thing that could happen to an author.

My friends Beryl and Sam Epstein have let me talk *oil* till it gushed from their ears, and still had the patience and fortitude to read every word of the manuscript and make good suggestions.

The war between the sexes is unflagging but it has its lovely moments, and so does the eternal conflict between Publisher and Author. In a flush of unusual candor, I must admit that Bennett Cerf and Hiram Haydn of Random House have been downright helpful. I have accepted their generous cash advances in a friendly spirit, and I have even accepted some good editorial advice, with grudging respect or occasional loud screeches. A wounded Lady Author is more dangerous than a charging wounded rhinocerous, but so far the boys at Random House have never shot to kill. This in itself shows a noble restraint, and calls for a hug.

Acknowledgments

My very warm thanks to Berenice Hoffman, who went over this manuscript with a fine Fowler-sharp tooth comb. And my admiration and gratitude to Regina Spirito of the Art Department, and Jean Ennis, Publicity Director.

For Diarmuid Russell, literary agent, friend and purveyor of Faith, Hope and Cheer, my love and hosannas, as always.

In the year and a half that I've been doing research into early oil days, and writing about them, I've felt a renewed and joyous sense of pride in my country and countrymen. And I hope this book will show why.

New York, N. Y., September, 1958   THE AUTHOR

CONTENTS

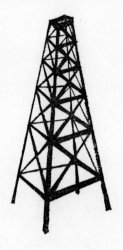

THE
GREAT
OILDORADO

O N E

Mr. Dickens' gorilla looms over a derrick

Unlike Texas, which has always been too big for its boots, the people of my home county, Venango, in western Pennsylvania, never expected the eyes of the world to be on them. After it happened, they were cocky enough, but I think their descendants have been entirely too small-mouth in bragging about it. I have actually met people who think the first oil well was drilled in Texas, but the truth is that Texas was still a big ole dry hole when our quiet little farming county became an uproarious Oildorado, in 1859.

I have to admit that Venango-ites fought this off as long as possible. In my hometown of Franklin, for instance, a workman digging along French Creek in 1832, for the new canal, kept turning up thick black oil till he got so enraged at this mucking up of good dirt and water that he flung his shovel and his oil-spattered clothes into the creek, and marched off to get drunk. According to an old town ordinance, whosoever became publicly intoxicated had to do penance by digging up a tree stump from the town square. For all I know, the workman doing penance with a hangover and digging down to hell-and-gone to uproot an old elm stump may have dug up oil again and been so irritated he went off and got drunk again.

3

Not that I mean to imply Venango-ites were a roistering lot, Heaven forbid. People went to church twice a day on Sunday, and read their Bibles every night by the stingy light of a tallow candle or lard lamp, and they drank mostly good cold well water. Whenever a man dug a new well in his yard and the water tasted oily, he had his neighbors' sympathy, if he went so far as to mention his bad luck in striking oil. There was a brilliant judge who moved to the county seat, the leafy little town of Franklin, about 1840, and hired a laborer to dig a water well. After getting down thirty feet, the workman struck a vein of oil that flowed in so fast he went hollering for the judge, to come help stem this calamity. They did everything they could think of to stop the oil flowing, but finally had to abandon the well. A friend of the judge said that this dignitary expressed his indignation pretty freely, "in very choice language," over "the nasty stinking Seneca oil."

So western Pennsylvanians didn't exactly stride toward their destiny, or even like the smell of it coming. In the summer of 1859, the belligerent editor of the Venango *Spectator,* the only newspaper in the county, heard that some ex-railroad conductor named Drake was deliberately trying to drill an oil well twenty miles away, near Titusville. He refused to report such foolishness in the columns of his four-page weekly, which erupted every Wednesday in Franklin. Instead, during those August dog days, he foamed and raged in print over his giant rival, New York *Tribune* editor Horace Greeley, who was bent on putting a subversive new party, the Black Republicans, into power, and to that end, "has used Kansas the way the wolf used the goat." Thanks or no thanks to Greeley, Kansas had recently been admitted as a free state to the Union.

The farmers who read the *Spectator* were more concerned over the Black Frost than Mr. Greeley's dark machinations. It had been the worst June frost in the county's history, blighting the oats, wheat, potatoes and rye that normally harvested a yearly income of around $250. A farmer could raise a family quite comfortably on that much cash, in this up and down country where hills crouched protectively, hills dark with pine and hemlock, leaping with game, from fat rabbits and wary-footed deer to timber wolves that brought a state bounty for each pelt, and screeching wildcats. The sawmills screeched too. Next to farming, lumbering was the main business; the logs were hauled to the nearby Allegheny River and floated by raft a hundred miles down to Pittsburgh. Many of the farmers made extra cash by selling off timber, or using their team and wagon to haul for the most prosperous lumber concern around, the Brewer, Watson mills below Titusville. It was on a piece of Brewer's land that the "crazy Yankee Drake" had erected a weird wooden structure, tapering to the tip thirty feet high, which he called a derrick. The amused gawkers that summer called it plenty else. When a curious farmer asked what the thing was for, a local wag told him gravely it was a monument copied after the Tower of Babel; another said No, it was the wigwam of Black Republicans.

If travelers on the stagecoaches that jolted over the ruts three times a week from Titusville down to Franklin brought these latest witticisms to the *Spectator* office, the editor undoubtedly snorted and then went on using lead type like buckshot to blast Mr. Greeley's hide. Even when the Drake well brought in oil, on August 27th—probably the most important industrial event of the century and certainly the most spectacular news-gusher ever to hit Venango County—the *Spectator's* editor ignored it and continued to ignore it for twenty-five pandemonic days.

Perhaps he still thought striking oil was a damn nuisance, as the judge had when he swore over his polluted water well, but already our country and Europe had gone through the mysterious, multiple ferment that prepares the way for most great discoveries. A Scotsman had developed an oil from coal, as an illuminant; a Viennese had experimented with a new lamp, using an oily slime which Polish peasants scraped from the ground and greased their cart wheels with; Rumanians were scooping up bucketsful to sell as a crude lubricant and for lamp fuel; new American machinery demanded new lubricants; and the change had come not with the speed of light, but with the need for light. Of course there were still plenty of people who took a dim view, and it's rather embarrassing that one of these was an editor who refused to see the greatest scoop of his life.

The first week after the strike, while astonished farmers who owned land along Oil Creek were being courted with more waving greenbacks than they'd ever seen in their entire lives rolled together, the *Spectator's* front page was given over to a cultural account of the

gorilla as described by Mr. Charles Dickens in his *All the Year
Round*. Mr. Dickens admired the gorilla as "an amiable and ex-
emplary husband and father," but found him deplorably short on
looks, according to the *Spectator:* "The leg is destitute of calf . . .
The brain case is low and narrow and the brow forms a scowling pent-
house over the eyes." This description might have applied nicely to
some gorillas wearing shoes who were soon to prowl through the
buckwheat, looking for victims to squeeze.

The week of September 7th, the *Spectator* gave a generous spread
to a discovery presumably much more fascinating than Mr. Drake's:
"Cooking for Pigs— Samuel Clay II of Bourbon has been experi-
menting in feeding several lots of hogs, changing them from raw to
cooked. They fattened on cooked, three times as much."

Around that time, several farmers, feeding at the new trough, greedily refused to lease their lands to hurriedly formed companies for one-
fourth royalty on oil, and cunningly held out for one-eighth or even
one-twelfth because it sounded bigger.

On September 14th, the *Spectator's* editor was still biting off the
news to spite his face. He exhorted farmers to attend the County Fair,
because the Reverend D. C. Osborne would deliver an address upon
the subject of Agriculture, and a fair "confers benefits by inciting
laudable competition." (Most of his rural readers were too busy getting benefits from the competition for oil lands, which was, if not always laudable, at least loud.) The newspaper also ran a helpful little
tabulation that week on Who's Who and how old: *"Ages of Our Public Men*— President Buchanan will be 88 years old November next;
William H. Seward is in his 58th year; Edward Everett was 64 years
old in April last; Jefferson Davis is 45 years old." It was even more
helpful to learn from such an authoritative source as a rabid Demo-
crat that the Presidential candidates for 1860 would be Seward and
Blair. Nothing was said about one Abe Lincoln, who would eventually
be shot by an unsuccessful Venango oil prospector, an actor named
John Wilkes Booth. So far, both Lincoln and oil were beneath the
Spectator's notice.

It was word-of-mouth that spread the oil excitement, even along
the prison grapevine. Two crooks, Stover and Walker, held for larceny
in the county jail in Franklin, escaped that week, from a padlocked

cell with walls three feet thick and a sheet-iron ceiling. They set fire to the end of a plank and used it as a blowtorch to melt a hole in the ceiling to crawl through. Any petty crooks fired by that much ingenuity must have known exactly where they wanted to escape *to:* the sweet new land of larceny along Oil Creek. I doubt if they were caught again. In normal times, con men stood out in the peaceful little villages like scarecrows on Broadway. But with strangers now swarming in on every stagecoach—ranging from hoitily tailored Eastern promoters to gamblers fresh from the gold-rush country, and all soon spattered alike with greenish-black oily mud—searching for escaped prisoners Stover and Walker would have been like looking for a straw man in a haystack.

The *Spectator* simply noted their novel exit from jail. And finally, on September 21st, the editor mentioned in print what everybody already knew. Rather pathetically, he used a warmed-over scoop from his hated rival Greeley that had already appeared on September 13th in New York. It had been tucked away on page 5 of the *Tribune,* along with an item about a "Flying-machine man" named Cook who was building an "aerial car" and expected to "navigate the air at will with an inconceivable velocity."

Just below the Flying-machine Man was the story which the *Spectator* reprinted, without comment:

DISCOVERY OF A SUBTERRANEAN FOUNTAIN OF OIL

(From a Correspondent of the New York *Tribune*)

Titusville, Pa., Sept. 8, 1859.— Perhaps you will recollect that in 1854 there was organized in the City of New York a Company, under the name of the Pennsylvania Rock Oil Company, which for some good reasons, passed into the hands of some New Haven capitalists, and was by them removed to New Haven. In 1858 the directors leased the grounds and springs to Mr. E. L. Drake, well known on the New Haven Railroad.—He came out here, and in May last commenced to bore for salt, or to find the source of the oil, which is so common along the banks of Oil Creek.—Last week, at the depth of 71 feet, he struck a fissure in the rock through which he was boring, when, to the surprise and joy of every one, he found he had tapped a vein of water and oil, yielding 400 gallons of pure oil every 24 hours (one day).

The pump now in use throws only five gallons per minute of water and oil into a large vat, when the oil rises to the top and the water runs out from the bottom. In a few days they will have a pump of three times the capacity of the one now in use, and then from ten to twelve hundred gallons of oil will be the daily yield. . . .

The excitement attendant on the discovery of this vast source of oil was fully equal to what I ever saw in California, when a large lump of gold was accidentally turned out.

Medicus

TWO

———•◦•———

Fuel for the fires of hell

I<small>N ALL</small> the excitement after his well came in, poor Edwin Drake got shoved aside and nearly lost in the rush. He was the hero, all right, but one of those heroes who seems to have been chosen in a game of blindfold, like Pin the Tail on the Donkey. To tell you the truth, if this were fiction, I'd invent a new hero, more in the style to which we're accustomed in glossy biographical novels, with large, firm sins and virtues.

In my hurry to get past Drake now, to the people—some villains included—who interest me much more, I'm apt to shove him aside too impatiently, as his contemporaries did. And that isn't fair. He deserves his one chapter. But he'll have to share even that. It took an improbable trio of New Englanders—a hearty country doctor, a lawyer-promoter who looked like a benzedrined Greenwich Village poet, and a banker with a coating of ballyhoo—to propel the ex-railroad conductor into that one larger-than-life act.

In fact, there are still factions who say that the other three men were the heroes. Since 1859, there have been so many fierce arguments that played ducks-and-Drake with the question: Who really deserves credit for discovering oil? that it seems only sensible to point

9

out that nobody "discovered" oil. The truth is large enough, that Drake was probably the first man to carry through a practical method for drilling and pumping out of the earth mass quantities of the liquid wealth that had been collecting for a few million years, in the slow distillation of matter, animal, vegetable or mineral. Job, in the Bible, sounds like the best prophet of the lot, with his talk of the rock that poured out "rivers of oil."

The first writer to pour it on troubled waters was Pliny, the Roman historian: "Everything is soothed by oil, and that is the reason why divers send out small quantities of it from their mouths, because it smooths any part which is rough."

An indefatigably bright-eyed tourist named Marco Polo reported in the fourteenth century that oil from Baku on the Caspian was used as "an unguent for the cures of cutaneous distempers in men and camels."

A few centuries later, British and French explorers sent back eager accounts from this country of the oil pools that looked like water and burned like brandy, but nobody seemed to care. Lewis Evans, drawing a map of the Middle British Colonies in America, in 1755, carefully lettered "Petroleum in Pensilvania," near the spot where Seneca and Cornplanter Indians spread blankets on the rainbowed oily surface of the creek, then wrung out the slippery liquid into earthenware vessels, for liniment and medicine, and to mix with their war paint for glistening, waterproof make-up. The great chief Cornplanter left off his war paint and was friendly to our side during the Revolutionary War, and in gratitude our brand-new government gave him three hundred acres in Venango County. The settlement of shanties that clung onto the hills like barnacles, above Oil Creek, was called Cornplanter, long after the chief sold the land, in 1818, to two white-face settlers for $2,121 and no beads. Later it became Oil City, but nobody suggested giving it back to the Indians.

Making a survey of other Revolutionary land grants, in 1785, General Benjamin Lincoln reported:

> In the northern part of Pennsylvania, there is a creek called Oil Creek, which empties itself into the Allegheny, on the top of which floats an oil, similar to what is called Barbadoes tar, and from which may be collected, by one man, several gallons in a day. The troops,

in marching that way, halted at the spring, collected the oil, and bathed their joints with it. This gave them great relief, and freed them immediately from the rheumatic complaints with which many of them were affected.

Settlers in western Pennsylvania had already discovered this from the Indians. Almost every household had a supply of Seneca oil, skimmed up wherever it appeared, and used to enliven the joints of humans and horses. In hot weather, farmers lathered their teams with it, because the oil reeked so hideously even blowflies couldn't stand the smell and stayed at a resentful distance.

Druggists touted sarsaparilla "to cleanse your blood whenever it is foul, and to cure Scrofula or King's Evil," but most housewives thought Seneca oil was just as good. But even they didn't realize what a gamut of miracle cures it ran, until they saw the gaudy testimonials that Sam Kier put out with half-pint bottles of crude petroleum and sold around 1850. Kier was a big, brisk, curly-haired man who breathed confidence the way timider men breathe soot. He had already operated a successful chain of canal boats between Pittsburgh and Philadelphia, and owned a share of his father's salt wells. Like all the other salt-well owners around Tarentum, above Pittsburgh, the Kiers were plagued by the "ugley grease" that often appeared in their wells and polluted the brine. They cursed it and ran it off into the canal, until Sam Kier put it on the market as Kier's Rock Oil, "Nature's Remedy, from Four Hundred Feet below the Earth's surface." The accompanying circular flaunted pictures of Indian chiefs, salt derricks, health-flushed maidens, and stated lyrically:

> The healthful balm from Nature's secret spring
> The bloom of health and life to man will bring;
> As from her depths this magic liquid flows
> To calm our suffering and assuage our woes.

It cost fifty cents a half-pint, and Kier recommended three teaspoonfuls three times a day, surely enough to choke a horse or galvanize an invalid into leaping up and down. He claimed modestly: "The lame were made to walk. . . . Cases that were pronounced hopeless and abandoned by Physicians of unquestioned celebrity, have been made to exclaim, *'This is the most wonderful remedy ever dis-*

covered.' Ingredients blended together in such a way as to defy all human competition. . . . Several who were blind have been made to see."

It would have taken a blind man to miss seeing the gaudy gilded wagons Kier sent rolling through the countryside to peddle his balm, each with huge, hand-painted renditions on the wagon sides of a green and crimson Good Samaritan leaning over a wounded soldier lying under a palm tree, presumably offering the poor devil Kier's balm. In spite of these traveling sales-posters, inspired by Phineas Barnum's "bulletin" wagons proclaiming freaks, Kier couldn't unload enough of his fifty-cent miracle cure to get rid of all the oil turned up, and he soon had the dazzling idea of trying to refine it, as a substitute for the new coal oil, or the expensive whale oil used in lamps. There was certainly no problem in making it burn; the trouble was the smell. A nasty-smelling medicine may be reassuring, but an illuminant that smoked and stank so it drove the user out of the house with streaming eyes and distended nostrils wasn't too feasible. Kier consulted a chemist who advised him to distill the crude oil at high enough heat to remove the offending vapors, but when the still was built, at Seventh Avenue near Grant Street in Pittsburgh, it raised an even worse stink.

Outraged neighbors complained to a magistrate that even if they didn't expire of the foul odor, they'd be burned up by the explosive stuff. Kier had to move his still outside the city limits, but he kept on brewing. Soon he was selling a distillate the pale gold of cider, called Carbon Oil, at $1.50 a gallon. Although he'd muted the aroma, there were still customers who took one sniff, shuddered, and demanded their money back. The sturdier rural dwellers went right on rubbing Kier's Rock Oil, Nature's balm, on their aching backs and chilblains.

Ebenezer Brewer, senior partner in the lumber mill below Titusville, skimmed up five gallons from the seepage on his land bordering Oil Creek, and sent it by coach to his son Francis, a young doctor who was starting practice in northern Vermont. Ebenezer, a bossy father, said in effect, Prescribe this oil for whatever ails them. Francis Brewer may have groaned, as sons have always groaned over family advice delivered in the large economy size, but he tried the greasy stuff on his own lumbago, then on his patients. It proved to be exactly the sort of unpleasant medicine Vermonters were crazy about.

Young Dr. Brewer was so gratified he took a flask of the crude oil down to his old professor at Dartmouth, Dr. Dixi Crosby, who examined it and agreed it might be a pretty good thing. The flask was sitting on Crosby's butternut desk when another graduate, George Bissell, a young lawyer, came back to Hanover for a visit. He had already heard about Kier's lamp oil, and now as he listened to Crosby talk about the interesting contents of the flask, he quivered like a bird dog who's caught the scent of new game. Bissell, in his early thirties, had already hurtled through several careers, as reporter, professor of Greek, high school principal, and had come most recently to law. He looked like a cartoon of a poet or anarchist, with long black wind-tossed hair, a beard that looked pasted on, villainous scowling eyebrows, snapping dark eyes, and a hectic intensity. It was possible to imagine him performing at fever pitch for a jury, to defend a sorrowing widow who hadn't known the gun was loaded, but matter-of-fact legal duties bored him. He and his partner in New York, Jonathan Evelyth, hadn't so much practiced law as promoted the laws of chance, in handling stock for such firms as the American and Foreign Iron Pavement Company.

Now they leaped into action and bought one hundred acres of the Brewer, Watson lumber firm's land, the acres that had an oil spring, on the east bank of the creek. They agreed to pay $5,000, eventually, but it was a nice Bissell touch to blow up this purchase price to $25,000 in the prospectus, to sound more impressive. The company was capitalized grandly at a quarter of a million dollars on paper, and one share would sell at $25, if they ever found buyers. But even the most gullible refused to take a chance on anything so silly. Gold, yes. Or iron. But who wanted oil? Not they. Prospects for the Pennsylvania Rock Oil Company looked dim. Villagers back in Titusville dubbed it the Fancy Stock Company, and chuckled over what those fool city people could think up.

Old lumberman Ebenezer Brewer, having sent along the oil to dose patients, was outraged that his son seemed to have swallowed it the wrong way. He wrote his erring boy who had arranged the land deal:

> I always told you that I had no confidence in the men from the very nature of the transaction and all that you would ever get would be what you received in the sale. . . . Now mark well what I tell you, it is for your interest alone that I now say it. You are associated with

a set of sharpers and if they have not already ruined you, they will do so if you are foolish enough to let them.

A New York merchant whom Bissell and Evelyth had approached about buying stock, wrote the Brewers: "From what little I have seen of them and their transactions I have no confidence in them as business men and would not trust them without security."

The hectic, brilliant Bissell was shrewd enough to attach his kite to a solid base; he and Evelyth hired Professor Benjamin Silliman, Jr., of Yale, the top chemist in the country, to analyze the oil and make a detailed report of its potentialities, especially for lighting. Silliman worked on this for the next half-year. By then, Dr. Francis Brewer had left Vermont and medicine, to become a partner in his father's lumber business in Titusville. The firm engaged a local man, Jacob Angier, to dig a series of trenches to collect the oil, and it was already being used at the mill to lubricate the huge circular saw, and to burn in lamps there.

At the impetuous Bissell's urging, Dr. Brewer shipped three barrels of this oil, via canal from Buffalo, to New York. When a drayman brought the shipment to Bissell's office on the corner of Broadway and Franklin Street, both lawyers were away, so he dumped it on the sidewalk out front and drove off. The law office was on the second floor; it was the tenants downstairs, the publishers and booksellers D. Appleton & Co., who were left holding the barrels blocking their elegant doorway, sitting in the sun oozing. They had just opened their elaborate new store on the first floor of the building, with a display of rare books and fine prints that was attracting the carriage trade. It is alleged that publishers have hypersensitive nostrils, but it was the customers who came in past the barrels holding their noses, and the fastidious creature who brandished smelling salts and said she was nauseated by the vapors, that goaded Mr. Appleton into action. He rushed out, imperiously summoned a passing drayman, and yelled, "Take these away." The bewildered drayman obliged, so successfully that it took Bissell three weeks to locate the missing oil, in a dock warehouse. He brought one barrel back to his second-floor office, so that he'd have a sample for possible purchasers of stock. He may even have considered wheedling the prosperous tenants below to invest in a few hundred shares, but unfortunately the publisher approached

Bissell first, with apoplectic roars. The oil had leaked through the newly decorated white ceiling below, and dribbled onto some costly bindings. Appleton wanted damages; Bissell was so broke he was already dashing all over the city, trying to raise enough capital to pay Professor Silliman. The professor had cannily refused to hand over his lengthy, detailed analysis until he got his fee—$526.08—in full.

If for want of a horseshoe a battle was lost, then for want of $526.08, the future oil industry nearly got left at the starting post.

Bissell already had a hint, from Silliman, of the glowingly favorable results of the tests, and this whetted him into getting the money, or rather, persuading his partner to pay up out of his own skimpy pocket. The report was worth every penny. It gave the results of innumerable tests and comparisons, and a few sentences must have been enough to convince Bissell he could outshine Aladdin:

> I have submitted the lamp burning Petroleum to the inspection of the most experienced lampists who were accessible to me, and their testimony was, that the lamp burning this fluid gave as much light as any which they had seen, that the oil spent more economically, and the uniformity of the light was greater than in Camphene. . . . As this oil does not gum or become acid or rancid by exposure, it possesses in that, as well as in its wonderful resistance to extreme cold, important qualities for a lubricant. . . . In conclusion, gentlemen, it appears to me that there is much ground for encouragement in the belief that your Company have in their possession a raw material from which, by simple and not expensive process they may manufacture very valuable products.

Silliman himself was so enthusiastic that he consented, briefly, to be president of the company. Since he was one of Yale's most distinguished men, the citizens of New Haven began to look sharp. James Townsend, head of the City Savings Bank, slid suavely into the thick of Bissell's stock tangle, and eventually got a new company formed, the Seneca Oil Company, in his own state, taking over the same lease on the Brewer, Watson land, and with Bissell and his partner still holding a majority share.

In the antimacassared parlor of the New Haven boarding house where Townsend lived, he talked of the new scheme to a fellow boarder—(Look sharp. Here comes the hero)—a courtly, frail-looking thirty-eight-year-old widower, Edwin Drake. It's rather mystifying why a bank president should have scraped the bottom of the barrel so vigorously that he persuaded an ailing conductor on the New Haven railroad to invest almost his entire savings—$200—in the venture. (Professor Silliman had backed out hurriedly; he still thought the oil was valuable, but he must have analyzed the human element involved and found it had a more peculiar odor.) What's even more mystifying, at least to laymen unused to the shorn-lambs maze of dubious stock transactions, is that Drake was elected president of the company and given a startlingly large block of stock, then promptly relieved of most of it. Townsend, who wore high, stiff collars and kept his lips tight in public, later admitted that it didn't do for a banker to have his name attached openly to such a chancy project, but he was perfectly willing to own all the stock he could acquire cheap, behind the scenes.

On the letterhead of the Seneca Oil Company, the sublimely innocent new president-in-name-only wrote out a memo disposing of his stock to the directors:

> For value received I hereby sell, transfer and convey to Asahel Pierpont— Thirty-three hundred and thirty-four shares of the Capital Stock of the Seneca Oil Company— Also Twenty-seven hundred and Eighty-three shares of said Stock to James M. Townsend— Also Sixteen hundred and thirty-two Shares of said stock to E. B. Bowditch— Also Five hundred and twenty-one Shares of said Stock to Henry L. Pierpont now standing in my name upon the books of said Company.
>
> E. L. Drake

The "value received" was a job; Drake was to go to Titusville and act as "General agent of this company to raise and dispose of Oil with a Salery of One Thousand Dollars per annum for one year from the date hereof." (The date was April 1st—often known as April Fool's Day—1858.) In the minutes of that meeting, it was also stated: "Voted that the Treas be requested to procure without delay the sum of one thousand Dollars to be placed at the disposal of Said Drake to be used in conducting the operations of this Company."

A man already too ill with neuralgia of the spine to walk up and down the aisles of a train collecting tickets was now going off hopefully to an obscure part of Pennsylvania, to run a hellish obstacle race over a course that had never been tried out before. The one thing he knew for certain was that it was a hard place to get to, because he'd already made one quick survey trip, traveling free on his railroad pass. Now he was going to return with his new second wife, Laura, and his small daughter.

Fair Haven, Apr. 2, 1858

Dear Dr. Brewer

I think I shall get ready to leave this place about the 13th and I shall visit my father in Castleton, Vt. on my way; this will take up the time until about the first of May, when I think I shall make my grand entree into Titusville, if you think the mud will be navigable by that time.

Now I wish to make a few inquiries: First, whether navigation will be open between your place and Erie. Second, how shall I direct my goods, as I shall send some things direct from here while I stop to visit, and thirdly, whether you think the oil will continue to flow since the admission of Kansas under the LeCompton constitution. . . .

If you can give me any information about the best way of getting my family in there I shall esteem it a favor.

Respectfully yours &c.
E. L. Drake

Round-cheeked, beaming Billy Robinson, proprietor of the American Hotel in the snug little valley village of Titusville, was rather impressed when large vellum envelopes arrived on three successive days addressed to a Colonel Edwin Drake, due to arrive with his family that week. Townsend, who must have had a brash streak of press agent under his sober banker's garb, had pulled the title out of a hat, to provide an air of solid worth to his agent.

He may even have provided the tall silk hat the "Colonel" wore, as further window dressing, but the quiet dignity and honesty were all Drake's own. By the time the villagers discovered the title was phony, they respected the man enough to go right on using it.

Titusville, which is just over the border from Venango in Crawford County, had been founded in 1790 by Jonathan Titus, a civil engineer who had worked on surveys for the Holland Land Company and had spotted the lovely three-mile-long valley lying between round-shouldered hills, and taken a piece for a farm. Of the three hundred people living there when Drake came, most of them were German, English or North Irish immigrants. They were cautious, thrifty and stubborn, and they paid grudging tribute to Drake's own stubbornness in sticking to his project that next gruelling year, even if they thought the idea of boring for oil was plumb crazy. At husking bees and church socials, the word went around that the Colonel was a nice hard-working gentleman and it was too bad he'd been sucked in by the Fancy Stock Company to come and do a fool's errand. The poor man didn't look fit; he was a bad color, and spindly.

The meals at the American Hotel, where Drake paid $6.50 a week room and board for himself, his wife and daughter, were generously designed to fatten almost anybody: smoked pork and johnnycake, mutton and mashed turnips, pie three times a day. On the wide, shady front porch, wicker rockers creaked companionably behind broad white pillars, while the guests exchanged stories. Visiting lumbermen always called the American Hotel "the tavern." The proprietor, Billy Robinson, was an exuberantly hearty host who would referee the young mill hands' impromptu wrestling matches on his taproom floor, or preside genially over a round of tall tales. There was one other hotel in town, the Eagle, and a general store and a grist mill. An ambitious German immigrant had opened a butcher shop which failed miserably, because almost every man in the area cured his own meat. The only other store was Peter Wilson's—"Dealers in Drugs, Medicines, and Chemicals, Paints, Oils and Varnishes, Pure Wines and Liquors for Medicinal Use." The main street was a stretch of sticky yaller clay.

Drake soon adopted the natives' clumping high boots, but the rest of him looked forever foreign. He dressed in the somber black of a deacon, and his long thin legs and the overcoat that reached almost to the ground made him look much taller than his five feet, nine and a half inches. His beard was silky and dark; his thin face, strengthened and whittled by suffering, and his enormous, deep-socketed black eyes, gave him an ascetic look. But the men soon discovered that Drake could tell a good story, and enjoyed a nip of whiskey and a skinny long Pittsburgh stogie, when they sat around the fat-bellied coal stove in Reuel Fletcher's general store, or played pinochle on an overturned barrel. Drake had a New Englander's twangy humor and deliberate way of speech. He was proud of some ancestor of Revolutionary War fame whose sword he'd inherited, but his own life had had more the scope of a paring knife. He'd gone to public school in Castleton, Vermont, worked on an uncle's farm, been a hotel clerk and a clerk in a dry goods store, an express agent, and then a conductor on the New Haven Railroad at $75 a month.

The irresistible forces that gathered—Dr. Brewer, the rocketing Bissell, and pinch-mouth banker Townsend—propelled Drake into the starting position, but once started, it was Drake who had the deep, dogged drive and the staying power. Armchair aficionados who now sit back and belittle his grip on fame—"So Bissell told him to go bore a well like Kier's salt wells, and even then it took him over a year"— might try putting themselves in Drake's too-new boots, in the summer of 1858.

He thought the oil spring on a small, barren, artificial island created by the mill flow was "a rusty, disgusting looking pool." He insisted later, resentfully, that neither Bissell nor anyone else had told him how to get petroleum in quantities out of the ground, and that he had to try whatever came to mind. Hiring local workmen to dig around the seepage seemed a logical start, but even that wasn't simple. He could get plenty of men, but a mill hand remembered Drake saying incredulously, his second morning in Titusville, "You don't mean to say I can't even buy picks and shovels in this town."

The storekeeper, Reuel Fletcher, had the answer to this and a dozen other dilemmas. He was a kind, sensible man, cheerfully and warmly helpful in the best cracker-barrel tradition, and even if he didn't carry picks and shovels, he was quick to offer the loan of his horse, so that Drake could ride off and buy from Fletcher's nearest rival, at Hydetown. Drake got a pick there, in the tumbledown log-cabin store kept by Charles Hyde. But he had to go to Sam Brown's in Pleasantville for spikes, and to John Mitchell's in Enterprise for a chain. He had to send to Erie, forty-five miles away, to get two shovels.

All that summer, he kept borrowing Fletcher's handsome bay horse and rig, to ride off in all directions, assembling tools and machinery by the maddening process of by-guess and by-gosh. He made longer, two-day-each-way trips by stagecoach, to Erie, Pittsburgh, and to

Tarentum, where he consulted the owners of salt wells and hired a borer who promised to arrive in July and never turned up. Drake, who had been frightened by tales of the salty thirst of borers, had told the man sternly he would receive only board and tobacco, but no cash wages, until he'd drilled a hole one thousand feet down. No salt well had ever been dug anywhere near that deep, and certainly never under such Spartan conditions.

This probably clinched the driller's suspicion that Drake was crazy, and he told friends he'd promised to work for the lunatic just to shut him up and get rid of him. A second borer had good intentions but itching feet; Drake traced him to Pittsburgh and learned he'd headed west.

The workmen Drake had hired, at $1 a day, dug trenches and finally a hole, but Drake wrote the directors of his company:

> In sinking our well last week we struck a large vein of oil but the same thrust of the spade opened a vein of water that drove the men out of the well and I shall not try to dig by hand any more as I am satisfied that boring is the cheapest. . . . I have contracted for an engine to be ready for boring by the first of Sept. The engine will cost five hundred dollars in Erie which is about one hundred dollars less than the same or one like it would cost in the East. . . . Now I think you had better make a loan of $1000 and place it in bank there where I can get at it as I need it & I assure you there is no risk whatever for I have got as far with five hundred dollars as any other company have with five thousand and further than some have with ten thousand dollars. . . . Money is very scarce here. The lumbermen could not sell their lumber for cash this summer and the people all depend upon the lumber trade, so money is as tight here as it was in New York last fall. The old lumber company begin to think they did not retain the best of the property when they sold out the oil springs. Old Mr. Brewer is here now and says he is sorry they sold that piece of land or gave that lease, but let them whine.

Ebenezer Brewer's partner wasn't a whiner, more a shouter; Jonathan Watson was a bluff, rough-grained lumberman with a craggy, big-nosed face, and a voice fit for yelling "Timber!" He took Drake's specifications for timber for an engine house, and told his head sawyer boomingly, "He says it's for a derrick and he's going to drill a hole through the rock and find a big body of oil even if it takes a year. I have no faith in the project myself." His nickname was Jonah.

Drake entered the Brewer, Watson bill for $36 on his expense sheet in writing as cramped as his budget, along with: "Poor Tax, .16 . . . Tinkers Bill, 1.24 . . . Trip to Erie for Pump, 6.63 . . . Carpenter on Engine House $8 . . . Liddell Hershey & Co., on Engine, $100.

The $100 was a down payment to the Erie firm for the six-horsepower engine and stationary boiler recommended by salt men, a Long John, the kind used on steamboats.

Even when all the machinery finally arrived, nobody around there knew how to operate the new gadgets, but Drake was as anxiously hopeful as a child who has written to Santa Claus for a mechanical-minded elf; he had been promised still another borer, due in September. Waiting that great day, he told cheerful jokes on himself and "Drake's Folly," quoting with relish the farmer who'd remarked he could always use the oil for syrup on buckwheat cakes.

When the fall bonfires sent up their nostalgic aroma, Drake told Reuel Fletcher one night about a queer dream he'd had as a child, on his father's farm in Vermont. He dreamed that he set fire to a pile of stubble, and it got out of control and spread frighteningly. He woke from the nightmare screaming, and his mother had soothed him by saying, "Why, that just means some day you'll set the world on fire."

The nights were already closing in early and frostily, and while Drake waited, the villagers went about their business and pleasures. At apple-paring bees in the big, pleasantly shabby farmhouse kitchens, the young men sat beside their best girls, and used a pocket knife to pare and quarter the tart, rosy fruit, while the girls strung the quarters together like yards-long necklaces and draped them around the fireplace to dry. Attics were heaped like squirrel caches. Rifle shots pinged in the thick woods, and the men brought home big, plump wild turkeys, and cut strips of venison from a fine buck, to store up for winter.

It was mid-November when Drake finally realized the third borer was as ephemeral as the others. He wrote his company directors sadly that salt man Lewis Peterson had told him he'd have to give up until spring. With his engine sitting mute and swaddled inside its new home, Drake reported, "I set myself down verry uneasy, to wait for Spring. . . . I never saw such winter weather as they have in that part of Penn."

His neuralgia was bad, and his constant worries about money enough to finish the project were achingly real. By the time another April Fool's Day had come—and that was technically the end of his contract—Drake was informing the Seneca Oil Company that at last he had a lead on a dependable man, a blacksmith who had often made tools and lent a hand on salt wells—but the directors no longer cared. Why should they pour more good money down the hole? Townsend must have been gladder than ever he'd kept his spotless banker's reputation intact, but he sent Drake a few small token loans, before he finally urged him to give up the whole scheme and come home. Of the lot, Drake was the only man who showed the single-minded passion and faith and curiosity that marks your real pioneer—and the wildcatters who've risked their necks and careers ever since, to find oil. He had to finish the well.

Later, the villagers said that Drake's sweet-faced wife was his "good angel" during those close-to-starving times, and that she kept buoying the hope in the pain-racked body, "his staff and his light in adversity." But it was the people of Titusville who gave practical comfort. Even if they couldn't believe in the wild and woolly venture, they had come to have a rather exasperated affection for Drake. Jonah Watson looked sheepish when a mill hand saw him give Drake a credit slip for the grist mill to get a 100-pound bag of flour for his family. The lumberman muttered, "Anybody who has the nerve to go ahead under these circumstances deserves some help."

Reuel Fletcher risked a good bit more than a bag of flour. He let Drake run up a bill of over $300 at the little store, and went on believing loyally that his friend would succeed, but he was frankly puzzled as to what on earth anybody would *do* with a vast lot of oil, even if they ever got it out of the ground. In spite of that, he and the lanky young druggist, Peter Wilson, Drake's only close friends, co-signed a personal loan for Drake of $500, at the Meadville bank that summer.

This time, Drake took no chances on losing his borer en route. He sent a local teamster to fetch blacksmith William Smith and his fifteen-year-old son Sammy, from Salina near Tarentum. Smith had agreed to work for $2.50 a day, with Sammy's services thrown in. Drake had also arranged with Smith to make a complete set of drilling tools before he left his forge, at a total cost of $76.50, and these, weighing one hundred pounds, were packed into the wagon, along with Smith's pretty oldest daughter Margaret, who was wearing a new brown calico dress and an uneasy look. She had promised to come and cook for her father and brother, and keep house in the engine-house shanty, but her mother, who had to stay at home with the youngest children, wailed that up there in the backwoods anything might happen.

On the blossoming May day the wagonload pulled up before the Drakes' little rented house (they had long since moved out of the hotel), Drake was too ill to take Smith to the well, but he sat up in bed talking feverishly to the solid-as-a-barrel blacksmith. Later he said thankfully, "I could not have suited myself better if I could have had a man made to order." They must have made a strange twosome; Smith, called "Uncle Billy," was a short, broad, hefty, laconic man who might have posed for Longfellow under a spreading chestnut burr. Whether or not he really believed in the project at first, he soon felt a protective devotion for Drake. When he was offered a smithy job in Franklin at $4 a day, he told his son, "I can't quit Drake now."

From the time he arrived, things throbbed. The derrick went up one afternoon in early June. All the men at the Upper Mill, a few hundred feet away, came down with their pike poles to help raise the pine-timber rigging, and they acted as if they were having a half-holiday. Pupils from the nearby one-room schoolhouse wandered past, and two twelve-year-olds stayed to join the fun. At least a dozen townspeople were there, including Reuel Fletcher. Chunky Dr. Brewer handed out cigars to the spectators, saying jovially, "Have one on me. They didn't cost me a cent. I traded oil stock for them."

Inside the twelve-foot-square base of the derrick, the walking beam, propelled by engine like a giant jerky grasshopper, sent the drilling tools down and up. But the soft earth still kept caving in. Drake, watching, got the one brilliant, inventive idea that even carping historians can't take away from him, and that drove the project through, literally. He went off to Erie again, got fifty feet of cast-iron pipe, in sections, and had the jointed pipe driven down through sand and clay, till it hit rock at thirty-two feet. Then the drilling went on steadily, three feet a day.

On a brilliant Saturday afternoon, August 27th, at sixty-nine feet down, the drill suddenly dropped six inches into a crevice. Uncle Billy fished it out, wiped it off carefully and knocked off for over the Sabbath. But by then the big, stolid blacksmith-turned-driller had a touch of the fever that keeps a man restlessly seeking the shade of a derrick that covers the Lord-only-knows-what. Monday seemed a long way off; by Sunday, Smith was back at the well, peering down the pipe, wondering if he really saw something glistening on the surface below. He grabbed a leftover end of pipe, plugged it up like a dipper, and thrust it down on a stick. It came back up filled with oil, to the brim. A wild shout brought several mill hands running. Young Sammy shot off to town, making a record run in bare feet, to notify Colonel Drake.

And it's at this point that I find Drake most irritating. What kind of hero is this, who not only isn't on hand to witness the famous strike, but doesn't even bother coming down to take a look, till the next day?

The whole village was buzzing; even townsmen who still couldn't imagine what in tarnation might come of the find were eager to see it. A Franklin man who arrived there the next day, joining the crowds streaming in on every road, in wagons, on horseback or on foot, reported, "It comes out a flowing dark grease with a heavy white froth."

By then, the few pine barrels Drake had provided were already full. Drake, the calmest man around, took Margaret Smith's washtub from the engine-house shanty (she complained later she never could get it clean after that) then commandeered old whiskey barrels and sperm-oil containers. And still Uncle Billy kept pumping and the oil kept coming; so did the crowds.

In New York, George Bissell, the bouncing promoter, received the word over that newfangled contraption, the telegraph, from Dr. Brewer, who was already regretting the stock he'd traded for cigars, and was ready to buy it back. Bissell, in turn, rushed around the city buying up all the shares of the Seneca Oil Company he could get his hands on. Four days later, he was in Titusville to grab leases. But already the rush was on.

One of the would-be deals Bissell panted over, that fall, was to lease the Story Farm on lower Oil Creek. He persuaded the owner, all right, but the farmer's dumpy little wife was unexpectedly stubborn. Perhaps she'd caught some subversive shift in the wind, generated by Susan Anthony, Lucy Stone, and other woman's rights devilish advocates. Whatever her reason for balkiness, even Bissell's hair-tossing eloquence couldn't budge her. She'd think it over, but as co-owner, she wouldn't sign any lease yet. Come back tomorrow. Bissell went back, but a wily agent for a group of Pittsburghers had been there before him. He had offered the Storys $40,000, and when Mrs. Story still placidly refused to sign, he had won her over, lock, stock, barrel and feminine foibles, by writing into the contract—"And for Mrs. Story, one new silk dress." She signed then, contentedly.

The stockholders of that Pittsburgh company, including a young steel man, Andrew Carnegie, made a pretty packet out of that deal, enough to pay for Mrs. Story's silk dress (even studded with diamonds) plus Carnegie's new steel mill, and whatever else their happy hearts desired.

Even before the Pittsburghers sent in their silken-tongued agent, the local boys were onto a good thing, and fast. They had all known vaguely of Silliman's report on the value of oil, but now suddenly it hit them head-on. If the sickly, citified Drake could drill a well that produced enough to make real money, then so could they. At 7:30 the Monday morning after Uncle Billy hauled up the first big dipperful, Jonah Watson rode up to the mill on horseback, and called his head sawyer, William Kirkpatrick, outside. This was the same sawyer he'd told, "I don't have any faith in Drake's project myself." Now he explained with a straight face that some urgent business had come up (he didn't add, "Out of the ground") and that he'd have to be gone for a few days, so would Kirkpatrick look after things? Then he went galloping off like a Paul Revere, but not to warn the inhabitants, only to lease their land before they knew what had hit them.

The head sawyer looked thoughtfully at the vanishing rear end of his employer's horse, then called the tail sawyer, a lusty, loud-voiced, bull-necked young fellow named James Tarr, and told *him* to look after the mill. Then he too leaped onto a horse and went off, to get two leases of his own by sundown.

The tail sawyer, James Tarr, went back into the mill and cheerfully oiled the circular saw. He owned two hundred acres on the creek, so poor for farming that he'd taken the job at the mill to help eke out a living for himself and his wife and child. Within three years, he would eke out gold the equivalent of two million dollars from leases and outright sales of his land, and at the most conservative estimate, another million in royalties. When he took his daughter to a fancy finishing school to enroll her, and the headmistress murmured snobbishly that she was afraid the girl didn't have the capacity, James Tarr pulled out a roll of bills as thick as his neck, and roared, "Then buy her some."

If Jonah Watson had stayed at the mill that first Mad Monday and made a friendly deal with his tail sawyer, he might have done even better. But he had his mind's eye on Ham McClintock's farm, twelve miles down Oil Creek, where an oil spring even larger than the lumber mill's had been a matter of general knowledge for years. Ham McClintock had often collected oil from the seepage, for medicine. The only people who'd been really excited over it were scholars like Timothy Alden, the president of Allegheny College in Meadville; he had delivered a paper in 1820, entitled "Antiquities and Curiosities of Western Pennsylvania," in which he marveled over the old oil pits around McClintock's spring, cribbed with logs, and bordered by mounds of the earth removed, in which grew trees hundreds of years old. Alden concluded they must have been dug before the French, even before the Indians, perhaps even by the ancient Mound Builders. He had also suggested briskly, "By extending the operation, this oil might be collected so as to become a profitable article of commerce."

Jonah Watson didn't give a hoot who had cribbed the old pits, but now he, too, thought oil might be a profitable article of commerce. Before 9 A.M. he was already hitching his lathered horse by McClintock's barn, and urging the owner to lay down his haying pitchfork and listen.

Within an hour, the lumberman had a lease on three hundred acres, agreeing to give Ham McClintock a twelfth royalty of whatever was dug up, such as salt marsh and other minerals, and even oil. All that day, as Watson went on leasing land clear to the mouth of the creek, he sprinkled mentions of salt to tame his prey. By the time he and his horse limped home, he had laid the groundwork for becoming the world's first oil millionaire—in a mansion with carved wooden moose heads, a little garden fish pond one hundred and ninety feet long, and twelve gardeners.

With booming good humor, Watson made several attempts to initiate Drake into this jolly sport of making a fortune. But Drake and money were forever at odds. Having brought on the deluge, he simply stepped aside and let it flow past. He bought a pair of loud checked pantaloons, and a horse from a hard-up, newly shingled country doctor, Dr. Albert Egbert, who was scratching around desperately for $200 to pay down on a farm that turned out to be the most fabulous producer of the lot. At least Drake had the horse. And he didn't neglect his company's business. Although within a year there'd be a dozen little makeshift refineries around Oil Creek, the nearest then was Sam Kier's, in Pittsburgh. Drake arranged with Kier to buy the well's first shipment of oil, at sixty cents a gallon. Then he took a day off, and went fishing.

One of his best stories that fall was about the Crawford County preacher who cornered Drake on the street in Titusville and told him furiously to stop taking oil out of the ground. "Don't you know," he thundered, "that you're interfering with the Almighty Creator of the universe? He put that oil in the bowels of the earth to heat the fires of Hell. Would you thwart the Almighty and let sinners go unpunished?"

The next years were golden for sinners, in the early-burly on Oil Creek.

THREE

---●●---

The boomer
brigade

Forty-niners who'd panned through the gold rush and now swaggered to Oil Creek expecting a rather panty-waist operation with effete Easterners and rubes, complained that conditions here were crazier than anything they'd ever seen. One miner said that if a new well brought up huge gold nuggets, the owner would throw them back in and go on drilling—for oil. This may have been a slight exaggeration.

But it was true that the great open desert spaces, the frontier stretches and mountains, couldn't have produced this fiercely concentrated frenzy, squeezed as it was, those first years, into a greasy mud furrow not more than twenty miles long, on Oil Creek. Rich men, poor men, speculators, thieves were all packed together like oily sardines in a barrel. The two little villages Titusville and Cornplanter, each at one end of this main furrow, this suddenly most-crowded, most-coveted land on earth, were entrance, exit, base of operations or bottleneck, and they swelled like frog ponds in flood time.

Between the two towns, derricks were going up so fast you couldn't see the trees for the wood. Wild turkeys took to the far hills, clucking in fright. The once-serene valley, with its few remote farms and thick timber, was parceled off in patches, a huge, vibrating crazy quilt, with the wooden structures stuck on like clothespins. Axes whanged; trees fell and were hauled off green to slap up into new houses and

28

free-and-easies where gamblers and "soiled doves" were already setting up shop.

Saloonkeepers who'd cut their eyeteeth or their whiskey in frontier
towns where polished six-shooters and dandified gamblers were stock
equipment didn't so much mind doing business in shanties, but the
mud drove them crazy. Customers wore thigh-high boots that oozed
at every step, and even when a man sat down, he left an oily imprint.
The more genteel proprietors tried valiantly to keep up appearances;
some of them wrapped the legs of the piano in old newspapers and
rags, like gouty bandaged limbs, to protect them from filthy kicking
boots.

Drillers' apprentices, tool dressers—toolies—wore railroad boots
that cost $1.50 and could thump to a fiddle and foot a fast hoedown
to the music of "Chase the Squirrel" or "Money Musk." Most of the
toolies were as lively and agile as monkeys; one of their chores was
to climb up to the top of a derrick to grease the crown-pulley, and it
was toolies who rigged up the pennants that floated and flapped from
the derricks derisively: Big Bologna, Old Misery, Scared Cat, The
Vampire, Sleeping Beauty.

Toolies made $2 to $3 a day, for a twelve-hour shift, and spent it
as freely as oil. To accommodate the day and night shifts, saloons
kept jumping around the clock, and there were always self-styled
ladies handy, in what a preacher called "suspicious houses." But the
soiled doves' patrons—rig-builders, toolies, teamsters, drillers—even
when they came away with cleaned-out pockets, weren't suspicious;
they seemed to feel they'd got their money's worth, and they drowned
out Methodist dissenters with their roar of approval:

> "The Oil Creek girls are the dandy girls
> For their kiss is most intense.
> They've got a grip like a rotary pump
> That will lift you over the fence."

It was said that the amorous Frenchified arts of one of these girls
could make even a teamster blush, and this was considered going
some. Raftsmen had prided themselves on their toughness, but oil-
hauling teamsters were tougher. For years, raftsmen running logs
downstream to Pittsburgh had stopped overnight at the riverside

Moran House at Cornplanter. In logging season, the rafts tied up
there stretched a half-mile above and below Moran's, while the pilots
and raftsmen rollicked inside to their favorite tune, "Hell on the
Wabash." Now their main cargo was oil, but they were a drop in the
bucket compared to teamsters, who swelled to four thousand in number. Day after day, wagons loaded with oil barrels stretched in an
endless chain along the quagmire roads from the wells to the nearest
railroad depots, Garland and Union, about twenty miles from Titusville, or Corry, twenty-seven miles, or to the waiting barges at Cornplanter. Every piece of furniture, and even the coal for engines and
the engines themselves, had to be hauled in to Oil Creek by teams,
through the mud that was

> Wholly unclassable
> Almost impassable
> Scarcely jackassable.

There's the story about a stranger who was slogging along and
kicked what seemed to be a man's hat lying in the middle of the mud.
From the depths a voice came angrily: "Say, that's my head in that
hat. Don't you kick it again."

The traveler peered down, horrified. "You'll be buried alive," he
screeched.

"Never you mind, stranger. I've got a good mule under me, and
he's got to the second sand rock."

It was the philosophic custom for many teamsters to carry a keg
of beer along, and when their wagon wheels sank to the hub, they
wet their outsize vocal cords between cursing the poor struggling
horses. Teamsters had an awesome vocabulary, "blasphemous, brim-
stone-tongued," and they were the meanest fighters around. In saloon
brawls, a teamster often bit off an opponent's nose, a portion of the
upper lip, or a chunk of ear. And I don't say he chewed it like tobacco, but he didn't apologize either. This disgusted and baffled the
transplanted Westerners: imagine biting a man instead of shooting
him neatly.

One driver who owned his own team swore bloody murder when
the owner of a well going down explained he was so broke he'd have
to give a one-twelfth share of his well, in lieu of the two weeks'

charges he owed for machinery and lumber hauled in. Probably no would-be producer ever studied the contents of the sand pump more prayerfully, watching for signs of oil, because if this well came in dry, the enraged teamster might bite off his ears or worse. Fortunately, the well flowed in the nick of time; the mollified driver's one-twelfth share amounted to $30,000.

Word of the teamsters rolling in money brought plenty of hopeful beginners to join their league. One of these came from downstate, and on his first morning of hauling oil, his wagon bogged down at the bottom of a steep hill on the way to Titusville, and it took him all day to pry it loose. He had just reached the top of the hill, at dusk, when the endgate broke and all the barrels rolled out and downhill. The infuriated teamster yelled after them, "You can go to Hell. I'm goin' back home to York."

The teamsters who stuck it out got arrogant on power. During their heyday, they had well owners over the barrel, and they gouged exorbitant fees. Once a group of teamsters made desperate producers bid at auction for their services, and the highest bidder got his oil hauled at $5 a barrel, for a six-mile trip.

Even drillers, a new breed of master artisan, made only $4 to $5 a day. On the job, on the high stool in the derrick called the Driller's Throne, they were highly responsible, proud of the tricky skill of handling the tools and cable. The best ones had a tactile intuition that made them know in their fingers what was happening underground, and whether they were close to a strike. For celebration, when a good well came in, the producer would buy his driller a fancy new outfit, like a winning jockey's silks, with $12 Wisconsin boots, and the wide-brimmed hats that distinguished them from ordinary men in inverted soup-bowl derbies. Right off, the driller would take his pristine new hat to the well, and initiate it with a few daubs of oily slush from the sand pump. If there was anything that marked a man as an amateur, a nonbelonger, in Petrolia, it was to be too immaculate, too slicked up with water, unoiled, not a mudder.

A visitor to Cornplanter wrote home despairingly, "How shall I describe this place unless my pen is dipped in mud?"
Another dubbed it "Sodden Gomorrah."

There was one main street, "filthy and snarling," with piles of barrels in lurching pyramids wherever you looked, and a welter of garbage, ashes and herring boxes dumped by the new hotels and groggeries lining the street: Petroleum House, Sheriff's, Jones', Parkers', Adamson's, Crapo's. This was the main shipping point of the oil region, where sixteen hundred teamsters brought their loads every day, and the river was teeming with flatboats and barges, all greasy, all with barrels banging around. The reek of petroleum hung like a mist over the village, and even the hitching posts were oily. The walls of each shanty were slimy to touch, inside and out. Because the town had no place to spread except up, with a steep hill on one side and a rocky cliff on the other, dynamiters swarmed laying charges, to gouge out niches for yet another rickety building.

A bystander hearing a shout of "Blast!" barely had time to leap before the boulders came tumbling down. When the frame went up, three-inch battens were slapped over the gaps between wall timbers; nobody thought of plaster or paint. Everything had a flimsy, improvised air, because whatever was put up one week would be outgrown by the week after. In the Williams Brothers' store, a bunch of the boys sat around on molasses kegs one night and decided that the Indian name of Cornplanter was much too old-fashioned for their bustling metropolis now. Who planted corn any more? Every square inch of farm land was being leased, and the ground was dug up so fast that one corpse had been accidentally dug up three times, before his indignant relatives shipped the remains off to Rochester, New York, so he could lie in peace. Definitely, Cornplanter needed a new name worthy of this high-powered tussle and hustle. The boys settled, not too deviously, on Oil City, and Doc Christy brought over a bottle of medicinal whiskey from his drugstore, to christen the borough-to-be. Next they rushed through a new post office, set up on the cliff side on spiles, but nobody was surprised when it collapsed and tumbled into the creek. Newcomers, after they'd been in the oil region a week, were beyond being surprised at anything.

Reporters who tried to convey what it was like, in their dispatches sent back to papers all over the country, were doing their best to record a phenomenon they didn't quite believe themselves. More than one editor those first months, receiving an on-the-spot account of a new well, sent back a stern warning to the writer: "Sober up. Enough of this nonsense." To combat this, and to assure their editors, their readers, or even themselves, reporters constantly prefaced an account with some such touching appeal as: "We shall ask you to believe that we are neither drunk nor crazy, though we shall hardly expect strangers to oil diggings to believe all we tell you."

The first man who wrote any sizable account of the early wells was Thomas Gale, and he too was nervously asserting his sobriety, in the pamphlet that appeared in June 1860, *The Wonder of the Nineteenth Century: Rock Oil in Pennsylvania:* "One is almost constrained, from his intuitive notion of the natural world, to suspect such a story is a *whopper;* and that the man who talks in this manner of oil flowing up, has been drinking poor whiskey. But good vouchers are at hand."

The vouching eyewitnesses included city promoters like Bissell who were rather miffed, in the midst of their frenzied large operations, their leasing and lawyers and hirings and engine-haulings, to see the village shoemaker quietly get his foot in ahead, by kicking down the very next well after Drake's without a smidgen of imported machinery, that fall of 1859.

If this caused consternation among the mighty, it didn't surprise the people of Titusville in the least. William Barnsdall was as good a shoemaker and tanner as you'd find in ten counties, a member of the town council who said little, and what little he said made pure sense. He was a tall, sensitive-faced, fine-boned man with the hands of a craftsman and the reticence bred in the English countryside. Born in Biggleswade, Bedfordshire, he had come to America with growing pains, and founded what was called by the natives the English Settlement, outside Titusville, in 1832. Soon he moved into town, and began making and mending shoes, sticking to his last until Drake's well galvanized the countryside.

Barnsdall's brother-in-law, James Parker, had a farm a few hundred feet from the Drake, just over the line in Crawford County, which the shoemaker began drilling on. He used a crude hickory spring pole, with stirrups operated by foot like a treadle to supply the power. It was hard work, but it was a good cheap way to drill, when a man couldn't afford an engine. To finance the cost of the tools, made by Titusville blacksmith Locke, Barnsdall took in two partners, Boon Meade and Henry Rouse. When he got down a few inches below the depth of the Drake well, the watching crowd of villagers and strangers, the first ever engaged in what was later known as "sitting on a well," were ready to give up their places at what seemed to be a flop show. The hole was dry, they croaked. It was deeper than Drake's, and no sign of oil. There was no sense in going on. It is worthy of "Quotes we doubt ever got quoted" that Barnsdall is supposed to have said, "Well, it's still a long way from the bottom of this hole to China, and I'm bound to find tea leaves if we don't get to the grease sooner."

He got the grease, at eighty feet down, and the new Barnsdall well was "the lion of the valley." Crowds lined up at the creek bank waiting their turn to pay a dime to be ferried across by flatboat to see this stupendous ten-barrel-a-day * marvel. One visitor wrote:

> A ladder was provided for our party to go up and see the oil spout out of the pipe. When we got up on the little platform, it was coming up gently enough. But soon it commenced throwing up the greasy and odorous substance far above our heads, and sprinkling us in a manner which was death to white vests and black pants. We were amused at one gentleman, who did not appear to like that kind of bath, and undertook to get away by going down the ladder. He started as though he would go down a pair of stairs, but fell through between the rounds and barked himself considerably!

The next well, kicked down by Titusville blacksmith David Crossley, made an even bigger splash on white vests. The pudgy-cheeked, iron-muscled Crossley had been pointed out to visiting lumbermen respectfully for years, because he was the only settler around who had walked all the way from New York. As an adventurous twelve-year-old in England he had run off to Liverpool and stowed away on a ship sailing for America. Once there, he located relatives in New Jersey, and bound himself out to learn blacksmithing. Looking for a likely community to set up a smithy in, after he married, he walked 450 miles to Titusville and the English Settlement there, and liked what he saw. Then he walked all the way back, and collected his wife.

---

* A barrel then held about forty gallons. Oil men got together a few years later and decided on a standard forty-two-gallon barrel to end cheating, and that is still standard.

Having developed his calf muscles in these marathons, he was in excellent shape to kick down the deepest well yet, to 124 feet. It was on the creek bank near Drake's, and sightseers nearly swamped the flatboat ferry, in their eagerness to get close to the well they called the Elephant.

Skeptics, among them some Wall Street men, stood by with watches in hand and timed the well like a race horse. They were openmouthed at the yield, fifteen quarts a minute. A representative of a Chautauqua County journal, reporting this, forestalled any suspicions of his own liquid content by explaining hurriedly that the men who had timed it were "well-known and reliable citizens. . . . The greatest excitement exists in that region, and fortunes are made in a few minutes by sale or lease of lands. . . . Wells are sinking in every direction and strangers are flocking from all parts of the country."

Pamphleteer Gale wrote with starry exclamation points, "A splendid thing is the Crossley well! A diamond of the first water! Enough of itself to silence the cry of humbug; to create a sensation among rival interests; to inspire hope in many toiling for the subterranean treasure, and to make every son of Pennsylvania rejoice in the good Providence that has enriched the state . . . with *rivers of oil.*"

Drake, who was placidly putting down a second well for his employers, wrote Townsend, "The Town is full of anxious seekers all determined to make a fortune or bust in the attempt."

The serene little village of Titusville now looked as if some shanty town had been wrenched up in a hurricane and flung down here helter-skelter among the prim white clapboard houses. Sidewalks were narrow planks in a sea of sucking mire, and newcomers walked the plank in more ways than one. Land sharks lurked in offices that didn't yet have a roof, and seldom a solid floor for their high-sounding propositions. "The mouths of speculators yielded more oil than the best wells on the creek."

You could buy one-sixteenth, or even a sixteenth of a sixteenth, of the greatest money-maker since Croesus, a well that was due to pour out wealth any day. Look! Look at the map and see how it sits in the juiciest strip of creek land. On paper, it all looked foolproof. Nobody had yet discovered that one out of every three wells was a duster, or dry. And the boomers, the shady speculators who moved in to make a fast killing, needed only a handful of blank leases and revenue stamps to be in business.

Every newcomer, whether honest buyer or boomer, had maps bulging in the breast pocket of his long-waisted frock coat, purporting to show just which choice leases were still available. Some of the maps were as near accurate as anything could be in that Sinbad bedlam, done by the civil engineers already sent out by responsible companies acting on solid fact: oil is getting popular as an illuminant and lubricant, so we'll invest in oil lands. But facts had almost no connection with the mass buying hysteria, the grab for whatever was offered. Prettily tinted stock certificates, marked "$10 a share of property," carefully didn't say what property; it might have been in Timbuctoo or Cuckooland. The filled-in stubs of an old stock book of this ilk show that a sucker who bought, say, $150 worth of these pieces of paper often rushed back and bought $200 more the next day. The fear of being gulled wasn't as acute as the fear of being left behind.

An Erie man plagued by prudence wrote apologetically to a reputable land agent and lawyer:

> Dear Sir:
> I have been trying to make up my mind definitely on the subject of your note and to screw up my courage for another visit of observation. . . . It is the bent of my brain to investigate and deliberate— even to a fault. If I think too long, will only have to regret I did not promptly embrace opportunity.
>
> Very truly yours,
> William W. Wallace

Opportunity, or a flashy facsimile of it, was knocking at every door and window. The town or crossroads that didn't have its own stock company with a highfalutin' title was considered too dead to skin. By summer of 1860, there were six hundred companies incorporated in Pennsylvania alone, and probably four-fifths of these were phonies.

During the peak of the boom a few years later, a Boston paper ran a straight-faced announcement on the prospectus of a new company:

THE MUNCHAUSEN PHILOSOPHER'S STONE AND GULL CREEK GRAND CONSOLIDATED OIL COMPANY

Capitalized at $4,000,000,000
with a working capital of $37.50.

Wells produce not just oil but cod-liver oil, quinine, ale, and the milk of human kindness. Last Wednesday at 2 P.M. . . . struck a large vein of quinine. This is generally administered without charge to any of the stockholders seized with fever, or shaky about the value of their shares.

The farmers on Oil Creek were almost the only people involved who didn't need quinine. From the start, they fared remarkably well, against city financiers, boomers and local tycoons like Jonah Watson. Most of their land along Oil Creek was already leased on a royalty basis, and those who weren't satisfied with the original deal had a forthright way of airing their grievances. The second lease Jonah Watson gulped up was on John Rynd's farm, and if he rubbed his big hands and chuckled over getting a bargain, granting a royalty of only one-twelfth, he must have been staggered to read the large public notice John Rynd inserted in the Venango *Spectator* afterward:

IMPORTANT NOTICE ABOUT OIL LAND

Whereas on the 1st of September 1859, certain parties by misrepresentation procured from the subscriber a lease for his land on Oil Creek, in the county of Venango. Therefore he hereby notifies all whom it may concern that as said interest of lease was procured as above stated, he is determined that the said lessees or their under lessees shall never take possession of one foot of said land or operate for oil or salt under said contract. Upon this all may depend.

John Rynd
December 21, 1859

John Rynd was the grandson of an Irish woollen factor, and he still owned three hundred acres his grandfather had bought from the Holland Land Company in 1800. He also owned a loaded Irish temper, and a shotgun. Within three weeks after his boldface roar of protest, Jonah Watson gave in. He was proud of his reputation in the lumber business as a shrewd bargainer, but he wasn't a crook; he was like a big-game hunter who creeps up on his prey *pour le sport,* and not because he needs the meat. Now that his kill turned out to be only nicked, and as cross as a wounded rhinoceros, Watson retreated cheerfully. The lease with John Rynd was changed to a one-fourth share of all royalties on oil, and salt wasn't mentioned.

The farmer Watson had tackled first of all, Ham McClintock, did very nicely too. Jonah subleased large chunks of this land, and each lessee subleased part of *his* piece, to get money to put down a well. Ham McClintock didn't bother putting down many wells; let others take the risk, and pay his royalties. He simply put down mattresses all over the floor of his house, five to each room, to bed down these benighted souls. For seventy-five cents, they could sleep in the hayloft without a blanket. There were sixty wells going down there, with engine houses and lean-tos scattered around like peanut shells, so that McClintock always had plenty of paying guests. He was still so conditioned by his sparse farming days that charging $3 a week for board (at a time when eggs were eight cents a dozen) seemed suitably steep. One guest said that when a farmer's daughter waited on you around McClintockville, you were never sure whether she was a milkmaid or an oil heiress or both.

A waif of fourteen, whose tattered, patched pants were held up precariously by one frayed suspender, poled a visitor across creek on a raft slightly larger than a breadboard, and the newcomer was so paternally moved by the lad's obvious poverty that he gave him a nickel tip and a kindly pat on the head. He was somewhat discomfited to learn that the waif was a brand-new oil heir.

To confuse outsiders even more, some of the newly wealthy farmers went right on living in their same dilapidated cabins, with rags and quilts hung at the windows in place of panes, and a limp calico curtain partitioning off a sleeping cubicle from the sitting-room-kitchen. They got up at cockcrow, as always, and plowed and planted as if their lives still depended on it. And in the best sense, perhaps they did. One farmer refused to lease another five acres, at a plump figure (the sum quoted now is a round million, but it probably got rounder with each retelling) until after he'd got in his buckwheat crop. "Ain't gonna have it tramped on," he said.

Old John Buchanan complained piteously to a newcomer that he had been taken advantage of, in leasing to sharpers, and left a pauper. His listener's eyes misted in sympathy, and he pictured the poor old fellow trudging over the hill to the county almshouse, until Buchanan finished sadly, "So here I am a poor man—worth barely a hundred thousand."

With a hundred wells drilled on his farm, and his royalty share one-fourth on each, he may soon have been complaining, "Worth barely half a million."

When one of the soundest companies that had a sublease on the Buchanan property asked a neighboring farmer if he'd like some stock, he said courteously, Wal no, he guessed he already had aplenty —three horses and a yoke of steers.

I think it was farmer John Rynd who, once he'd bested Jonah Watson and made him raise the ante, sat on his front porch rocking, day after day, sardonically observing the antics of the outlanders who kept arriving "by rickety coach or rickety mare or on rickety legs."

They came by water, too. Steamers like the *Allegheny Belle,* chugging upriver from Pittsburgh, were loaded like cattleboats. A tiny steamer renamed the *Petrolia,* once accustomed to carrying about a dozen farmers from Franklin up the six miles to Oil City, now carried at least a hundred passengers each trip. On deck, a dapper gambler would unroll a large piece of checkered red and black oilcloth, each square numbered, and urge listeners in the jolly tones of a neighborhood bingo announcer to invest fifty cents in this great Havana lottery. For only fifty cents, you had ten throws of the dice, and if the numbers you rolled matched the numbers on the oilcloth, you were $150 richer. It was understood, of course, that you'd multiply this sum a thousandfold, once you reached oildom, but this was your starter. The percentage of winners in the Havana lottery was even lower than Oil Creek's.

If you covered the last lap to Titusville by huckleberry coach, you arrived with a sore, bruised behind (the springs were stiff and sharp as a fakir's bed of nails) and with your pantaloons mud to the hip, what with leaping out along the way to help pry the coach out of sock-holes or push it up hills. When you staggered finally into a lobby and asked a hotel clerk for a room, and he said he'd try to squeeze you in, you discovered he meant just that, in the tightest sense of the word. Eying the guests sprawled on the floor snoring, he'd push and nudge two recumbent bodies till he cleared a space narrower than a coffin, or, as one victim said, "We were hung two on a peg." Luckier arrivals paid $1 to spend the night on a billiard table, or sitting up in a barber chair, or lying behind a counter wrapped in a buffalo sleigh-robe or his own rosy dreams of riches. "The most favored individual accepts with grateful joy the offer of a one-twentieth interest in a bedroom."

Tenderly reared, well-to-do business men from Boston, Philadelphia and Manhattan slept on half a straw pallet and scratched like commoners. Often the stranger who shared a bed insisted on describing, feverishly, his trials in drilling to the second sand rock. Or he'd moan in his sleep, ". . . sucker rods drawn . . . high driller . . . spud in . . . stratigraphic . . . surface indications."

Meals were even worse, served in three or four shifts, with mobs of hungry men crowding impatiently, waiting their turn. An observer wrote, "When you see a man who wouldn't sell for half a million trying three times in vain to get to the table while a poor digger who happens to understand the ropes gets comfortably fed, you are apt to inquire What's the use?" At first, the more gentlemanly types nearly starved to death, in the wild push by heartier comers for food. But the outdoor life of the oil region (even traveling around on horseback inspecting wells was rugged work) sharpened their appetites and their elbows, and they soon learned to shove and grab.

What they got might be half-baked water biscuits with salt pork, or a few pallid beans swamped in molasses. Steak was so leathery that the uninhibited stood up at table, braced their feet against a chair, and got a purchase on a dull table knife, "whacking the meat like a shoveler dealing with frozen cod." Aficionados carried their own well-honed knives stuck in their boot tops, and after using them to cut up an indigestible hunk, tucked the blade back tidily in their boots.

For all this discomfort and near-hunger, guests were permitted to pay through the nose, as high as $4 a day. If anyone dared to complain, the clerk told him coldly, even scornfully, "This is the oil country, you know."

Anybody who didn't know it must have lacked all five senses. It was a world so foreign that visitors talked constantly of "returning to the States."

No customs or castes were familiar. It was as if a portion of the earth had turned upside down and produced this bewildering new democracy, where no one could be judged by appearances. One critic snapped, "They don't have time to be aristocrats. They don't even have time to change their sheets." Another wrote a few years later:

> That individual right in front of you, this greasy specimen could by one stroke of his pen produce a paper of more value than all your worldly possessions, and that would be honored quickly by any great banking institution. That little man to the left, nearly over his boots in mud, with hands covered with "crude" from the barrels which he is filling, handles more money than you ever saw, and beneath that covering of dirt and oil on the hand which you would now scorn to grasp, there glitters a little sparkler that would delight Tiffany or dazzle the eyes of many a Flora McFlimsey of Madison Square. For the individual is the possessor of a piece of land nearby which monthly returns him an income larger than that received by the President of the United States each year.

Experts (this now included anybody who'd been there a week) sat roasting their boot heels against the box stove in smoky, crowded taverns, while they gave their geological opinions on what caused petroleum, and where it was found. Some explained learnedly, between spurts of tobacco juice onto the muddy floor, that you had to go by "the dip and lay of the land." They said all oil ran downhill underground, and was therefore found only by "criks." Even more interesting, oil was a perennial, like daisies, and would rebloom every year till Kingdom come. Another sect of believers said oil was produced by the steam from buried volcanoes of the carboniferous age.

A grizzled old whaling captain from New Bedford, now living in the oil region, had perhaps the most ingenious theory of all. He always expounded it at Crapo's, because another ex-whaler tended bar there, and the captain emphasized the points of his talk by pounding on the bar with his blackthorn stick with the whalebone handle. Every newcomer who would stand still long enough to listen got an earful of the theory: a large shoal of whales had been stranded in Western Pennsylvania at the time of Noah's flood, and left high and dry there, and the oil borers were now drilling into that blubber.

Even the staunchest whalers seldom accepted this as bona-fide blubber. They were already coming in shoals from Nantucket and New Bedford, to try their luck in the oil country. Melville's *Moby Dick,* published early that decade, was fiction following fact; the catch was getting scarce, and had to be sought too far. As one reporter said, "Now they have come to harpoon Mother Earth."

Animal similes were also dragged in forcibly, to describe the newest oil spouters and show that they were even more dramatic than harpooned whales: "The earth seems to bleed like a mad ox, wrathfully and violently."

The editor of the new Titusville weekly, the *Gazette,* managed to bleed pretty violently himself, in crimson prose. Soon after Drake's strike, this young newspaperman, Jim Burchfield, had moved over from Meadville with a second-hand printing press, and set it up on the second floor over one of the new slapped-up stores, Peter Miller's on South Franklin Street. At nine o'clock one pleasant summer evening, he was working in his office there, correcting proofs, when what sounded like a lynching mob pounded up the stairs and burst in. They had come to tell him that the Williams well, one of a dozen or so Jonah Watson owned a slice of, had been drilled down to a new vein, and had struck, at 145 feet, an absolute sensation. Everybody babbled at once, trying to tell Jim Burchfield, with gestures, what the new well was like. They were proud of having a newspaper at last, and they were noisily determined to help the editor do a proper job, even if they had to bang him over the head with a big story. Like any good newspaperman, he grabbed his hat and took off, with several of his babbling informers.

The Williams-Watson well was next to shoemaker Barnsdall's "lion of the valley," and on the way there, Burchfield passed returning throngs who shouted after him of what they'd just seen. Arriving at the well, the editor became rather gibbering himself: "The coolest nerve could not witness the scene without excitement."

He mentioned the streams of oil overflowing the vat and running along the ground, and then went on, panting:

> We have no language at our command by which to convey to the minds of our readers any adequate idea of the agitated state at the time we saw it. The gas from below was forcing up immense quantities of oil in a fearful manner and attended with noise that was terrifying. . . . When the gas subsided for a few seconds, the oil rushed back down the pipe with a hollow, gurgling sound, so much resembling the struggle and suffocating breathings of a dying man,

as to make one feel as though the earth were a huge giant seized with the pains of death and in its spasmodic efforts to retain a hold on life was throwing all nature into convulsion. During the upheavings of the gas it seemed as if the very bowels of the earth were being all torn out and her sides must soon collapse. At times the unearthly sounds . . . drew one almost to sympathize with earth as though it were animate.

A year or so later, newsmen were doing their pop-eyed best to describe the first real gushers, 3,000 barrels a day, "higher than steeples." They'd be accused of drunkenness or even insanity a good many times, as one improbable event followed another.

But that first year, the baby industry was still so freakishly new that each little well was touted like a three-headed cow. In fact, the first well drilled off Oil Creek got more headlines all over the country than a good many gushers later, because there was a pretty girl involved. A blacksmith in my hometown of Franklin found oil right in his own back yard.

And with that, our town went crazy.

FOUR

————◆◆————

How does your garden flow?

THE EVANS back yard was on the bank of French Creek, a few hundred feet from the spot where a young surveyor named George Washington crossed in December of 1753. Of course he crossed the Delaware too, but the difference is that he didn't fall in there. He fell into French Creek when his canoe overturned in the icy water, and it's a wonder we didn't lose the Father of Our Country right then and there, at the downy age of twenty-one.

He had been sent to western Pennsylvania by Governor Dinwiddie of Virginia to find out what the French were up to, in their forts Le-Boeuf and Presque Isle (later Erie) sixty miles above Franklin, and he was on his way there when he got the dunking in French Creek. He dried out his clothes and spent the night in the only cabin in Franklin. It had been built a few years before by an English gunsmith, John Frazier, who traded with the Seneca Indians and kept records of sales that look slangily up to date now: "Sold Eight Bucks worth of Goods Today." It's still good deer country.

When the French troops moved into the area, Frazier left hurriedly to join the British army, and his cabin was taken over by Captain de Joncaire, who flew the French flag from the ridgepole and soon founded Fort Machault. As Washington's host overnight, he assured the young lieutenant, perhaps a bit condescendingly, that the French would keep on holding this territory.

After the Revolutionary War, the settlement of Franklin was built up around the American fort there, and Commonwealth surveyors laid out the town, handsomely, in 1795, with an extraordinarily wide main thoroughfare worthy of being called Liberty Street.

The town lay mostly in the valley, "a rich bottom abounding in clover," curving around French Creek where it flows into the Allegheny River, encircled with gently rounded hills. The Commonwealth sold off pieces of Franklin's rich bottom quite reasonably; for instance, an Indian, Silver Heels, snapped up three town lots for $29.

I don't know where Silver Heels went, although with that name I assume he went far, but I do know that another resident at that time was a young fellow who later traveled under the name of Johnny Appleseed. He's listed on the Venango County census of 1801 as John Chapman. At the Franklin courthouse, he signed two notes saying:

> For value received I promise to pay Nathaniel Chapman or order the sum of $100 in land or apple trees with interest till paid as witness my hand.
>
> John Chapman

A local Presbyterian minister, Dr. Eaton, who wrote the history of the county, dealt with Johnny tartly: "Of a thriftless disposition. With a few other spirits as restless and discontented as himself, drifted further westward."

Let him go, good riddance to that seedy character, seems to have been Franklin's attitude toward Johnny, and it's true that they already had more trees than they knew what to do with.

By 1859, the pretty public square in the center of town had already been cleared of unwanted stumps, but with plenty of elms left to spread their dappled green shade over anyone strolling across to Elk Street from the United States Hotel or the courthouse. As the county seat, Franklin already had a population of 936, and a settled, respectable air. It looked rather disdainfully on hovel heaps like Cornplanter, six miles up the Allegheny. As a mark of cosmopolitan elegance, Franklinites could even rent a light-trotting sulky at Pinney's Carriage Repository. Several daughters of local merchants and lawyers went to Olome Institute for Young Ladies at Canonsburg, which cost $56.50 a term, with pew rent seventy-five cents extra, and "Each lady will find her own light."

Jimmy Lamberton, one of the half-dozen dry goods merchants in town, advertised such citified wares as Fancy Cold Taffeta Eugenie, Black Shotted Silks and Lace Vizettes, along with Curry Combs. He enticed farmers in by announcing, "Highest Prices Paid for Sheep Pelts." Jimmy was a fine big figure of an Irishman, flamboyant as a shamrock, with the shiniest silk hat and fastest twirling cane around. It is claimed that when he first came to Franklin, he pointed his cane at a turtle ambling along in the mud and roared, "Shure, and what manner of country is this, where a cow turd walks?"

In September of 1859, there were still plenty of turtles on the banks of French Creek, approaching the Evans back yard almost as meanderingly as I do. In the small frame house, James Evans lived with his wife, his son Henry, and a quartet of delectable daughters. Anna, the oldest, was as blond and blue-eyed as her lean, handsome father, but without the blacksmith sinews. All the Evanses complained mildly in dry weather that the water in their back-yard well, seventeen feet deep, tasted of oil. During that summer's fierce drought, it was especially annoying.

But with the news of Drake's well—and every customer bringing a horse to be shod talked of nothing else—Evans thought of his oily-tasting water, and decided to try his luck on something larger than horseshoes. If Uncle Billy Smith could make Drake's tools, then Evans thought he could make his own, but a blacksmith with five children had no cash to spare for materials. William Phipps, who stocked the local hardware store with a jolly, helter-skelter array, everything from nails to accordions and blue vitriol, agreed to furnish the iron on credit. Evans hammered out a set of rough drilling tools on his forge, and he and his son rigged up a spring pole. Henry did the springing or kicking down, and his father guided the drill.

At seventy-two feet down, they struck rich, heavy oil, "black as a stack of ebony cats."

That was just after ten o'clock on a cold, raw November morning.

With four daughters around, and neighbors already watching out the windows, the news went streaking through town like a bevy of greased pigs. Everybody came running. The tanner, Andy Bowman, up the street from Evans, was out in the back alley about to dip a hide, and in his excitement he brought the large hunk of cowhide along, waving it like a battle flag. Reverend Eaton's old sexton at the Presbyterian Church saw Andy charging down the street, heard the yelling, and got so carried away he rang the church bells wildly. (People said afterward he thought the Irish were coming.) By that time, the place was bedlam. Children came tumbling out of the one-room school near the church, followed by little Mr. Dale, their teacher, and a pack of barking dogs. Dr. Robinson rushed to the scene in his stockinged feet. "Women deserted their households without fixing their back hair."

At the courthouse across the town square, Judge John McCalmont was sitting in November session, but when the whoops and hollers penetrated the quiet, oak-paneled precincts, court adjourned "in half the number of seconds that Sut Lovingood's nest of hornets broke up the camp meeting." One of the lawyers who broke out of court that day was a beau of pretty Anna Evans, and when Anna spotted him charging toward the house, she screamed, "Dad's struck ile!"

The whole crowd picked it up, "Dad's struck ile!" And the whole country picked it up almost as fast. This was the first quotable line to come out of the backwoods boom-land, and journalists latched onto it happily. Newspapers extolled blacksmith Evans as "The lucky disciple of Vulcan," and placed Anna's remarks in a tender romantic setting: her simple, devoted, village bumpkin suitor had proposed, and she had turned him down airily, as befitted a new oil heiress, with a shake of her curly blond head and the terse, "Dad's struck ile."

The *Spectator's* editor ignored this prettily curved human-interest angle, although he reported, in one niggardly paragraph, that the Evans well was pumping steadily "at the rate of 50 barrels per day. *This is no exaggeration.*" He was concentrating his news fire that fall on John Brown, who had been captured by the U.S. Marines at Harpers Ferry, after he tried to take over the arsenal. John Brown had been a tanner in our part of the state just above Meadville, for ten years, and as he once wrote his father:

> I have aroused such a feeling toward me in Meadville by shewing
> Anderton's statement [anti-Mason] as leads me for the present to
> avoid going about the streets at evening and alone.

He had moved away in 1834, but older people still remembered
him and the commotion he'd caused, so ordinarily local feeling about
his raid on Harpers Ferry would have run strong, for and against.
But news of one captured Abolitionist couldn't compete with the
frenzy over our brand-new home-grown oil boom. While the editor
thundered that the Black Republicans had built John Brown up as a
liberal hero, and then dropped him after Harpers Ferry, that Black
Republican Horace Greeley was building up our local heroine Anna,
in his paper. A crack New York *Tribune* feature writer, Edmund
Morris, came out to Franklin and wrote, "We had the pleasure of
seeing the young lady whose independence was secured by 'Dad striking ile' and can assure the reader that, from appearance, the unlucky
suitor not only lost a fortune in oil, but a treasure in herself, in being
rejected by the lady; for she seems to be a sweet-tempered and oblig-
ing blue-eyed village belle, an oil princess par excellence."

Fifteen years later, when Anna and her husband, a Franklin furniture dealer named Miles Smith, visited England, some Londoners,
discovering they were from western Pennsylvania, asked eagerly if
they knew the origin of "Dad's struck ile." They knew, all right. By
then, Anna was long since tired of the whole thing, and explained
she'd only said it for a joke. A few catty neighbors insisted it hadn't
been a joke, but that Anna, once her father made money, wanted
to disown her provincial past.

At least three popular songs had been dinging in her ears and
everyone else's. One was "Pa Has Struck Ile":

> I once was unknown by the happy and gay,
> And the friends that I sought did all turn away;
> Our dwelling was plain, and simple our fare,
> And nothing inviting, of course, could be there.
> But now, what a change! Our house is so grand,
> Not one is so fine throughout the whole land,
> And we can now live in the very best style,
> And it's simply because my "Pa has struck ile."

'Tis strange what attention a fortune does bring,
At home or abroad how friends to one cling;
And now even strangers are courteous and bland,
To pay their addresses or take by the hand.
When before, on a walk if a neighbor I'd meet,
Cold was his look and quick his retreat,
But now in my carriage he greets with a smile
And it's simply because my "Pa has struck ile."

Another of the Anna-inspired songs was more rock-and-roll-out-the-barrel:

Pe-tro-le-um
Pe-tro-le-um
We must all have some.
Fill our barrels up to the top!
Hurry up! Don't stop!
They say all round where you may go
Just give a tap and oil will flow
Best of all, it's worth your while
To come where I've struck ile.

But it was Anna's dad who made what is still my favorite remark. When a wealthy Ohio lumberman who had rushed over to see the excitement offered to buy out the blacksmith for $40,000, James Evans said sturdily, "This is my well. If you want one, go dig your own."

At least half the townspeople were already doing just that, or trying to. Derricks went up in gardens and barnyards. Quite a few Franklinites still kept chickens or geese, a cow and a pig out back, but the beasts and fowls were shoved aside ruthlessly, as their owners dug. The pigs must have been confused to see people rooting around even in public spots, because they themselves had been restrained by a town ordinance from running hog-wild. Several pigs had ignored this and gone to dig in the park, and the *Spectator* reported, "The proper officers, armed with the authority of the commonwealth, made a descent upon the swinish multitude. After sundry evolutions, which seemed like a mixture of light-horse and infantry tactics, they succeeded in forming a line of march. The pigs became desperate and the scene highly exciting. Some half-dozen of the swine made their escape and three, better calculated for bacon than a footrace, went to the 'pound.' "

Now the pigs had to watch resentfully while amateur operators dug any old place, even in the park. They had barely scratched the surface when the Hoover well just outside Franklin came in, the third week in December, and envious townspeople longed for a Christmas present just like it.

By then, John Brown's body was quiet in death after hanging, and the *Spectator's* editor had time to focus his sights closer to home. The first local company, the Franklin Oil and Mining Company, "which comprises the leading business men of our place," had already been formed, and solidly, with ex-Congressman Arnold Plumer as president. Plumer had been one of the behind-the-cloakroom powers who arranged old James Buchanan's nomination, so the little matter of sinking a well must have seemed simple. The *Spectator,* noting the activities of Plumer and his colleagues, called attention to A. N. Hood's advertisement for an engine, "Just the thing for boring," and added approvingly, "The Company in this place have ordered an engine from this establishment. . . . They have secured an experienced operator."

Their well, drilled beside a black walnut tree almost on top of Evans', and four times as deep, came in early the next year, 1860. Stock in the company went from $100 a share to $1,000, in a week. One of the original stockholders, John Hanna, was also a land agent, and on behalf of Western clients, he put a notice in the *Spectator* that still makes me swagger almost a hundred years later:

**6,400 ACRES OF LAND IN TEXAS
FOR SALE OR EXCHANGE.**

It pleases me mightily, pardner, to think of Texans who were hankerin' to git up to Pennsylvania and strike oil.

The small garden variety of operators in Franklin had already discovered that drilling a well wasn't like digging for fishing worms; it took a good bit more money than they'd bargained for. Now everybody was trying to raise cash. Merchant Jimmy Lamberton, in place

of his usual affable advertising of "Highest Prices for Sheep Pelts,"
took a larger space in the *Spectator* to dun his delinquent customers:

LOOK HERE—I Want Money and Must Have It

> All persons indebted to me by Judgement, Note or Book Account
> will please call and pay up. Those having unsettled accounts must
> *immediately* settle same. If this Notice is not attended to, I shall
> force payment without respect to persons.

The townspeople were used to Jimmy Lamberton's florid ways, and
were in fact very fond of him, but it was another, less loud Lamberton, no relation by blood or begorrah, whom they trusted with all
their cash. Suddenly citizens like blacksmith Evans, and the farmers
leasing their land along Oil Creek, and the proprietors of swarming
hotels, found their hands full of unaccustomed money, and a need to
keep it handy. Even the well-to-do citizens like Arnold Plumer wanted
their funds where they could grab them in a hurry, to buy up a lease,
instead of going by coach to the nearest bank, twenty-five miles away
in Meadville. In this emergency, they turned to Robert Lamberton,
who presided over The Cheap Store, a sturdy calico-and-galluses sort
compared to silk-hat Jimmy's Fancy Cold Taffeta. A few customers
asked the quiet, dependable proprietor to keep their cash, as a favor,
in his big safe. Soon a steady stream of people from all over the
county were bringing their money to The Cheap Store, to stow in
Robert Lamberton's safe and be credited for the sum on his books.
But everybody had so much money, including the proprietor (he was
a stockholder in the first oil company) that he built a fine new brick
house and used one room of it for banking. Finally he had to give
over a whole building to a bank. One of the most dashing local oil
men, Thomas King, used to ride past on horseback, fling a wad of
greenbacks or a fistful of gold pieces in through the door of the bank,
then ride on without bothering to wait till the scurrying clerk had
picked up the deposit and counted it. This was probably the first
drive-in bank, millionaire style.

One of the earliest and biggest depositors on Robert Lamberton's
books was the rocketing lawyer-promoter, George Bissell, who had
deserted, forever, his New York law office over Appleton's bookstore.

(Mr. Appleton must have been happy to see him and his leaky barrels go.) Bissell had managed to get good leases in Venango County even if he did miss out on the silk-dress deal, and had settled in Franklin and started the first big barrel factory, across French Creek from the cemetery. Unlike that crude village Cornplanter—alias Oil City—Franklinites didn't go around digging up bodies, even in the midst of the boom; the cemetery was one of the few places they didn't plant derricks in. Of the hundred wells drilled in and around Franklin that year, not counting those scratched at the start of the race, fifteen were producers. Most of this oil was hauled by teamsters to Erie, and shipped from there to New York. Already, fifty or sixty refineries throughout the Northern states that had been distilling coal oil for lamp kerosene were switching to the new petroleum. It had to travel to them in barrels, and coopers couldn't begin to keep up with the frantic demand. Bissell, as usual, had sniffed the need and acted at the right moment. When oil was selling for anywhere from $14 to $20 a barrel, the barrel itself cost $1.50 to $3.

When other producers were screeching in frustration because they couldn't get barrels at any price, Bissell the manufacturer supplied Bissell wells with his product, so that he met himself coming and going. In fact, the ex-lawyer was becoming involved in so many operations that he seemed to split like an amoeba and multiply. One of his new leases was in partnership with the wealthy Ohioan, Frederic Prentice, who had been told by James Evans, "Go dig your own."

The Dad's-Struck-Ile well was a steady customer for Bissell barrels. James Evans retired contentedly from blacksmithing, and although he never made much more than the impetuous lumberman had offered him in one well-swoop, he had the satisfaction of having dug his own, and tended it lovingly. With profits from his first sale of oil, he had paid back storekeeper William Phipps and bought an engine for pumping. But what exasperated his envious neighbors was that he never kept the pump going at night. They wanted him to work the well fast and hard, for all it was worth. Instead, he treated it like a good horse, giving it a nice rest between runs. The well seemed to appreciate this considerate, tranquil treatment, and although it eventually dropped to a tenth of its peak yield, it was still a good provider. This was the first of the heavy black petroleum that is still famous as the best lubricating oil in the world. The Galena Refinery, started in Franklin later, had a cheery way of acclaiming its virtues:

> Have you a somewhat cranky wife
> Whose temper's apt to broil?
> To ease the matrimonial strife
> Just lubricate when trouble's rife—
> Pour on Galena oil!

Opposite the Evans back yard, on the other side of French Creek, there was a forty-acre, scrubby evergreen tract called Hill Point that nobody wanted, least of all the owner, Lowry De Woody. Lowry was a big man with long red hair he tossed around like a lion's mane, and a roaring voice. When he tried to persuade Frankliners to buy his land for $1,500, he was eloquent, all right, but he didn't have the glib persuasion of a promoter. Once he served a term in the State Legislature at Harrisburg, as a Democratic Greenbacker, and horrified ward heelers by blurting out the truth about bribes and tricky deals. When the Vagrancy Act, more casually known as the Tramp Bill, was up for passage, he went rushing down the center aisle of the State capitol hollering, "If Jesus Christ were on earth today, this monstrous bill would jerk him as a vagrant and dump him into the lockup."

With that same directness, when he was trying to sell Hill Point, he admitted freely that he wasn't offering it as fine oil land. Hell, no, he was simply trying to dump it as timberland and get some cash so he could lease a piece of low-lying creek property to drill on. But at that stage, everybody knew oil ran downhill, so they too wanted low-lying acres, and the outspoken Lowry was out of luck. Several years later, he sold it for the original low price, to some operators who were buying everything up or down dale, and the fact is that Hill Point turned out to be oozing with the wherewithal for a dozen oil fortunes. James Bleakley, Daniel Grimm and William Mattern were three of the Franklinites who got a rich slice of Lowry De Woody's hilly white elephant.

One well eventually drilled there created the oddest sensation of all. What happened was that the driller felt his tools drop suddenly, down, down, down, six or eight feet. He was pop-eyed, thinking that with that deep a crevice before he'd even gotten down to the first sand rock, it must mean a whole lake of oil. He drew up his tools, sniffed, and was even more pop-eyed to smell not oil, but beer. He tasted the amber stuff; it was beer. Ten times he ran the sand pump down. Ten times it came up foaming with beer. A toolie ran to tell the owners, who ordered the tubing put in, and began dreaming of how they'd be the first beer barons in all Venango. It was true they had wanted oil, but this strike was so deliciously different it would make them famous, beer with a headline on it.

They were already at the well with a whole crowd of enthralled and thirsty spectators, watching the treasure foam up, when a puffing German, as fat and red as a sausage, came clambering up the hill shrieking, *"Gott in Himmel.* You vas broke ober Grossman's vault."

Brewer Phil Grossman had cut a tunnel into the hillside, to store his stock in a cool place, and the drilling tools had stoved in the head of a vast tun of beer.

For the owners and their well-wishers, this discovery was worse than flat beer. When two weeks afterward, drilling in a slightly different spot on the hill, the owners only struck *Oil,* it must have been quite an anticlimax.

The most unusual saloon in town was under Hill Point too, called the Cave. Unlike those pseudo pirate dens and nautical bars that try whimsically to look like their names, this saloon didn't try for atmosphere; it *was* a cave, deep and dark, with subterranean refreshments served by the watchful-eyed proprietor, John Minich.

I wish I could say it was the toughest joint in the whole oil region, but as a loyal ex-Franklinite, all I can say is that it sounds like the toughest. Actually, our town never achieved any such rip-roaring rowdiness as Titusville and Oil City (before their indignant citizens formed vigilante committees) and it never came within a wicked mile of the wide-open boomtowns that mushroomed around the big wells. As the county seat, it was the nesting place of lawyers; no gamblers or pimps felt at ease doing business in such a law-infested town, and they soon moved on up to Oil Creek.

Our local rivermen weren't by any means Fauntleroys; one night they tossed John Wilkes Booth out of a dance hall down on the Allegheny, because he came there slumming and they thought he looked too dressed up and smarmy. When his accomplices in the assassination went on trial a year later, the testimony contained depositions from Franklin men who had treated him more tenderly.

Even when we did get a criminal to hang in Franklin, it was always some other town's villain. In our town, to get to a hanging you had to be invited, and very politely, too:

OFFICE OF
THE SHERIFF OF THE COUNTY OF VENANGO

Franklin Pa., Oct. 22

Sir:

You have been selected as one of twelve men to witness the execution of Thomas McCarty sentenced to be hanged on the 28th day of October agreeably to the seventy-sixth section of the Act of the General Assembly, approved March 30th, A.D. 1860, entitled, "An Act to consolidate, revise and amend the Penal Laws of the Commonwealth relating to Penal Proceedings and Pleadings."

Please notify me as promptly as possible of your willingness or unwillingness to attend said execution.

Respectfully,
P. R. Gray
Sheriff

The tower which still rises above our jail was built especially to accommodate early hangees like McCarty. A friend of my father's, Frank Williams, had the Ford agency and garage in town when I was a child, and he said that when he was sheriff he'd presided over the last hanging in the county. With real thrift, he had saved the rope, and was using it to tow cars.

To get back to the first victim—McCarty was a mean, grubby, kill-for-money man who murdered a farmer named Barry up French Creek, but Franklin saloons were full of transients who would have done almost anything *but* kill, for lease money. They crowded into the Cave, the Cornucopia, and the Terrapin on Turtle Street which was faster than it sounds. But the Keystone, kept by Henry Dexter, was the worst dive of the lot, at least that's what the son of an early oil man tells me his father told him.

His father was a New Englander named Henry James (no, this is another Henry James) who gave up whaling and came to the oil region early, and became a well-known operator. When I asked the son, Frank James, if his father had described specific deviltry at the Keystone, he looked at me thoughtfully, decided I wasn't up to the kind of revelations I was asking for, and said with finality, "Just say it was tough." To distract me from further foolish questions he described how Henry James' partner, Reuben Painter, got caught in the bull wheel at a well, and whirled around like some poor wretch in the Spanish Inquisition. He was dead before they could get him off.

The other Henry James was linked to our section in a more tenuous way. He is supposed to have based a character in *Portrait of a Lady* on a beautiful Meadville woman, but he only knew her in Paris.

When the non-lit'ry Henry James came to Franklin, the Kinnear House on the square and the Mansion House at the far end of French Creek bridge, were two of the respectable inns strangers were crowding into. The Rural House down on Liberty Street didn't look rural any more; both it and the United States Hotel had their corridors jammed with cots, like a hospital in plague time. The Lamberton House (Cheap Store Robert had branched into innkeeping, as well as banking) advertised, "Careful hostlers always in attendance," which makes me suspect horses got better treatment than humans, and better beds.

If you rode into town from the north or Meadville direction, the first place you came to, after crossing the bridge, was Levi Dodd's store. He had been a farmer and he still catered to farmers, with a large supply of churns and buskins. So it's suitable that when he formed the second oil company in Franklin, he called it the Farmers and Mechanics Company. What seems more surprising is where they struck oil: in the yard of our Common School. Probably the school children didn't get much work done *that* spring.

Pamphleteer Thomas Gale saw this well around April of 1860, and he was much more delighted with the educational aspects than the well itself; one-tenth of the yield went to the support of Franklin's Common Schools:

> By making this provision, the city, or rather Borough Fathers, have evinced in the best manner their *fatherly* care for their children and for succeeding generations. Many a child will rise up and pour its gushing gratitude upon them.

By the time I went to school in Franklin, nobody told us we should rise up and pour our gushing gratitude. The well was long since buried and forgotten, like part-owner Levi Dodd, but that wasn't the way Pamphleteer Gale had envisioned it in 1860, when he wrote:

> At its present rate of yield, the well will give the schools a barrel of oil every day it is operated. This ought to net $5000, or $6000, per annum. The prospect therefore is, that Franklin will enjoy as good educational advantages as almost any other place in the state. This of itself, and especially in connection with its beautiful situation, the good morals and intelligence of its citizens, must render it a desirable spot to those seeking a place of residence for their families.

The man responsible for the school's tithe of royalties, Levi Dodd, was one of the most fiercely moral men who ever settled their families in Franklin. He started the first Presbyterian Sunday School and poured large, forcible doses of religion into his children like castor oil. His son Sam was one of the brightest pupils in the public school —ten years before his father drilled for oil in the playground there. I doubt if Sam played even Blindman's Buff, because he was a dud at sports and games. What he did best was debating. After graduating from Jefferson College below Pittsburgh (now Washington and Jefferson) he had studied law with James Kerr and been admitted to the Venango Bar just in time for the oil boom, at the age of twenty-three. He was a big, clumsy, overgrown bear-cub of a man with a funny little mustache that would have better fitted a poodle. Townspeople agreed he was smart as a whip, but too free-thinking, and at first they felt safer giving their business to old, established law firms like Church & Heydrick.

Judge Heydrick watched out for his oil clients' interests with a wily eye, as shown in this letter from an exasperated man who was trying to arrange a deal:

Franklin, April 18

Dear Alf,

I brought Sam McTate down here today to get the two deeds from him but could not get one made that I would accept. Heydrick would not let him sign one that would specify the particular well from which he should receive the tenth of the oil, but rather claimed that it called for one-tenth of the whole. . . . Heydrick says he sold 47/50 of 2/5 of that property for $60,000. . . . It is not necessary for Mother to sign a deed made by us.

In haste,
J. Lamb jr.

Reading it, I had a feeling that this little Lamb needed his mother along, in dealing with Heydrick. Any lawyer who can sell 47/50 of 2/5 of a property for $60,000 is pretty clever, but there's a local legend about the time Judge Heydrick outsmarted himself. At the height of the buying frenzy, he and his brothers were offered one million dollars by a feverish New York syndicate, for the family farm at Utica on the way to Meadville. It was called Custologa Town because Chief Custologa was buried there, and there's also an indestructible rumor that Chief Geyasutha, whom Washington called the Hunter, was buried in the same lot, with his camp kettle filled with soup, his much-used tomahawk and his rifle, all placed beside him in his grave. When Judge Heydrick turned down the chance to sell this place for a million, I doubt if he was too sentimental to allow the Indian chief (or chiefs) to be dug up or drilled on. He just thought he'd hold out for a better price, and that's where he got fooled, because Utica, Pennsylvania, proved dry territory, and the buying fever moved to richer fields.

The Judge's brothers did very well in oil anyway, with their Wolverine company, in less haunted spots than Indian burial grounds. But to get back to young lawyer Dodd (Stick with me. I've laid a modest time-fuse that won't go off for another few paragraphs) Sam never bought so much as a square foot of oil land. If Judge Heydrick was a Pillar of Society, Sam was a blaster of pillars. It was whispered that he helped slaves on the underground railway get through Pennsylvania on their way to Canada. It was also said that Levi Dodd had given his children such an overdose of religion Sam had turned atheist in rebellion. He even wrote poetry. When his parody of Byron's "Isles of Greece . . ." appeared in the *Spectator,* townspeople were divided on whether it was comical or shockingly disrespectful. It began: "The land of Grease! The land of Grease, where burning oil is loved and sung; Where flourish arts of sale and lease"—and got even closer to home in stanza four:

> I sat upon the rocky brow
> Which o'erlooks Franklin—far-famed town;
> A hundred derricks stood below
> And many a well of great renown.
> I counted them at break of day
> And when the sun set where were they?
>
> They were still there. But where art thou
> My dry-hole? On the river-shore
> The engine stands all idle now,
> The heavy auger beats no more;
> And must a well of so great cost
> Be given up and wholly lost?
>
> 'Tis awful when you bore a well
> Down in the earth six hundred feet,
> To find that not a single smell
> Comes up your anxious nose to greet;
> For what is left the bored one here?
> For Grease a wish; for Grease a tear! . . .
>
> Place me in Oil Creek's rocky dell,
> Though mud be deep and prices high;
> There let me bore another well
> And find petroleum or die.
> No more I'll work this dry-hole here;
> Dash down that cup of lager-beer.

He was odd for sure, by town standards. When a fellow lawyer ran into his office to tell him jubilantly that Cyrus Field's transatlantic cable had finally been laid successfully, he was startled at Sam's bitter reaction. "Life's already too harried," Sam said. "It won't be worth living unless we stop making inventions to annihilate time and space. Why do we have to tie continents together with electric bands? Why can't we get along the old way?"

Even his most clacking critics agreed he didn't care a hoot about money, that he practiced law and took all kinds of cases for the sheer love of it. When the big railroads began moving in, to carry oil freight, and took right of way through farmers' property willy-nilly, Sam Dodd handled so many cases for farmers he was called the Poor Man's Friend. Just the same, his practice swelled so lucratively that when he was still paying $8 a month rent for his house, he paid six times that for a new office to hold his onrush of clients. Frankliners always called him by his first initials—S.C.T., Esseeetee—which had a hissing sound in the mouths of those who still considered him too radical. I mention this because later Sam Dodd became the head counsel for Standard Oil, and drew up Standard's first trust, on one sheet of paper.

A young Cleveland produce-commission merchant, John D. Rockefeller, had become interested in oil, as you may have heard. After he and a partner started a Cleveland refinery in 1863 (more about this later. It became Standard Oil in 1873) he was often in Franklin, and had a shipping office down by the French Creek bridge. One of the places he boarded at was Anderson Dodd's—Sam's brother. Nobody ever accused Mr. Rockefeller, as they accused Sam, of not caring a hoot about money. And he could spot a good man early, radical or no, from the opposite side of the fence.

Mr. Rockefeller had one old, shabby suit of clothes he kept just for visits to the oil region, and he'd even pitch in and help load barrels. But on the Sabbath he refused to have anything to do with business; he dressed up in his non-oil suit, and went to church. One Sunday morning in spring, as he was putting on his black frock coat, one of his employees came running in to Mrs. Sarah Mayes', where he was boarding that visit, to tell Rockefeller the river was rising and threatened to carry all their loaded barrels away. All the townsmen concerned with oil business, and some who were just concerned in lending a neighborly hand in emergencies, were already down on the riverbanks, helping move the barrels to higher ground. Panting, the man urged his employer to hurry down there. Mr. Rockefeller put on his Sunday hat calmly and said No, he was going to church. What really irritated the town was that although plenty of valuable oil was lost that day to the rampaging river, not one barrel of Mr. Rockefeller's was touched. If this was God's reward for his righteous Sabbath ways, several Franklinites thought that God should have taken a sharper look around on weekdays. But Mrs. Mayes and Anderson Dodd's wife both liked their boarder fine. Anyone who only wants bread and milk for supper—and that's what Mr. Rockefeller asked for—is apt to please overworked landladies.

At least half the townspeople opened their houses and made a tidy income on paying guests, during the jam-packed period. One of these was Widow Sarah Webber, the postmistress. In the spring of 1860, four years before John Wilkes Booth took over her front bedroom, Franklin was already so crowded that the Widow Webber, as post-mistress, was listing dozens of unclaimed letters in the *Spectator*. When I look over those names now, names so unfamiliar to Franklin —Catherine Boozer, Sophia Brig, Jasper Slaymake—I long to know what happened to them. Did Miss Boozer and Miss Brig really start for the oil country, and get lost on the way? Or lost more hopelessly in a free-and-easy? But weren't they rather doomed from childhood, with names like Boozer and Brig? And Jasper Slaymake? I have learned from an unreliable source that he changed his name to O'Shaughnessey, and drilled happily ever after.

While the *Spectator* was listing the unclaimed letters of oil drifters, suddenly the editor himself decided that oil was almost as newsworthy as Black Republicans. More than that, he now acted like the proud manager, or even the inventor, of the oil business. A large bland an-nouncement under the paper's masthead stated: "Persons leasing or sub-leasing Oil Lands will find the best printed forms at the *Spectator* office."

He printed a pleased account of the superiority of Venango oil over coal oil: "The lamp burning the Venango Oil will give a light equal to *Seven* candles, while the lamp burning the Coal Oil gives a light equal to only *five* candles." When this was picked up and reprinted by other papers, without giving credit, he blasted these snip-and-paste rivals in a snappish editorial headed:

RENDER UNTO SCISSORS
THE THINGS THAT ARE SCISSORS

He was even fiercer in defending the reputation of the infant prod-igy, more like an aroused mother tiger. When the Pittsburgh *Dispatch* announced: "The Oil fever is said to be subsiding very rapidly. Parties are terribly scared if not badly hurt who but a little while ago were perfectly sanguine of large fortunes," in answer he snarled editorially: "These stories are doubtless started by those who are deeply interested in the manufacture of Coal Oil. . . . Instead of being pumped dry, the Wells are now improving both in quality and quantity. Oil is now a fixed institution. It presents to all an avenue of wealth."

In the adjoining column, he made it clear that the Black Republicans were the avenue to the poorhouse, if by any horrible mistake they got into power in the coming Presidential election of 1860. As their convention opened that summer in Chicago, he commented, "The collection of animals in Noah's ark falls far short of the collection of animals that will be exhibited at the great Chicago Sanhedrin. . . . There will be Mr. Seward, the originator of all the political platitudes of his party, and whose doxology commences with 'the Irrepressible Conflict' and ends with John Brown. If the nomination is disposed of at auction, Mr. Seward will be the highest bidder."

Two weeks later he had to comment through clenched teeth on the nomination of Lincoln:

> One of the most delightfully bewitching romances of the day is presented in "The Life and Doings of Abe Lincoln." It is beautiful, excelling anything from the pens of Cobb, Ned Buntline, or any of the writers of flash literature. A poor little "orphling" without any father or mother or anybody else, starts out in life with nothing to get a living with but his axe, and mauls and splits enough rails to make himself famous.
>
> Then he quits the rail business and becomes a lawyer. He makes the bar split its sides laughing at his jokes.
>
> He goes to the Illinois Legislature and rails at the Democratic party.
>
> He runs for the Senate, and "goes down" with a heavy fall.
>
> He is nominated for President and anxiously awaits the results.

The editor, now a good bit more anxious than Mr. Lincoln, was impatient with men who didn't see their country's danger, and wagged their tongues on nonpolitical subjects. After an overnight tour of new wells, he complained, "We laid our course for Cherrytree and the

house of Richard Irwin. The conversation here, until the hour for retiring, was all about *oil,* with now and then some side remarks about
oil, by way of preventing the talk from being too monotonous."

But he was a loyal enough home booster to take a pot shot at
Titusville, which, as I've already mentioned, lay just over the bound-
ary in Crawford County: "It is a thriving little village, and owes its
progress to *Venango* oil." (The italics are mine, but I feel sure he
would approve the emphasis.) "The town is irregular and lying
around loose."

In August, he reprinted a piece from the Auburn, New York,
Advertiser, datelined Franklin, Venango County, and headlined:

A YANKEE EDITOR VISITS YE OIL REGION, TAKETH YE FEVER AND WRITETH A LETTER

I hardly dare to record what I have actually witnessed for fear
our readers will charge me with an attempt to practise a fraud
and deception upon them. I will, nevertheless, proceed to note down
what I know from *personal* observation to be *true.* Arriving in
the village of Franklin on Thursday, the 12th inst., I have spent
five *working* days in visiting the various wells in successful operation . . .

Two wells have favorably developed themselves since our arrival
here. The owners had reached to nearly the depth at which oil is
found, and trembled with anxiety as to the result.—They were men
in very moderate circumstances, and if they failed after spending
three or four hundred dollars in boring it would be a serious loss to
them. Their anxiety, therefore, for the result, may be imagined.
On Friday morning the owners of this well would not have been
considered responsible for a debt of five hundred dollars. On Friday
afternoon they could have obtained credit to the amount of
Twenty Thousand Dollars.—They had found oil, and in a moment
had stepped from *Poverty to Wealth.* . . .

California never, in its palmiest days, offered as great induce-
ments to men seeking fortunes as the oil regions in Venango
County.

Probably California never slapped down its *nouveaux riches* as
hard as one Franklin storekeeper did. This was George McClellan, a
burry man whose grocery was on Liberty Street facing the square's

watering trough. The wife of a new oil king came in one day, rustling her city-bought bombazine, and with her nose very high and dainty, she asked for a dozen eggs.

"You get most of your groceries in Pittsburgh now, don't you?" McClellan asked.

The lady nodded haughtily.

"Then go get your eggs in Pittsburgh," George snapped.

It was quite a deflated oil queen who slunk out of there.

The *Spectator* was concerned with a different kind of royalty, the summer of 1860: "It is rumored that our Borough Fathers are going to give the Prince of Wales an invitation to visit our town and see the oil operations, when he arrives in this country."

Not even Mr. Greeley of the New York *Tribune* ever claimed that the Prince of Wales might come to Oil Creek.

The one night the spirited young Prince of Wales got loose from the British Minister, his chaperon in New York, it is rumored he paid a visit to John Allen's house on Water Street, acknowledged on all sides to be the raciest place in the city. But I think the Prince might have had more fun if he'd got to the oil region's honky-tonks. When Petroleum Centre mushroomed a year or so later, halfway between Oil City and Titusville, a visiting reporter said that "dance houses there, where sharpers and prostitutes flourished with no fear of human or divine law, in the metropolis of rum and debauchery, made John Allen's Mabille and Billy McGlory's Armory Hall [a Bowery dive] look like Sunday School models."

The *Spectator's* editor had no time to brood over the Prince of Wales avoiding us, because he was following the Presidential campaign tensely. His only comment on Lincoln being elected was:

> Our Black Republican friends look joyful—something like a boy who has just found a three-cent piece. It is not true that barbers in town charge Democrats any more for shaving than formerly. The length of face is compensated by a corresponding reduction in width. It may not be out of place to state here that there will be another Presidential election in 1864.

The Republicans were in! Oil prices tumbled. But nothing could keep down so lively and upshooting an industry, not even Republicans. Wells kept on going down—eight hundred by the next summer —and oil kept coming up, more lushly than ever dreamed of. Even the Civil War didn't stop it, for more than brief emergency periods. And oil was to be an economic lifesaver, as exports boomed. Instead of sending our much-needed gold abroad, to buy war materials, we sent oil. At home, perhaps it was most important as a morale booster, a spectacular new lottery, buoying war-torn Northerners with hopes of a golden prize. When Methodist Bishop Simpson of Washington preached on American Progress, Lincoln said to him afterward, chiding him teasingly for an important omission, "Bishop, you didn't strike ile."

So Lincoln knew it was one of the country's great blessings, but the editor of the oil county's paper certainly didn't return the compliment. He regarded the new President as an unnecessary evil. The week war was declared, in April of 1861, the *Spectator* said, "Our country will be a hissing scorn in the eyes of the world. Could we not have lived together in peace? We could have retained the border States and still been great and powerful." Brooding over the surrender of Fort Sumter, the editor went on, "The Flag of the Union is dishonored at the hands of this wicked and feeble administration. If Mr. Lincoln esteemed it his duty to reinforce Fort Sumter, he should have done it at whatever cost or sacrifice. There should have been no child's play."

For weeks, he ran this ominous masthead: "Our Platform—Mr. Lincoln is not the U.S. Government. The government is ours and we do not owe allegiance to him. Mr. Lincoln's term of office is short and fleeting; the government, we hope, will last forever."

Most of the townspeople couldn't have felt so virulently, because the *Spectator* had terse notices of mass meetings "of citizens patriotic to the Union."

The President called for sixteen regiments from Pennsylvania, the highest of any state but New York. Fifteen hundred men from Venango County alone went to fight, for $16 a month plus food and clothing. But the wartime government was still so disorganized at the start that our county, like many others, raised money to buy uniforms and pay a soldier's bounty, usually several hundred dollars. Oil men gave lavishly to these funds. Some of them, with even more willingness, paid a $300 exemption fee or hired a substitute to fight. Whether they knew it yet or not, they were serving in an essential industry.

But from the fall of Fort Sumter on, Pennsylvanians took their share—and more—of the fighting. It was remarked cheerfully that recruits from the oil regions would make the best soldiers because they were already so used to drilling.

FIVE

The big squirt

THREE days after the fall of Fort Sumter, a small, lively man with stick-out ears, cowlicked brown hair, and a shy, enchantingly sweet smile, sat having supper in the shanty-like hotel of a new oil settlement that would one day be named after him. Henry Rouse was thirty-seven years old, a bachelor, with the biggest following of children of any man around. The pockets of his rumpled suit bulged stickily with licorice and peppermints, and small friends surrounded him like a Good Humor Man. They scrambled up for rides on his big black mare, tagged him on foot, and listened saucer-eyed to his stories. With grownups, he was still bothered sometimes by the stammer that had made him give up a law career, but with children it vanished magically.

Stammer or no, Henry Rouse had done brilliantly in business and politics. He'd had a flourishing country store at Enterprise, five miles from Titusville, and later became Jonah Watson's chief rival as a phenomenally successful young lumberman. With confidence bolstered by lumber wealth, he licked his stammer enough to run for the General Assembly, in 1858. His loudest, bitterest opponent was Jonah Watson. Jonah didn't want to run himself, but he didn't want that bantamweight Henry getting more kudos.

In spite of all Jonah's in-fighting, Rouse was so popular he won the election by a fat majority. His constituents, seeing the new schools and bridges he brought them, were of the gratified belief that here was one politician who performed more than he promised. The blunt Jonah decided he'd made a bonehead mistake in opposing so good a man; when he ran into Henry with a group of friends, in Titusville, he came up and offered his big hand, towering over the slender, boyish Rouse. "Let's forget the old score," he boomed.

Henry said, "I can f-f-forget and f-f-forgive all b-b-but one thing."

"What's that?" Jonah asked.

Henry, with a quick wink at the bystanders, said, "Your s-s-story b-b-before the election, that I was a c-c-crazy spiritualist. If I find you s-s-set that story in mmmm-motion, I'll never f-f-forgive you." Then he grinned and held out his hand to the chastened Jonah. Their circle of listeners grinned even more broadly, enjoying a private joke. Of all the unfriendly stories Jonah had circulated about Henry, at least he wasn't responsible for that one. As everybody in town knew, Jonah's wife was a fanatic about spiritualism, and dinned it into her husband so constantly that to humor her he sometimes consulted clairvoyants about where he should drill his next well. Once he told a throaty Oil City spiritualist that if she persuaded the spirits to pick him a good spot, she would get, as her bonus, the first day's receipts from the well. She got $2,002. But with all Jonah's successes, he eventually earned the dubious reputation of drilling more dry holes than anyone else in the business, and it may have been because the spirits moved him too often—in the wrong direction. Or his wife's spirits, rather.

Henry Rouse was never guided by any spirit but his own, and it seemed to be infallible. He had taken a share of shoemaker William Barnsdall's well, the next strike after Drake's, and had been rolling up lucky hits ever since. His largest leased holdings were on the Buchanan farm, four miles above Oil City; two of Rouse's partners in this venture were storekeepers Sam Brown and John Mitchell, who had sold Drake his first spikes and chain.

The slapdash settlement that had grown up near the wells was named Buchananville, after the farmer, but nobody wanted to board with him if they could help it. Rouse lived with the family of the storekeeper, Thomas Morean, whose small daughters Maggie and Eva were envied by all their playmates because they had Henry right in their house, and could even wangle more stories from him at bedtime.

They weren't going to get any stories that April evening, because Henry was having supper in the village at the Anthony Hotel, with his cashier George Dimick. The first real details on Fort Sumter had appeared in the Titusville *Gazette* that day, and the two men were discussing Major Anderson's surrender. Rouse, with his usual warm perception, said that Anderson had been put in a terrible fix, a Southerner loyal to the Union but dreading to fire on compatriots even in defense of a crucial Southern fort.

They had just finished supper when a worker came in, oil splattered and panting, to tell them that the driller of the Little and Merrick well, in which Henry had a large share, had struck "a monstrous vein of oil."

George Dimick went off at a run to get teamsters. If the flow was as big as it sounded, there'd be plenty to haul away. Henry Rouse and several other men hurried to the well, and joined the jubilant crowd gathering there. Rouse went into the derrick to congratulate the driller, Mr. Page, on his spectacular strike. Mr. Page estimated they'd have 2,400 barrels in the next twenty-four hours, and Rouse said gaily to the friends nearest him, "Well, I'm a dang sight richer tonight than I was this morning."

In the murky, humid April dusk, as they stood watching the golden geyser, a streak of flame leaped from a nearby well. There was an explosion that sounded like a barrage of heavy artillery. (Villagers who heard it from a distance had a bewildered notion the Civil War had already moved onto their soil.) Instantly, fire engulfed an acre of oil-soaked ground. Two wells and their wooden vats blazed up. A hundred just-filled barrels burst. Farmer Buchanan's barn, where more oil, and grain, were stored, blazed next. Oil from the well spurted seventy feet into the air, a pillar of flame topped by a weirdly white light, and kept spraying fresh fuel. Of the hundred or more people there, at least thirty were caught within the blazing circle. George Dimick, who arrived just after the fire started, wrote later: "So numerous were the victims and so conspicuous as they rushed out, enveloped in flame, that it would not be exaggeration to compare them to a rapid succession of shots from an immense Roman candle."

Henry Rouse, caught at the white-hot center of fire by the derrick, managed to stagger far enough away to throw some valuable papers, and his wallet, to safety. He took a few more steps, collapsed, and buried his face in the mud, to keep from breathing the fumes. Then he got up, a human pyre, and walked another six feet, before he fell again.

Most of the onlookers in the outer circle had been knocked down and stunned by the force of the explosion, or seared by the far-reaching oil spray, but they forgot their own injuries in heroic, frantic attempts to reach the men trapped in flames. Some had died instantly. One of the dead carried out was identified by the gold watch melting in a stream down his side. Another poor wretch thought he was already in Hell, and screamed out delirious warnings before he died, calling friends by name and begging them never to sin again. "You must listen," he moaned. "Take heed from one lost in eternal hell-fire."

Two workers dragged Henry Rouse out, and carried him to a toolie's shanty. Most of his body was burned to the bone. Only a few shreds of his clothing were left, and parts of his high boots. For the next four hours, he lay on the cot gasping for breath and dictating his will, an extraordinary, moving document of a man's courage and loving kindness.

George Dimick, who was a cousin of Rouse's as well as an employee, sat beside the cot taking dictation; after every few words he gently put a spoonful of water between the blackened lips, so that Rouse might go on speaking. In clear, simple terms, the man who had given up the law because he stammered, directed the intricate division of his entire fortune and his belongings. He bequeathed the bulk of his estate to the Commissioner of Warren County, half to be used for the poor of the county, and half on roads and other improvements. He made generous bequests to friends and relatives, arranged a monthly income for life for his father, remembered "my hired boy" with five hundred dollars, and lifted burdens from struggling young neighbors:

"Rouse and Mitchell hold the notes of A. Skinner and Allen Wright for twenty-five hundred dollars. My half I bequeath to them; they are having hard enough times, without having to pay the notes."

He left his black mare, which had carried so many children, to his partner John Mitchell, and made loving provision for his landlord's little daughters:

"I have the Sheriff's Deed of the Store and Dwelling House occupied by Thos. Morean. I bequeath said property to his two youngest children, Eva and Maggie. Their father to have the use of it until they come of age."

All this time he was in such agony, although he never cried out, that the friends in the little shanty could hardly bear to watch him. Just once, pain clouded the brilliant lucidity of his mind, and he left a bequest to a godchild—"I cannot think of his name." But he mentioned the child's mother, a relative, and minutes later he remembered that the little boy was called Harry.

His thoughts must have kept going back to the storekeeper's family who had made him feel so affectionate a part of their life, and he remembered to leave $300 to Maggie and Eva's mother. Each word he spoke now was a heart-breaking struggle, but he went on dictating, and a half-hour later, in one of the last bequests, he left Mrs. Morean his wardrobe, so that she could cut it down for her sons.

"Two gentlemen carried me out of the fire. I bequeath them each one hundred dollars.

"Let my funeral be without display. No funeral sermon to be preached. Bury me by the side of my mother in Westfield.

"I bequeath my library to my father.

"I have a beautiful picture, an engraving, in Herstfield's store at Pittsburgh. I bequeath it to William Hirst of Meadville. . . .

"I authorize all who are here present to witness the foregoing as my last Will and Testament."

Dr. Christy of Oil City, one of the physicians who were working over the victims all that night, had been in and out of the shanty. Now he signaled that Henry Rouse had only a short wait, to be freed by death. A well-meaning friend fetched a minister who began to pray unctuously, petitioning God to forgive transgressions and receive this soul. The charred, dying man on the bed waved him away: "My account is already made up. It would be cowardly to ask for credits now."

George Dimick wrote afterward that his cousin Henry had "exalted ideas of the Creator and Ruler of the Universe but he deprecated the popular forms of worship. Fear of the present or of the life to come had no place in his heart."

I don't think the brave, gay, compassionate Henry had to be afraid, when he went to meet his God.

Eighteen other men died, besides Henry Rouse. A dozen more were maimed. At least twenty of the seriously burned men who had been carried that night to the nearest beds were cared for tenderly for weeks by the village women, in their already overcrowded shanties.

The fire burned three days and nights, while workmen fought it desperately, before it was finally smothered by dumping on wagon-loads of manure and earth.

One eyewitness to the first night wrote, "It was the most frightful and yet the grandest pyrotechnical display ever vouchsafed to a human being."

Several newsmen, with kindled imaginations, said the fire had started because Henry Rouse walked into the derrick house smoking a cigar. That was idiotically untrue. Because of the gas spewing out, and the humid air, every fire in the area had been put out. A smouldering coal in a nearby boiler sent off a spark that ignited the gas. Ironically, Henry, who didn't smoke himself, was stern about only one rule with employees: No smoking or drinking around a well.

His friend Allen Wright, whose note he'd canceled "because they're having a hard enough time as it is," had stationery made up headed *Rouseville,* and Buchananville was Rouseville from then on. Even in its days as a boomtown, it stayed surprisingly free of vice. The villagers who had known and loved Henry Rouse were a sturdy-minded lot, and they had forthright ways of dealing with flotsam. Ida Tarbell, who was born four years before the fire and lived in Rouseville till she was thirteen, told with amused satisfaction of the time a houseboat loaded with gamblers and prostitutes docked on the creek near her town, and let it be known they were in business. That's what *they* thought. The villagers, especially the women, thought otherwise. In the night, an impromptu committee of six crept down to the boat, cut the mooring rope, and away it drifted. When the gamblers woke up the next morning, they were floating down the Allegheny, twenty miles away.

A few miles above Rouseville, an oil village sprouted that was so moral and tidy and well-managed it was like one of those model villages displayed at world fairs. This was on the Story Farm, which had been bought with the silk-dress bonus by Pittsburghers. In May of 1861, they formed the Columbia Oil Company, with Andrew Carnegie one of the biggest stockholders. Shady speculators were never allowed to get so much as a foot in here. The Pittsburghers hired an efficient superintendent, George Bancroft, and put down wells in a systematic, well-spaced manner. They built cottages for the workers, a machine shop, and an impressive library open to any man, woman or child who came with clean hands. This must have been Andrew Carnegie's special pet, and I suspect it sparked his library philanthropies to come.

The villagers' own special pet and pride was the Columbia Oil Band. Its members, all oil workers, wore uniforms braided like musical-comedy generals' and topped by high-spiked steel helmets. The prancing drum major was "an acrobatic revelation," and the band itself "could have given Sousa's points in ravishing music," one writer declared later. He thought the profits of the Columbia Oil Company were even more ravishing. Estimating that the deal consummated with a silk dress had yielded over ten million, he exclaimed, "The long-haired novelist who soars into the infinite and dives into the unfathomable, may try to imagine what the addition of a new bonnet would have accomplished."

Andrew Carnegie, on his first visit to this beautifully managed bonanza, was appalled at the casual wastefulness of other producers along Oil Creek. He arrived in May, in time to see the most uproariously inefficient procedure of all: sending oil to market via the spring fresh, or pond freshet.

Horses were involved in the first act of this spectacle. Four to a team, they pulled barges and towing boats up the shallow Oil Creek, leaving them at the creek banks nearest the big wells. Barrels were loaded on, but most of the oil was run in bulk, through crude troughs, into the boats' leaky wooden vats. In preparation for the great day, water had been stored up in lumber millponds on the creek all the way from Hyde town, above Titusville, to Oil City. When the boats were ready, the dams were opened and the wild rush was on. Hundreds of boats of all shapes, sizes and fighting conditions spilled down the crooked creek together, sideways, endways, in a wham-bang free-for-all. If one boat hit a rock, a dozen crashed on top of it. Barrels toppled into the water; oil from the vats spurted and dribbled. (Andrew Carnegie estimated, in horror, that one third of all the oil was lost in the smashups, and another third leaked away in the wooden vats, before the surviving boats ever reached Pittsburgh.) Each freshet cost oil men several hundred dollars paid to mill owners, but it raised the level of the creek twenty to thirty inches.

A Reverend Dubbs, one-time minister, was in charge of the operation, that is, he supervised the unleashing of waters in each dam, and supposedly signaled the boats when to fall into orderly line. But the result was crashing confusion, and the boatmen cursed so feelingly that the Reverend's ears must have been scorched. Sightseers crowded the creek banks and hung over the Oil City bridge to watch the slam-jamboree, screaming advice and cheering their favorites.

The boats that weren't smashed to tinderwood proceeded down the Allegheny, leaving an oily green trail, and unloaded their cargo in Pittsburgh. Then the boatmen collected their pay and celebrated at Ben Trimble's, a variety hall and saloon (next door to Horne's store). It was here that they'd picked up the song "Hell on the Wabash," from Ohio rivermen who had never experienced the tender frenzies of a spring fresh on Oil Creek.

Which brings us to a riverman who made a fortune on land, during the freshet season of 1861. This was Captain Andrew Funk, who looked like a Viking mariner, six feet of him topped by a thatch of sun-washed hair. He must have dreamed big even as a very young man, when he built and ran small lumber steamers on the Youghiogheny River downstate. In 1848, he built his dream ship, a large side-wheel steamer, and I think he must have pictured himself as the dashing captain of the biggest boat on the river. Unfortunately, when his impressive vessel was launched in the Youghiogheny, it nearly got stuck for life, because of its heavy draft. The Captain had to change plans in midstream and move her over to the Ohio and Mississippi rivers, which were big enough to hold her. He spent several years navigating his oversize boat there, then sold it to buy a lumber tract in western Pennsylvania. (Jonah Watson must have been crosser than two sticks, at all the new rivals who appeared in his province in the mid 1850's.) Captain Andy Funk kept a decent distance away, at Steam Mills in Warren County, where he ran a lumber mill. But right after he heard about Drake, his Viking spirit took over, and he was off to the oil region, to snap up one of the bargains Jonah Watson had missed: David McElhenny's farm, one hundred acres for $1,500 and one-fourth the oil. It was on Oil Creek a few miles above Henry Rouse's settlement, and at the time of the fire, Captain Andy's well was looking very dry indeed, at three hundred feet down. The Captain got so disgusted that he announced one April day, "I'd trade this hole for a yellow cur."

Luckily, nobody had a yellow cur handy, to take him up on this deal. His son persuaded him to get an engine, and the well was drilled down to almost five hundred feet, the deepest yet, to the third sand rock, when it came in so lavishly that suspicious natives called it the Humbug, figuring *that* couldn't last very long. But it lasted fifteen months, at 300 barrels a day. Captain Andy, who had once built a boat before trying it on for size, now had a well worthy of his largest wishful thinking. Speculators came scurrying to buy up leases on his farm. The town of Funkville sprang out of the mud. And the fifty-year-old captain retired serenely from the race. It wasn't that he had more money than he knew what to do with. He knew exactly.

He went back to the tiny, poverty-ridden village of Steam Mills and paid every penny of the cost of building a church, which he presented to the Methodists with five acres of ground. Next, he built a library and school, but his favorite young schoolteacher had already gone, with the Captain's hearty blessing and help, to make *his* fortune.

The two men had first met in 1858, when twenty-one-year-old John Fertig came to teach "reading, writing, cyphering, syntax and grammar" at the tiny (red, of course) schoolhouse at Steam Mills. Most country people liked a "loud school," where their children recited constantly, good and loud. It was said that the scholarly, bony young Fertig taught "quiet," and kept his charges using their heads more than their lung power. For this, villagers rather grudgingly paid him $18 a month and board, for the four winter months when the school was open. Out of this sum, John Fertig paid his tuition so he could go to school himself the rest of the year, at Neilltown Academy. As one of twelve children of a Venango County farmer, John had only been allowed the luxury of schooling two months each winter until he was sixteen. Next, he had worked as a farmer's hired hand, at $8 a month, and as a sawyer, but at the age of nineteen he had the formidable idea of "reading enough books to learn to be a teacher."

A year later, he was teaching the lower grades and cramming himself through the upper ones. When Captain Andy Funk heard about this, he added $18 a month to John Fertig's salary, out of his own capacious pocket, and loaned him books. The young man who protruded from his shabby clothes with such calm self-possession amused and pleased the Captain. The boy was stubborn, too. No nagging or nudges from pupils' parents would make him teach "loud." Once he told the Captain, "They want a talking parrot. But owls are better. Even hoot owls."

One of the books he borrowed was Mr. Longfellow's newest and most popular work, *The Courtship of Miles Standish*. Captain Funk teased the forthright Fertig about that other, diffident John, and said, "Nobody'd ever have to tell *you* to speak for yourself, John."

When the Captain leased the farm on Oil Creek, John spoke for himself in a hurry. He came back from a visit to Oil Creek glowing, and announced he intended to drill a well. Captain Funk gave his protégé five acres of his own land, and said in effect, "Go to it, lad."

John went to it, as soon as his winter term of teaching "quiet school" was over. To ease the cost of drilling, he took two partners, a Steam Mills farmer, Michael Gorman, and young David Beatty of West Hickory. They hired a contractor to kick down a well by spring pole, at $2 a foot. Then John Fertig promptly asked the man, "Now will you hire me to work for you at a dollar a day?" The contractor was understandably a bit confused at hiring the man who'd hired him. Anyway, what did a schoolteacher know about kicking down? This teacher learned fast. But after a whole spring and summer, the well was abandoned as dry. The resourceful John immediately bought a set of tools on credit, and contracted to put down three wells above

Oil City for another producer. When Captain Funk's well came in, in May of 1861, John rushed back to his own abandoned well and drilled it down to almost the depth of the Captain's. It came in, about one-fifth the yield of his patron's, in time to celebrate the Fourth of July.

The country that had cherished its independence was sorrowfully divided and fighting against itself, in the two bloody battles at Bull Run. But early that fall the oil region had its first really rip-snorting gushers, so sensational they blotted out war news, in western Pennsylvania. The Empire well, drilled by two Cleveland men at Funkville, spouted with a stupendous 3,000 barrels a day, ten times bigger than the biggest yet. (Henry Rouse's well, born in fire and tragedy, had never lived up to its first torrential flow.) The bewildered owners of the Empire were swamped by this embarrassment of riches. No coopers could keep up with the demand for barrels; the oil wouldn't shut off; it overflowed tanks and the hastily built dams and ran loose. Families for miles around came running, with dippers and pails and wash buckets. Children ran barefoot through the onrushing streams of dark oil.

The market was glutted and the price of oil plummeted, till it was down to ten cents a barrel. The owners of the Empire were so desperate they arranged to sell one month's yield to a Cleveland firm for $500. It came to five cents a barrel.

When the next tank-buster struck that October, even bigger than the Empire, nobody knew what to do. But here I want to backtrack downriver and bring the owner, William Phillips, up to meet destiny in a ramshackle houseboat.

William Phillips had been a pilot on the Allegheny River, a hearty, loud-laughing man, as solidly dependable as an anchor. Soon he owned his own boat, the *Orphan Boy,* and with the profit made carrying freight, he drilled several salt wells below Pittsburgh. When the Drake well oozed out its first bucketfuls, Phillips, who had the clear-charted mind of a good river pilot, instantly remembered a spot on Oil Creek where the greasy scum was thickest. He talked to his friends John Vanausdall and Captain Kipp about taking a lease there. They collected two other friends, Charles Lockhart and William Frew, who were very junior partners in a Pittsburgh store, McCully's. Lockhart had already had dealings with Sam Kier, in the Nature's Remedy and Carbon Oil period, so that he knew something about marketing. And Will Phillips, having drilled salt wells, knew what tools to collect in a hurry. The quintet bought an ancient keelboat for $20, and ceremoniously repainted the name on its peeling hull: *Crystal Palace.*

Horses towed them upstream, with their equipment and provisions, to anchor by the Downing farm on Oil Creek. For months, the five men lived on the boat and cooked their own meals, mostly pork, beans, molasses and coffee, but with homemade bread. Charles Lockhart, a cherubic, radiantly friendly man who could have unbent even a wooden Indian, was the one who sweet-talked a farmer's wife into making bread for them. Compared to the thin fare fought over at hotels, meals on the *Crystal Palace* were a banquet. Homesick oil men angled like small boys for invitations to come aboard and share a man-sized meal washed down with beer, where no second shift breathed down their necks.

Will Phillips' hunch about the greasy scum was right; their well, the Albion, came in modestly in March of 1860, and they shipped their first oil on the steamboat *Venango* to McCully's store.

Two of the quintet, Charles Lockhart and Frew, now left the floating bachelor life to concentrate on building up markets. (Eventually they split off amicably, and formed a firm of their own.) The other three men were still rarin' to go farther on Oil Creek. Phillips went to see James Tarr, the tail sawyer at Jonah Watson's; the two men liked each other instantly. Both were bluff and lusty, honest and direct, with no fancy double talk. Tarr agreed to lease a large piece of his farm, stretching the length of the frontage on Oil Creek, and "inland five rods," for a royalty of one-fourth the oil. In the summer of 1861, the well called Phillips No. 1 flowed handsomely. Or at least it seemed handsome until Phillips well No. 2 roared forth in October ten times as big, a staggering 4,000 barrels a day. It set up a record that wasn't to be broken for twenty-three years.

Will Phillips was too independent to beg a city firm, as the Empire well owners had done, to "come and take it all at $500 a month." He and his partners devised the astonishing method of selling "by the hour." Boats backed up to the troughs that ran from the well to the creek bank, to take on "an hour's flow," or two or three or four. If

the boat's vats were full before the time was up, the rest of the oil—
say, nineteen minutes' worth—cascaded into the creek.

The owner of a Boston coal-oil refinery, Sam Downer, who was inspecting the area with the plan of converting to petroleum, rode by
the Phillips well and gaped at the great stream of oil going to waste.
As a New Englander, he was horrified, and as a refiner, he was genuinely concerned. He got off his horse, a stout, dignified Bostonian,
and waded through the slime till he found Will Phillips in the engine
house.

"Sir!" he said. "Do you know that a hundred barrels an hour are
going to waste out there?"

"Yup," Will said. "But what should I do with it? You'd give me
five cents a barrel for it, and I'd rather stand a loss of five dollars an
hour than let you have it for a nickel."

It was Sam Downer's introduction to oil-country philosophy, but
by nature he belonged there, and not in rock-bound New England.
Two years later, his new refinery at Corry, the City of Stumps,
twenty-seven miles from Titusville, was the largest and finest around,
with fireproof brick buildings and mammoth stills of heavy copper-
plating. When a friend scolded him for putting $250,000 into a re-
finery for an industry that might be a flash-in-the-pan, Downer answered his critic boomingly, "The Lord Almighty doesn't like things
done in a small way."

Neither did Will Phillips, but he hadn't bargained for anything
quite so monstrously big as well No. 2. He and his workers built
great underground wooden tanks, the tops just level with the earth,
to hold the oil against a happier day and higher prices. The tanks soon
covered three acres, and were such a hazard they had to be tightly
covered, to keep innocent passers-by from falling in and drowning
in oil.

Late that fall, Phillips and his two current partners, plus other
leading producers and some of the worried farmers who shared royalties, met in conclave at Rouseville, to discuss what to do about the
glutted market. Words flowed almost as excessively as oil, but plenty
of sense emerged, finally. For a long-range plan, they wanted to get
a railroad built from Oil Creek to some nearby depot, to speed up
transportation and cut down teamster overcharging. A Mr. Struthers

of Warren got up and said simply that he and a group of friends were already working on this, and had had a survey made, for a possible route. Labor and materials were scarce, in wartime, but he thought the line could be operating within a year.

That settled, the immediate problem was to regulate the supply of oil, and set up a system that would benefit large and small producers. This was tougher. The Venango *Spectator* reported rather dubiously that "articles of mutual agreement . . . were presented for consideration, but held over to the next meeting." The writer added shrewdly:

> It is to be hoped that some means may be adopted which will secure to operators and owners of land a fair price for oil. We think this object can be accomplished by regulating the supply; but we have our doubts whether there is enough of unity and faith in men who are working for the "almighty dollar," to prevent underselling, or looking out for self first when an opportunity offers for a "big thing." If there is, and our oil operators are true to each other, the matter is un fait accompli, which in the vernacular means, it can be did.

The solution was the Oil Creek Association, which included all operators on the creek and down to five miles below Franklin. A hired inspector and two assistants visited all wells and regulated the flow. No oil was to be sold for less than ten cents a gallon at the wells, or $4 a barrel. All money was to be paid into a common fund, to be held for each seller. And for big producers this worked fairly well; they turned the stopcocks and held tight, all through the ruinously low prices that spring. But dozens of small operators, with no resources but their own courage, were wiped out. And most of them accepted failure with the cheerful fatalism of the oil region. Already inured to violent shifts in luck, they despised sniveling. Their attitude was summed up by a famous oil scout later, who bellowed, "Hit the calamity howlers in the solar plexus."

Some of the operators shrugged and walked off forever, leaving their machinery and derricks behind. Those who had the real oil bug got laborers' jobs in the area, to hold on till the depression was over and they could drill again.

But Congress, trying anxiously to raise money for the war, proposed a bill to put a thumping tax on crude and refined oil. The alarmed producers met in Titusville in a noisy mass meeting, and sent representatives to petition Congress against bleeding an already ailing industry. (They've never minded calamity howling to the government.) Congress listened, and settled for a duty of only ten cents a gallon on refined petroleum. That was July of 1862, and the government must have begun to realize that it would be short-sighted to kill off this strange juicy fowl that might conceivably lay golden eggs abroad for its country.

One of the first men to take samples of oil to London was Charles Lockhart, the beamishly friendly partner of Will Phillips on the first well, who had wangled homemade bread for the *Crystal Palace.* Charles was a born good-will ambassador and salesman; "his compliments had the juiciness of a peach," and his talks with English dealers eventually bore fruitful contracts. But the first real shipment was sent by a Philadelphia export firm, Peter Wright & Sons, who chartered the brig *Elizabeth Watts* and loaded an entire cargo of oil, ready to sail for England. This was a few months after the horrible fire at Rouseville, and Philadelphia papers had been full of it. As a result, the crew refused to make the trip with so inflammable a cargo. I don't know who got them drunk, and I'd hate to imply a Mickey Finn was involved, but the not-so-sober truth is that the crew was hustled or carried aboard one dawn in too sodden a state to argue. The brig *Elizabeth Watts* sailed at once down the Delaware River. There is no record of what the sailors said when they woke up, and perhaps it wouldn't have been printable anyway. At least, they didn't jump overboard, or toss over the barrels either. Their ship landed its cargo at an English port in the fall of 1861.

Because a Scotsman had developed the first coal oil, and refining it was now a flourishing industry in England, these manufacturers did their wily British best to discredit American petroleum, and managed to get a tax of one cent a gallon put on. English newspapers were almost as rabidly against our oil as they were against Mr. Lincoln. They fanned public hostility, played up the dangers of fire—all too true—and even attacked the oil simply as a bad smell:

> Unless some means can be discovered of overcoming the miasma an American and a Canadian will be detected in society by his scent as easily as a musk deer or a civet cat. . . . Their produce in crude emits so foetid an odor that everything that comes within its influence is rendered so noisome as to be almost unendurable. A truck, a cart, a waggon, a ship which has been employed in carrying petroleum is thereby rendered forever unfit to carry wine, flour, bacon, cheese or any other article of human food.

But there was no stopping the bull-wheels of progress. Back in Meadville, the president of the Atlantic & Great Western Railroad, William Reynolds, was champing with eagerness to build up the foreign markets for oil, so that his line might be extended from Meadville to Franklin, and from Corry to Titusville, to carry freight. He sent 12 barrels of oil as samples to London, to his chief contractor there, James McHenry, and just after the great Empire well spouted, he wrote him:

> The quantity now sent daily from the wells exceeds 2,000 barrels, and I am assured this does not exceed one fourth part of the quantity actually yielded by the wells, the other three fourths being stored in tanks in the ground awaiting better prices. . . . It may from eighteen months' experience be safely assumed that this business is perminent and may enter into future estimates of the profits of the road. Each month has produced wells surpassing those previously drilled until many of these a year since considered a fortune are now regarded as small affairs. The yield of some of the late wells is truly wonderful, forcing from a depth of 600 feet . . . with such power as to throw the oil and water like a vast fountain to a greater height than the surrounding forest trees.

His contractor, McHenry, passed out samples, smelly or no, to the portly members of London's Board of Trade, and tried it on chemists in France. He wrote Reynolds from Paris in June of 1861, "The Gas Company considers it better than anything they know of for the fabrication. . . . If the oil comes cheap the trade will be fabulous." He was a good prophet.

By the end of that year, the London *Times* was worrying whether "American hostilities" would hold up oil exports, and giving what amounted, for the conservative *Times,* to a rave review of the new petroleum's by-products: wax; a substitute for spirits of turpentine; naphtha and benzole for "the fashionable dyes Magenta."

Our new U.S. consul at Antwerp, A. W. Crawford, wrote home eagerly to the Secretary of State, "Some of the numerous oil springs of the Allegheny Valley might profitably let their lights shine in this direction."

The Secretary of State being otherwise occupied with a Civil War, the ebullient Mr. Crawford had samples of refined petroleum sent over at his own expense. Then he went calling on Antwerp merchants. It's gratifying and even startling to read now that one bustling U.S. consul touted an odd, smelly new product to such good effect that the following year a million and a half gallons were sold in Belgium alone. Up to then, Belgians had preferred something called rapeseed oil, which sounds pretty dangerous.

In Italy, people soon found that petroleum was cheaper and burned brighter even than olive oil.

Russians had begun to drill their own wells, but the only refinery there charged such a stiff price per gallon ($1) that only capitalists could afford it, and the flow from Oil Creek soon spread over that country. Our consul at St. Petersburg reported, "The people are becoming accustomed to it, and they will not do without it." I mention this in case the Russians claim they invented the art of drilling.

The man who did drill the first well, Edwin Drake, had long since been heckled by his employers to send samples abroad. Asahel Pierpont, Secretary and Treasurer of the company that had first sent Drake to Titusville, wrote him a letter early in 1860 that sounds as if it were addressed to a ten-year-old halfwit:

> Townsend wishes you to select the very best Barrels (*your new ones*) paint and dry the heads thoroughly and nicely put on the Plate with the *Trade Mark* in the most skilful manner, hoops &c thoroughly secured, and well fitted for a voyage to Europe, Wm. Townsend wants them thus prepared and sent forward *soon as you can,* he is going to send them to London, (England).

James Townsend, the tight-mouthed banker who had sold Drake the first oil stock, in New Haven, was now busily providing his whole family with jobs, promoting oil abroad. A few months before, he had written in a twitter:

> Dear brother Charles,
>
> . . . Everything looks very prosperous, but I don't calculate any upon it, may all fizzle out but so far it works well. I hope to get the agency . . . in New York for brother William to manage. I am also managing to hire him to the other concern. If I do both sides will be nicely fixed I think. (Keep dark.) Then if it continues to work well, there will be some opening for George [another brother] to manage I think, so that he can get out of the ice trade. But Charles this is all talk, for it may "fizzle." Now remember this, I don't count anything upon it . . . so that if it all fizzles don't laugh at me. . . .
>
> Your affectionate brother,
James

None of the brothers was laughing; William went as a salesman to England; Charles, a steamboat captain with a run to Le Havre, was sent to Paris. George reported happily, "We have hired the whole of the store where our ice office is and we are going to enlarge [it] and make room for the oil company with us, and make it appear more respectable."

Drake wrote Big Brother James Townsend, in the spring of 1860, enclosing the names of London commission merchants who had written him:

> If your brother William . . . is in Europe write him to call and see these folks. At last I have recd a small Order from the Cleveland & Erie Rail Road. . . . Mr. Ferris [an important New York refiner] was here and offered the enormous sum of 20¢ per Gall for the Oil at the works. He did not call upon me at all but devoted his whole time to Brewer and Watson but it did not amount to any thing he is a gas Bag I have been shut up in the House the past 5 days about half sick shall get out as soon as the weather clears up it is storming now.
>
> My family all got colds but not sick.
>
> Yours &c
E. L. Drake

The oil was winning much more recognition than poor Drake. The government was already using it in lighthouses all down the eastern coast. Factories were enthusiastic about it as a lubricant, although a Chicago man reported his machinists objected violently to the odor. An Erie merchant wrote a staunch testimonial:

> A lamp holding 1/2 a pint, will burn in our dwellings at this season of the year, every evening till 10 o'clock for a week. We judge the cost to be about 1/2 a cent per hour. Some of our customers . . . say a lamp full will burn with a full head of blaze, without cessation and without smoke, through 14 hours.
>
> W. Murphy

Thomas Gale, in his *Wonder of the Nineteenth Century,* was skittishly eloquent on this:

> Its light is no *moonshine.* . . . For the Christian by means of it to peruse his Bible, is no infliction. It never causes the politician to weep, when he reads at night in his favorite newspaper, the victories of his own party; nor the merchant to shed tears over the *price current,* showing a turn in trade which puts money into his pocket. In other words, rock oil emits a dainty light; the brightest and the cheapest in the world; a light fit for Kings and Royalists, and not unsuitable for Republicans and Democrats. It is a light withal, for ladies who are ladies *indeed,* and so are neither afraid nor ashamed to sew or read in the evening. An oil man, without any risk of a breach of *promise,* may warrant them, that by this light, they can thread their needles the first time, and every time they try.

Another writer, marveling at our far-flung exports, wrote fulsomely:

> Upon the romantic *boudoir* scenery of Spain it falls blushingly. . . . And in the wilderness of Paris, where the gamin throws his cap aside to fling the gay grisette above his head and kiss her ere she falls, the naptha flings a witch-like gleam about her carmine gaiters, dazzling the vulgar glances of the crowd.
>
> Across the sea, from the summits of cliffs, from the binnacles of ships, it shines, a beacon seen and blest of mariners in storms. And on the new continent [America] at night its glow will leap like magic from coast to coast, illuminating cities, villages, railroad cars, farmhouses—a golden web woven over all the land.

Drake had once written his employers cheerily, "It takes time and work to introduce it, but I shall succeed, I know." But the qualities that had made him drive the well to completion—stubbornness, for one, and a single-minded faith—acted against him later. He wasn't a good business man; he wasn't shrewd about money, and I think once he began to take his nominal title of President seriously and make marketing contracts on his own, he was blundering out over his depth.

It's obvious his wrangling employers in New Haven thought so too. At a meeting of the company in the spring of 1860, the minutes show:

> Voted: That for certain reasons the President E. L. Drake and Secretary and Treasurer A. Pierpont be requested to resign their several offices.

Drake was still to serve as an agent, but at least one director, William Ives, wanted to boot him out altogether. He wrote another official, sputtering with exasperation:

> The failure of our Co to make money hitherto has been the inefficiency of our agent & the divided Councils of our Board & if these causes continue the same effects will follow & all the money we may hereafter raise will be lost. . . .
> I beg of you to appoint some other one (not Drake) but some *honest* man. . . . I will bear my share of the burden if there is the *least* prospect of success, but you must excuse me for saying that if Mr. Drake is continued I can do nothing. *If* I do *anything* I Should propose to . . . take Mr. Root to Titusville, enstall him in the best & most economical manner, make arrangements for freight to come forward at regular & low rates—and as for Mr. Drake's affairs I want nothing to do with him or them. . . . If this had been done a few weeks ago it would have prevented Drake from making his last return in his own name & thus *undoing* all we had been so careful to accomplish.
> I tell you my friend these things are important.
>
> Yours
> W. A. Ives

And on his side, Drake was getting understandably resentful. By the summer of 1862, when oil exports were booming (up from zero to $15,727,881 at the end of the war) the man who'd put down the first well wrote banker Townsend bitterly:

> You all feel different from what I do. You all have your legitimate business which has not been interrupted by this opperation, which I staked everything I had upon the project and now find myself out of business and out of money.

In his next letter, he said:

> If the Co will work the Wells so that I may receive something to live upon I should be glad for you know I have nothing only what is in that property. If I was worth what you or Bowditch are I would not care whether they were worked or not. I could stand back and not work myself or let another do it. The Rail Road is completed to Centerville ten miles from this place and most of the grading is done to here, intend to come in on the 20 Sept.

The Oil Creek railroad reached Titusville that fall, on schedule. A farmer in the hills, hearing the first high-pitched wail of the locomotive, grabbed his shotgun and rushed out to shoot "the goldarndest wildcat I ever heerd."

Villagers sat on the roofs of their houses to watch the "neighing monster" approach. As it chugged into the lean-to depot, a cornet band fronting the welcome committee burst into "Ain't I Glad to Get Out of the Wilderness."

The little railroad was a screeching success from the start. It took on passengers at Corry, which was a junction of the Philadelphia and Erie line (later the Pennsylvania) and the Atlantic & Great Western (later the Erie), whose president had so truly predicted oil was "perminent."

Men from the cities who had reached Corry on their way to the oil fields got a first taste of the roughhouse life to come when they tried to board the cars of the little Oil Creek line, for the last lap to Titusville. Passengers overflowed the seats, aisles and platforms, and crouched on the roof of the cars. One witness claimed, "The gripsack brigade even swarmed up and sat on the locomotive." Strong men used umbrellas to battle their way inside. Women and children didn't stand a chance.

By spring of 1862, the Atlantic & Great Western had been extended from Meadville to Franklin, but it wasn't until two years later that the neglected people of Oil City could join us in singing "Ain't I Glad to Get Out of the Wilderness." Before that, greedy stagecoach drivers practiced a kind of highway stick-up, in charging as much as five dollars for the six-mile ride. Now it cost thirty-five cents to go in plushy ease, "on the cars."

The railroad soon did away with one of the most unusual conveyances on the creek, a scow canopied like Cleopatra's barge, and drawn by horses. All along Oil Creek, the captain steered this odd craft and blew a horn as reedy as the Pipes of Pan. Whenever he spotted passengers waving on the banks he would "Whoa" the horses and stop. At the mouth of the creek, if the water was high enough, the horses were unhitched, and the craft floated back down with the current to Oil City. The biggest excitement was to race with the Rouseville stagecoach headed for the same place. If the scow won, the captain used his horn to crow triumphantly of victory.

But if the railroads dispensed with some of this local color, they also cut down on hauling charges, and speeded the flow to the big refineries. By 1863, oil was $7 a barrel, and climbing even higher the year after. In view of this, the claim of the men who fired Drake—that their company never made a cent—is rather confusing. But then, it was always a confusing company. (George Bissell finally bought up all the stock.) The two wells drilled by Drake were puny, by the new gusher standards, and fell into neglect like Drake himself. The people of Titusville, considerably more loyal than the Seneca Oil Company, appointed him a justice of the peace, and it's a wry twist that in this role he notarized leases on some of the biggest wells.

He also served for a while as agent for a wholesale drug company, Schiefflin & Brothers, who had sent their best chemist, George Mowbray, to Titusville, to open a small refinery and laboratory. Mowbray and Drake were kindred souls from the day they met; they sat up that first night till 4 A.M. telling stories, discussing oil, and smoking almost an entire box of the firm's best Havana cigars.

Another crony who brought Drake good cigars and good stories was the first, and great, photographer of the early oil fields, John Mather, a gay, gregarious little man with a Barrymore profile and a

candor as sharp as his stickpin. When Mathew Brady was taking his
first photographs of Lincoln, young Mather was an itinerant photographer traveling merrily through Ohio, bubbling with music and high
spirits.

As the son of a prosperous paper-mill owner in Staffordshire, England, he had applied his deft hand and eye to every phase of that
business, but a strain of some wandering minstrel ancestor must have
been lilting inside. He had studied the violin, and played at many a
castle; Queen Victoria herself had complimented him. But Mather
Senior thought fiddling was a feckless way to make a living, or not
make one, and he wanted young John to take over the paper business,
because his two oldest sons had already emigrated to America. This
blueprint of the future sounded very solid, but not so exciting as the
letters that arrived from the United States to tingle a young man's
wanderlust. John's brothers urged him to come visit this extraordinary
country. At the age of twenty-eight, with his violin under his arm and
the respectable cushion of $1,000 in cash to fall back on, John Mather
set off.

At the summer hotel in the Pocono Mountains of Pennsylvania,
run by his brother Edmund, John met another Englishman, named
Johnson, who was seeing the country and paying his way by taking
pictures. Photography, as an art, wasn't even as old as John Mather.
He examined his new friend's camera, watched him take pictures,
and held his breath in the impromptu darkroom as the wet plates
were developed. It was affinity at first sight, and forever.

He begged to go along with Johnson as an apprentice, and he
learned so fast, as they traveled through West Virginia, that within
a year he was teaching his teacher. He had been earning $5 a week
and board, so he still had most of his $1,000, prudently salted away
in brother Edmund's hotel safe. (The prudence was probably more
Edmund's than John's. Mather was never one to save for a rainy day
when sunny ones were so much his meat and drink.) With this nest
egg, he bought his own equipment and a high-wheeled wagon, with
the back built up for a darkroom. Then he set out to see America
through his camera's eye, stopping in every town to photograph the
inhabitants. He had covered Maryland, and was in Painesville that
spring of 1860, when he first heard about Drake's well, and the spec-

tacular oil rush. As he said later, "I turned my horse's tail west and we both headed east."

A week after arriving in the teeming village of Titusville he had taken over half of a watchmaker's tiny frame building as a studio, at the inflation rent of $23 a month, and put in a skylight which the local children admired as "a glass roof to see birds through."

But like Brady, Mather was no see-the-birdie, smile-please sort of photographer. He advertised "Ambrotypes, Porcelains, Double Position (superior)," but his manner and methods weren't always guaranteed to flatter the subject. When an early customer brought in her small son with a bow tie stretched from ear to ear, she complained, after seeing the photographs Mather took of the boy, "They're homely."

"Well, dammit, ma'am," Mather said. "Look at yourself and your husband. What can you expect of that union?"

As a Titusville man said admiringly, "His insults cut to the bone."

He had the scratchy, driven restlessness of an artist, and a scorn for prettying up nature or people. His handsome head was perpetually cocked on one side, with ears as alert as an animal's, and wonderfully alive amber eyes, the kind that might glow in the dark. The unpredictable compound of mud and magnificence that was Oil Creek was made to order for his talents. The crudities and crazy paradoxes, the raw frontier harshness and beauty and squalor, disaster and the golden flow, are all there in his photographs.

One of his first pictures, which has been reprinted all over the world, was of Drake in his stovepipe hat and undertakerish garb, standing in front of his derrick. It's typical of Mather that he pulled Drake's friend, the lanky young druggist Peter Wilson, into the foreground for a villager contrast to the tall-hat formality, and set the men by a raggedy pile of lumber. Three oil workers lounge like cowboys in the background. In a later shot there, Mather caught Uncle Billy Smith sprawled on a wheelbarrow.

Producers with a new well were like proud parents; they wanted their baby's likeness, and at least a dozen prints to give away. Often, if Mather heard of a well going down that sounded promising, he'd rush off to be in at the birth. His small high wagon loaded with fragile glass plates jounced like a jeep over the ruts and around the stumps of destroyed forests. If there was no road to a well, he took the path teamsters had made before him by pushing down a farmer's fences and riding across fields.

At the well, Mather sensitized his plates carefully in readiness, often in the midst of the wildest confusion. Once he set up his tripod so close to a well that when it spurted up a gusher he was drenched. The happy owner gave him fifty dollars to get a new suit. Mather often retold this story in the poverty of his old age, enlarging it considerably with each telling, until he had the man handing over a five-hundred-dollar bill. But in those days, $50 bought quite a suit, and Mather loved clothes. He had suits made by a Pittsburgh tailor, and was known among oil workers as "a nobby dresser."

He also liked good brandy, good cigars, and the camaraderie of the oil-country saloons, where millionaires and toolies were all in the same greasy boots. In that congenial setup, the little Englishman would get out his fiddle and play till his listeners were stomping and shouting for encores. Playing for Queen Victoria was never like this. But the wives of those same oil men, when they came to his studio, didn't rate music, even as background. If they had what Mather considered high-toned notions on how they should be posed and rendered, he'd roar, "Then go to New York, dammit. If you're so rich, go buy a fancy retoucher."

Discussing one overbearing ex-customer, the wife of a teamster turned millionaire, he told a friend, "She can stick the money up her snotty nose and blow it, for all I care." But he kept on supplying Drake with prints, free, in his leanest days.

After Mather married, he went through the motions of settling down, but he was often out fiddling with a band he'd gotten up in Titusville, and every new oil strike, or rumor of one, sent him leaping. His wife complained, with some justice, that she almost never saw him, and he told an apprentice, "Remember, women are born crabs. A man has to get beyond clawing distance."

When the oil excitement moved down creek, Mather bought a flat-boat, with a built-on cabin darkroom, topped by a vast sign:

PHOTOGRAPHIC VIEWS—OIL CREEK ARTIST

He tied up at every new boomtown, Funkville, Tarrville, McClin-tockville, Rouseville, Petroleum Centre, and shot everything he saw, from the vast glistening mud holes piled with tanks and shanties and derricks, to primly hair-ribboned little girls watching their father kick down a well. His sardonic eye must have enjoyed the paradox of a squalid cabin in the mire, with an oil-man's wife standing daintily outside the door in sweepingly full skirts and tight-corseted bodice, like a figure cut out of *Godey's Lady's Book*.

Well owners paid Mather from $5 to $10 for a large "panoramic" photograph, but he took thousands of shots on his own. Most of his money went for new equipment; he even had a 16 x 24 camera, rare in those days, and bought all kinds of lenses to experiment with. Once he crowed over a new lens that caught gradations of light at sunset. Silas Eckstrom of Titusville, who worked in a studio when Mather was an old man, has said simply, "He was a real artist. There wasn't a young photographer in this part of the state that didn't come asking him questions."

As an example of Mather's talents, Silas tells the rather ghoulish story of the mother who kept grieving because she hadn't had a picture of her teen-age son taken before he died. Six months after the funeral, she was still brooding, and a relative said, "I'll bet Mather could do it."

The glass-topped coffin was dug up, and Mather, happy over this interesting challenge, ordered it propped up endwise, against a hitching post. Silas, who was there as helper, ends the tale, "And you know, he no sooner got a good picture than that corpse crumbled down into dust. That kind of bothered Mather. He said, 'I don't think I'll take another job like this—unless I need the money.' "

In the dank early spring of 1862, Mather drove down to Captain Funk's farm to photograph a dozen new derricks huddling around the juicy big Empire well. On his way back to Titusville, he stopped at the Foster farm, just above the Captain's, to see how Joel Sherman was doing. To Mather's experienced eye, Joel was in a bad way.

Sherman had come to Oil Creek from Cleveland the fall before, drawn by news of the mammoth gushers. His wife had inherited a few hundred dollars, and turned over the whole amount so that Joel could lease a piece of land. Her husband was a forty-year-old clerk, pathetically inexperienced in drilling, but he set up a spring pole and kicked down, with one helper, all through that miserable winter, until he was ready to drop of exhaustion. It wasn't just pluck that kept him going; there were definite signs of oil at the first sand rock, but by then his wife's money was gone. So was his strength. Joel Sherman wasn't a promoter; even if he'd known how to form a stock company, it was a bad winter for selling; even suckers weren't biting. Finally, he persuaded a native to part with a bony white horse named Pete, in exchange for a one-sixteenth share in the well. Pete was harnessed to the spring pole, to supply horsepower in its plainest form, for drilling. But after two weeks of this, Pete lay down, wheezing, and wouldn't get up again. Sherman found two disappointed owners of a dry hole who had a small engine and boiler. The men swapped these for another sixteenth of the well, in the spirit of "What have we got to lose?" But by now all four owners were so broke they had no money to buy a ton of coal to run the engine. Coal dealers had become wary, and would sell only for cash, getting as high as $1 a bushel.

That was the frustrating situation when Mather, sitting up high and natty on his wagon seat, pulled in his reins beside the well. Sherman, who now looked almost as gaunt and feverish as a prospector lost in a desert, begged the photographer to take a one-eighth share, in return for $75 cash. Mather refused, but he good-naturedly supplied the name of a farmer up country who'd made some money selling off timber, and was hankering to get in on the oil business. Sherman's horse Pete was too done in to make the trip to try for the loan, so Mather took Sherman himself.

The farmer said he could only spare $68 cash, for a one-sixteenth share. After some haggling, he threw in a shotgun, to complete the deal. Sherman bought coal and food, stoked himself and his boiler, and started drilling again. On March 16th, he had twenty-nine cents left; perhaps only the awful thought that he had to go home and tell his wife he'd lost all her money kept him going the rest of that day. At dusk, the well roared in, 1,500 barrels in twenty-four hours. Teamsters who were brought in that next morning, March 17th, celebrated St. Patrick's and Sherman's Day in high, liquid style.

The one-eighth share John Mather turned down would have earned him $175,000.

The little photographer thought it was a great joke on himself. But what seemed to amuse him most was that the farmer who'd taken the last share had been so reluctant. In his light, clipped British voice, that forty years of oildom never quite submerged, Mather would say, "He hated to part with that shotgun, you know. He couldn't be sure the barrel was loaded."

S I X

————————◆◆◆————————

Diamonds dunked in oil

IF THERE was any man around who knew the oil country as well as Mather, it was Henry Howe, a civil engineer who had opened an office in Titusville near the photographer's studio. In Howe's mind, and in his meticulous maps, the wild sprawling scene was reduced to neat squares or oblongs, and small inked lines curved or zigzagged toward the long black serpentine length of Oil Creek: Muskrat Run, Cherry Run, Hunters Run, Church Run, even a Bull Run. On each tiny section, the name of the farm's original owner, or sometimes the oil company that had taken it over, is delicately lettered, like engraving on the head of a pinpoint. If you examine a Howe map with a magnifying glass, the names of the only four women leap out as unexpectedly as a petticoat hoisted over a desert island.

Mrs. Richardson, Mrs. Fleming, Mrs. Foster—what on earth were they doing here? (To paraphrase a song of the 1860's: "Madam, does your husband know you're out?") But the fourth name, *Widow McClintock,* is as plain as a black crepe mourning band. And it's the Widow who was used by the fates—rather meanly, taking advantage of her truly Christian nature—to foster the most notorious playboy of the oil boom, Coal Oil Johnny.

I use the word "foster" because the Widow was childless. She adopted Johnny as a baby, a beautiful child with great dark eyes and long curving lashes, after both his parents died of diphtheria in 1843. And she brought him up with constant loving doses of bonset tea and the Scriptures, good for whatever ailed him. Her husband, Culbertson McClintock, was as devoted to the gay, affectionate little boy as his wife was, and Johnny adored his adoptive parents, whom he called Uncle and Aunt.

Their log cabin, surrounded by two hundred acres, faced the Buchanan farm across Oil Creek. Culbertson, who lived until Johnny was twelve, built on a frame addition for bedrooms, but the big central room with the huge stone fireplace that served for cooking and heating, festooned with strings of red peppers and dried apples, was the heart of the house. As a child, Johnny sat by the fire, cracking hickory nuts with a flatiron, or the wrinkly-burred black walnuts that grew around Buchanan's.

His uncle taught him to shoot when he was nine. The fresh scented forests were full of rabbits, quail and squirrels, and more dangerous game, wildcats and foxes. Rattlesnakes slithered over the paths and sunned on the rocks by the creek. Killing them was a favorite boyhood sport, and the high-spirited, adventurous Johnny was neighborhood champion. Years later, gulled and fleeced by sharpers, sucked dry by leeches, he was to remark bitterly that rattlesnakes were gentlemen because at least they gave warning before they struck.

Every Sunday morning, Culbertson McClintock and the strong, agile Johnny would finish up the farm chores early. Then they all piled into the lumber wagon, with a picnic lunch, and went off to spend the day at the little Seceders' church—a meeting house—deep in the woods. The Seceders were old style Presbyterians, and their services resembled the early settlers' "meetings." Farmers hitched their horses to trees around the grove, and the children played quietly while the grownups gossiped. Boys, their hair slicked down with marrow grease, eyed demure young girls in linsey-woolsey. Sunday School was from ten to eleven; for the next two hours, Elder Slentz hollered and pounded on the pulpit in the tiny church, in a sermon reeking of brimstone for sinners. Johnny, raised in the strict, devout McClintock household, had learned his Catechism, the first four Gospels, and most of the Acts, almost before he could spell. But the long Sunday sessions were hard on even the most docile children, and Johnny, an exuberant normal boy, got a warning pinch from his aunt whenever he fidgeted.

The picnic lunch was a blessed escape, but all too brief. Afterwards, men, women and children went back inside for another hour, or sometimes two, of the Elder's damning the Devil, and offering the Kingdom of Heaven like a bribe for model deportment. Prayers were a droning filibuster to keep Satan at bay. To please his aunt, Johnny, who could carry a tune about as well as a tree toad, even sang in the choir.

On weekdays, he went to the little country schoolhouse on the Blood farm, two miles away, and at night his aunt heard his lessons. When Culbertson McClintock died in 1855, he left the farm to his wife in trust for their adopted son, John Washington Steele.

It was soon after this that the Widow McClintock had her first inkling that when it came to money, Johnny didn't have the brains of a rabbit. Each week, the boy had put a big sack of grain across the horse and ridden up to Irwin's mill to have it ground. He had performed this errand so conscientiously that she didn't have any qualms about sending him off in the wagon to buy some eggs for cooking, at Merrick's country store, when her own hens weren't laying well. She was aghast when the boy came home with a hundred-dozen eggs, neatly packed in a wooden crate, and explained radiantly that the price seemed so low he had stocked up and put them on her bill.

She couldn't bear to scold him too harshly. Johnny was her comfort and her joy, especially now that her husband had died, so she put down the eggs in a crock of "water-glass" (a preserving method used even in my own childhood) and talked to him sweetly about thrift and responsibility, and the importance of education to prepare him for the day when he'd manage the farm. When he had finished "common school," she sent him as a "subscription student" to the Cherry Tree Academy, where old Mr. Crosby and his spinster daughter taught a sprinkling of gentlemanly manners over algebra and Latin gerundives.

The desiccated Mr. Crosby, fingering his birch rod as he listened to the Venango County youths' versions of Dido at Carthage and Caesar slicing up Gaul, couldn't have had a notion that his three most obstreperous students would be part of oil history, two of them honorably. Lyman Stewart became president of the Union Oil Company; Dan Scofield headed Standard Oil of California; the third was Johnny. But all Mr. Crosby knew about oil was that it was a homely remedy for rheumatism, denied to him because the after-scent stank in a stuffy classroom. His teen-age students, Johnny included, knew oil at first-hand. All of them had done the family chores of putting flannel rags on the creek scum, wringing out the greasy liquid in a bucket, and taking it home for medicine.

When the Drake well came in, Johnny was sixteen, impressionable as melting tallow. Watching the hordes of strangers, including the ones who came to the Widow McClintock offering what seemed insane prices for leases, he was hang-jawed with wonder. All the innocent pleasures of a life bounded by frugality, hard work and threats of hellfire seemed meanly little, compared to these scatterers of wealth. For the first time, he began to think about the world outside.* If these strangers were an example of how life was lived there, casually and splendidly open-handed, then he longed to see the cities they came from.

For over a year, the Widow McClintock refused to lease any land, although her brothers-in-law, Ham, George and John, were already making money in amounts that must have bewildered and worried her. I think it was an instinctive fear of the effect on young Johnny that made her hold off. And when she finally yielded, it wasn't for herself. She couldn't bear to cheat her boy out of a fortune, but she made sure he didn't get enough to hurt him. She sold leases for $500 down payment, with a royalty of one-eighth the oil, and promptly bought a safe to keep the money in. She kept out only enough to buy a cookstove, a new carpet, and a horsehair sofa, but she herself preferred the bare old stiff-backed wooden chairs, and the life that went with them.

It relieved and reassured her to see Johnny in love with the pretty, gentle girl he had first met at meeting house. Eleanor Moffitt was the daughter of a well-to-do farmer who had been a close friend of Cul-

---

* If I seem to barge into Johnny's mind rather frequently, from here on, it's not omniscience, but material drawn from his memoirs: *Coal Oil Johnny, His Book* (1902).

bertson McClintock's. The two families had always gone to the same church and the same harvestings. Johnny had taken Eleanor sleigh riding, and been her partner at paring bees. Now when he told the Widow McClintock excitedly of the money teamsters were making, and begged to haul oil so he could save enough to get married, she thought it sounded like a safe, sound ambition, and bought him his own team and wagon. Almost every farmer's son within thirty miles had come to the creek to haul oil, but their peers in the profession wouldn't tolerate any sissies. What surprised the older men was that Johnny, who looked like a pretty choir boy, proved to be the quickest study of the lot, when it came to cursing and drinking. He could down the slugs of raw whiskey—boiler-splitters—like a man, they told him approvingly.

And all the sucked cloves and peppermints didn't deceive the Widow McClintock for very long. She was lecturing him about this gently but anxiously at supper, on a humid April evening in 1861, when there was an explosion that rattled the windows. The sky was a thick orange color; swirls of black smoke and jets of fire were rising over Buchanan's, just across the creek. Johnny yanked on his boots and ran out. He didn't get home until daybreak.

The horrors of the fire in which Henry Rouse died that night must have scarred the memory of a seventeen-year-old, because years later he told a Franklin man, "Yes, I was there, but I still don't want to think about it."

The year after he and Eleanor were married, there was another spectacular fire. Three men on a flatboat moored in the eddy below Oil City were blasted out of sleep at 2 A.M. by an explosion that blew off the roof of their shanty and sent a shower of sparks into the next barge, loaded with oil. Within minutes, at least two hundred boats were a moving, blazing fleet swirling downriver, while the flames spread even to storage tanks along shore. Men leaped frantically from boat to boat, and most of them made it to land. Messengers raced their horses just ahead of the blaze, downriver, to arouse the citizens of Franklin. A crowd of hastily dressed men were at the river bank before 6 A.M. and made heroic attempts to halt the boats short of the bridge that was our town's main pride and glory. Only one boat, the largest, got through. The editor of the *Spectator,* among the watchers, wrote:

> No human efforts could save the noble structure except the land-ing of the burning boat, and all attempts at this failed. She passed under the bridge, the flames shooting to the very comb of the roof and instantly enveloped it in fire. A large crowd of people were on the bridge at the moment, several of whom made narrow escapes, so rapid was the spread of the flames. In thirty minutes this splendid structure was totally destroyed. . . .
>
> The destruction of oil is immense. This is the most serious calam-ity that has visited us yet.

Oil companies were now so frightened of fire that owners of several leases along the creek tacked notices on trees:

"SMOKERS WILL BE SHOT."

With derricks thrusting up all over the Widow McClintock's farm and some so close to the cabin that it echoed the engine throbs, she must have seen these posted warnings, but considering her careless-ness later, they couldn't have made any impression, or convinced her petroleum was inflammable. She was more concerned with the dan-gers of hellfire, for her carefree adopted son. At the age of twenty Johnny was already a father, and the Widow fretted over his not be-ing a sober enough family man. In an anxious attempt to get him away from teamstering and boiler-splitters, Mrs. McClintock, in the early spring of 1864, decided he should go into the grocery business with her nephew David Hayes, who already owned a small store. When she arranged to finance a partnership, Johnny remarked that he knew how much she loved him, to forget the time he'd bought a hundred-dozen eggs and believe he could make a go of the grocery business.

The first phase of the project enchanted him. He and David Hayes went to Pittsburgh on the steamer *Allegheny Belle*—the first time he had ever been farther from home than Oil City—and the *Belle* seemed to him incredibly elegant. But the hotel in Pittsburgh bowled him over. He couldn't sleep, what with constantly jumping up to ex-amine the heavy carved furniture in the room, and stroke the bell cord; could he really pull it and order something? He wished his wife and aunt and friends could see him in all this splendor. All through that night, he quivered with excitement, while the policeman on duty near the hotel shouted the hours, a human, hoarse chime-clock.

In the morning, Johnny was to go calling on wholesalers with David Hayes, but he slipped out early and saw his first streetcar. He was almost afraid to ride on anything so newfangled, but he watched Pittsburghers calmly stop the driver, who whoa'd the horses while the conductor took their nickel. The thing that terrified him most was showing himself up as a hick. To prove his nonchalance, he went into a saloon and had his initiation into something the bartender called a "cocktail." Compared to the boiler-splitters at home, this was delicious lemonade. He had several, and spent the rest of the day riding on every streetcar in Pittsburgh. By dusk, he reported, "quite a few of the conductors and drivers were calling me by my first name."

He spent the rest of his money fulfilling a dream he'd had since childhood: to own a whole barrel of maple syrup. He arrived at the dock with his barrel in a carriage, just in time to take the steamer home. I suspect his future partner must have had qualms right then, if he hadn't before, but if Mrs. McClintock had already invested in the store it would have been hard for Hayes to tell her the deal was off.

Back at the farm, Johnny contentedly poured syrup on everything he ate that week, and told of his fabulous trip, a slightly censored version. His aunt still thought he'd been meeting wholesalers with David Hayes.

About a week after his return, Johnny was out with his team, and came home to be met by a weeping Eleanor. His aunt, starting a fire in the cookstove, had tried to hurry the process by sprinkling crude oil on the kindling. She was horribly burned, and died the next day. Johnny, almost frantic with grief and shock, and with a memory inflamed by all he'd seen at the Rouse fire, kept saying to his wife, "But she was so *good*. She worked so hard. And she never had any fun with her money."

By the terms of the will, he didn't come into ownership of the farm until he was twenty-one, in another six weeks. But in the meantime, there was $24,500 in the Widow's safe.

It's a bit of irony that the first slice of that sum went to a lawyer Johnny consulted in Franklin, earnestly asking advice on how to handle business matters. During a half-hour talk, the lawyer advised the naïve young heir to let everything run along as before, and simply reratify existing leases on the farm when he came of age. For this less-than-Solomon instruction, the man's fee was $500.

The $24,500 was now down to $24,000. But Johnny's royalties from leases were running $2,000 to $3,000 a day.

And to focus attention on him, the Hammond well drilled on his farm spouted in late April, a gusher. It was owned by John Fertig, the young ex-schoolteacher who had taught "quiet," and his partner John Hammond, a big man with desperado mustachios who had been a frustrated Forty-niner in the gold rush. Stranded on the West Coast, Hammond had conceived the rather chilling idea of profiteering on ice needed for feverish victims of a cholera epidemic in Sacramento. He went up to the Sierras with a borrowed team, hacked a ton of ice from the mountain gorges, and arrived back in town with half of his wagonload still unmelted. He sold it for a dollar a pound. After his return east, some of these dollars-on-ice had gone into leasing, with John Fertig, a piece of the Widow McClintock's land. Their well wasn't in a class with the Empire or Phillips, but with oil prices now anywhere from $7 to $13.50 a barrel, the yield was a golden one. And Johnny's royalties zoomed. Newspapers played up young Steele's coming into his inheritance just as a new gusher hit, a sensational birthday present.

Johnny's wishful thinking began to soar beyond the barrel of maple syrup. If only he had a really fine team of horses. The team his aunt had bought him was the dray-horse variety, and he began to talk rather grandly about needing something better. One of the men who heard him was a slick-haired, slicker-tongued barrel salesman from Meadville, Dan Fowler. He knew just the team, he said.

The team, as a decoy, was good. Johnny, who had been a teamster long enough to have some knowledge of horses, was delighted to get them for $600. (He eventually sold them for $1,000, the only money he made in the whole comedy-tragedy of crazy spending ahead.)

Fowler, Dapper Dan himself, made Johnny feel he was "a greater financier than Jay Gould." After a heady dose of deference and drinks, he introduced his pleased victim to a friend, Horace Cullom, who also professed to be struck by Johnny's amazing financial acumen. Cullom explained that he owned a lot at the corner of Chestnut and Water Streets, and planned to build a business block there. He would allow Johnny, as a special favor, to buy a half interest. Johnny signed—the first of his foolish signatures—to pay $5,000 down and $5,000 a month for eight more months. Ah, well, now a brilliant young business man like Steele should own some residential property too. By a darling coincidence, Horace Cullom owned a fine house and lot on Crab Alley near Chestnut. Sold—for ten thousand. Before the day was over, Fowler had Johnny back at the place outside Meadville where he'd bought the team, buying the farm itself for a mere $7,000 more. Then Dapper Dan and Cullom let their golden goose go home. But they must have fretted at letting him get away so soon; a week later, they flattered him into buying three more lots, for $5,500. Each deal called for more drinks, before and after.

By this time, Johnny's pretty nineteen-year-old wife was in "poor health," and moderns weaned on psychiatric jargon would have wordy ideas why. A young Meadville doctor Johnny had met through Dan Fowler and Cullom came to the farm to examine Eleanor, and said a change of scene was all she needed. No, no charge. The doctor waved aside all mundane talk of fees, and Johnny was touched and grateful. But a day or so later, the doctor asked if he might borrow $600 to take a graduate course in medicine. He got the $600—for good.

Eleanor Steele must have been grateful for the "change-of-scene" prescription, thinking it would be an excuse to get Johnny away from Oil Creek and Fowler. After family consultations, it was decided the young couple and their child should visit in Philadelphia. Johnny's father-in-law had lived there before he came to Venango County, and the Moffitts must have thought their relatives in the Quaker City would keep an eye on Johnny. As it turned out, half the population of Philadelphia kept their eyes on him, in astonishment, disgust, envy or glee.

Just before the Steeles left for the east, William Wickham, a member of a New York investment firm, came to Oil Creek and offered to buy Johnny's one-eighth royalty interest in the Hammond gusher for $100,000. That was late one Saturday afternoon. They agreed to sign the papers on Monday.

On Sunday, after the tubing was pulled from two wells across the creek at Rouseville, the Hammond was suddenly flooded, and useless.

Johnny himself admitted cheerfully afterward that he had hoped to keep this news from Wickham till after the papers were signed, and he must have gone about it like a canary swallowing a cat. The wily Wickham, sensing something was up from Johnny's frenzied impatience to rush him to Oil City to sign, said, "No, let's go up and take another look at the well first."

Once Wickham had looked, and heard the gloomy prognostications, he called the deal off. But to Johnny's guilty wonder, Wickham was nicer to him than ever, and urged him to visit in New York on his way to Philadelphia.

Johnny thought it was a bully idea. He would go on ahead, and Eleanor and their little boy would join him a few days later. Until she arrived, Wickham showed him the sights, and they made the grandeur of Pittsburgh streetcars seem piddling. The two men drove in a smart hansom to dine at the new Fifth Avenue Hotel which had sensational innovations: private bathrooms for one hundred rooms, and an amazing "perpendicular railway intersecting each story." Johnny rode on this elevator to the dizzying top, six stories up.

Wickham, who years later became Mayor of New York, was a charming and knowing host. At the Astor House, on Broadway at Barclay, he introduced the young provincial to politician and journalist friends, and had him sample the famous free lunch at the bar that was the longest in town. Johnny sampled more than free lunch there. He had his first champagne on this visit, but to a man initiated on boiler-splitters, the "bubbly" was no great shakes, and although he was to buy a good many magnums for others, he went on preferring whiskey. It was just that now he wanted the best imported brands. And the finest Havana cigars were none too good, for the twenty-one-year-old whom Wickham introduced as "a great oil prince and a prince of a fellow."

At the end of three days of this treatment, Johnny was floating so high he resented being wrenched down to the humdrum level of family life. When Eleanor arrived, exhausted from an overnight trip on the cars with a small boy, and as shy as a sweet brown wren among peacocks, Johnny took her hastily to her relatives in Philadelphia. He didn't quite have the brashness to dump her there and rush back by himself to New York. Instead, he told Eleanor, in the virtuous, see-how-busy-I-am tone of a restless husband, that he must go back to Oil Creek at once and see to his affairs.

And it was on that trip home that he met the most plausibly helpful scoundrel of all, Seth Slocum.

Seth was the wolf-in-black-sheep-clothing of a good old Erie family, and he had come down to Oil Creek to see what he could latch onto. He was glib and worldly, at least by Johnny's standards, and although he wasn't especially prepossessing, he had an almost hypnotic charm for the boy.

Of the two, Johnny was far and away the more handsome: he was tall and innocently boyish looking, with beautiful dark eyes, the kind of hair women want to smooth tenderly, a sensual, almost Cupid's bow mouth, and a trace of baby fat around his chin. When the two men met, Seth explained easily that he was looking for congenial work. Most jobs were so boring, and Oil Creek was so crude; he was sure Johnny must feel limited here too. An oil prince of discernment needed a cosmopolitan city as a worthy setting. Johnny lapped it all up. This wonderful sophisticate understood him as no one else had. Seth was the one person who really cared about his happiness. When his new friend offered graciously to go back with him to Philadelphia and show him the town, for a mere matter of expenses, Johnny was overcome with joy.

In Philadelphia, Seth, the man of the world, said of course they would stop at the best hotel, the Girard House. They engaged—or Seth did—a suite, but Johnny was still enough himself to insist on rejoining his wife. He found an act-of-God excuse waiting for him at Eleanor's relatives: the house was quarantined because Johnny's little son had smallpox. He returned to the hotel anxious and depressed over his son's dangerous illness, and Seth prescribed a few drinks to ease his worry. And more drinks to celebrate when his child was out of danger. By then, Johnny was standing firmly on quicksand. His New York friend, William Wickham, had offered to buy his farm outright for a million dollars. Johnny, who had left an agent in charge at Oil Creek to collect the fat royalties, refused. He had loved and perhaps feared the woman who'd brought him up, and he didn't think he should sell her home. Seth Slocum thought otherwise. It was Seth who talked Wickham into raising his offer to one million two hundred thousand.

But by now the Widow McClintock's brothers-in-law had brought suit to break the will that gave the farm to Johnny, and until that was settled, Johnny couldn't make an outright sale because he didn't have a clear title. Never mind, Wickham said genially. He would pay $30,-000 cash down as rental for six months, and if by then the title was clear, he'd pay the rest of the twelve hundred thousand.

Johnny deposited the $30,000 in the hotel office, in a private strongbox urged on him by the galvanized manager. The entire hotel staff was laying itself out like a rosy red carpet for their prodigal guest. Rumors about him flew like mosquitoes, swollen with each new tidbit. Johnny had just got a million. He was to get a million more in six months. Other guests began to stare at him eagerly. At first, the boy so country-fresh and new to a city was embarrassed by all the attention. But soon he was swaggering up and down the corridors with Seth, courting stares.

The idea of moving back with a sorrowful-eyed wife and her relatives was too drab to contemplate. He took Eleanor and the small Oscar home to the farm, and then hightailed it back to Seth and Philadelphia. Now he was gloriously free to see the town. All he had to do for six months was to spend money, enjoy himself, and wait for his million-and-more from Wickham.

Wartime Philadelphia was crowded and hectic, and the oil hysteria was louder than ever. The City of Brotherly Love had 1,000 new oil companies incorporated or incubated that year. Fly-by-days who couldn't afford to open an office advertised:

A RARE CHANCE:

An oil company in order to organize without delay, will receive one or two original Subscribers. Prospects unusually flattering, every satisfaction given.

    For interview, address Reliable, c/o Inquirer office

Profits in legitimate firms soared; the Atlas Oil Company announced its third dividend within a month, out of net earnings. The Philadelphia *Ledger* exulted over the leap in export of coal oil (a term used interchangeably with petroleum), twenty million gallons in the first eight months of 1864. It assured readers: "There is no falling off in supply of oil, as had been previously feared and predicted by those who could not rationally account for the wonderful existence of oil so far below the surface of the earth." One well alone, the *Ledger* chortled, had produced more in a day than eight hundred whaleships had brought back to New Bedford in a whole year.

It all added up to the cheery thought, "Go ahead and invest. You can't miss."

When the stock of the Maple Shade Company was put on the market, men lined up for two blocks, holding their hands up and waving their money frantically, shouting their names and orders, terrified that they might be left out of the buying. In this atmosphere, the wildest rumors about Johnny's fortune were believable. And it worked both ways, because seeing Johnny in the diamond-studded flesh, and reading about his extravagances, ordinary citizens took him as an example of what oil could do for them, and bought stock more wildly than ever.

Thanks to Seth, the oil heir was seen all too clearly, on their debut in new suits. Seth had taken Johnny to a tailor, and wanting to show himself a man of uncommon taste, had contemptuously waved aside the bolts of fine dark cassimere the man showed them. Too plebeian, too dull. The tailor got his revenge; he pulled out a bolt of horse-blanket plaid, with reds, blacks and grass-greens that called for blinders.

Johnny protested timidly it looked "too much like a gambler," but no self-respecting gambler would have touched it. Seth Slocum told the tailor to make up two suits in a hurry.

With this horse-blanket finery, they wore high silk hats, enormous diamond stickpins, gold chains draped down their boiled shirt fronts attached to large gold watches, and they carried gold-headed canes. Their appearance in the hotel lobby caused such a stir that Johnny wanted to go back upstairs and change his clothes. Instead, they had a few whiskeys and set out again. Within two blocks, they had a chattering, giggling crowd of followers, and when a puzzled policeman stopped them, Seth, whose idea of wit matched the outfit, announced they were bounty jumpers. The cop didn't think it was funny; he hauled them into court, where a chastened Johnny explained to the judge they were visitors from Oil Creek.

The judge dismissed the case with a grin, but Johnny, still shaken by the humiliation of being arrested, turned on Seth bitterly. His ex-teamster vocabulary of curses must have startled Seth and sharpened his cunning. He gave the suits to a bellboy, poured drinks to toast "the best sport in town," and soon had Johnny exactly where he wanted him, in an alcoholic haze that never quite lifted. Whenever sobriety threatened to rear its ugly head and remind Johnny guiltily of his wife, Seth poured on more anesthesia. He soon wangled power of attorney, and the money gushered out in an insane flow.

They bought a large, elaborate carriage, and as an extra touch had Johnny's "coat of arms"—a derrick, tank, and flowing well—painted in crimson on the door. (Johnny remarked later, "There was nothing else quite like it in the Quaker City," which was probably the understatement of the decade.)

This chariot, with its occupants shooting off rays of diamonds, was the first thing that drew reporters to Johnny. One wrote wryly, "It would almost seem that the wand of the good fairy had been at work turning rags into robes, cabbages into chariots, and rats into jolly charioteers. . . . What may we not expect hereafter, if spontaneous combustion does not ensue from the too rapid development of inflammable materials raised so suddenly to the surface."

The driver of the chariot soon found that one of his extracurricular, non-Cinderella chores was to carry at least one inert form to bed at dawn. But it was gratifying to drive the flashy vehicle and flashier occupants through Fairmount Park and have the passers-by gape. Another excursion was to a restaurant just outside town that served catfish and waffles; Johnny gorged on this delicacy until he broke out in a rash.

Soon they were driving every day to the race track at Point Breeze. They bought an expensive "thoroughbred," hired a trainer, and swaggered out importantly to clock their horse's speed. In these solo tryouts, the animal went like a winged steed, so they entered him in a race and laid down large, confident bets. On the big day, Johnny was inspired to drive a sulky to the track, standing up holding the reins with one hand and a large cigar with the other.

The crowd at the track was enormous. And when it was time for the race in which Johnny's horse was entered, the derisive cheers sounded in the owner's ears like acclaim to a conqueror. But the horse disliked noise, and he disliked company on the track. He simply stopped running and disdainfully let the panting competitors go past him.

He ended up working for a streetcar company.

After that, Johnny rollicked and spent more frantically than ever. A bootblack near the hotel who reveled in this lavish patron was the first to hail him as Coal Oil Johnny. (Considering all the diamonds, Rock Oil Johnny might have been closer.) Newspapers grabbed the name and made it a byword, a synonym for playboy gone wild.

The "gutter press" described happily how Coal Oil Johnny walked down Broad Street with five-dollar bills tucked in his buttonholes, for newsboys and bootblacks to pluck. As if the truth weren't blatant enough, their accounts of revels in Coal Oil Johnny's hotel suite outstripped even Roman orgies. The Brussels carpets were soaked with champagne; silk stockings hung from the chandeliers in streamers, while the stockings' owners danced, dishabille, on the marble-topped tables, or hung out the window shrieking at the people on the street below. Comatose guests were strewn about the floor like empty bottles.

Another free-flowing yarn had Johnny miffed at the rudeness of a clerk in the Continental Hotel, and demanding that the offender be fired. The manager refused: "After all, you can't tell me what to do. Only the owner can do that." Johnny promptly offered to rent the place for one day, for $8,000. As a friend described it, "The doors were thrown open and every guest in the house had his fill of wine and edibles free of cost. A huge placard was posted in front of the hotel: 'Open house today; everything free; all are welcome.' It was a merry lark. The whole city seemed to catch on and the house was full. When Johnny thought he had had fun enough he turned the hostelry over to the landlord."

Steele said he never rented the Continental, he just went on a hat-smashing spree there, in the bar. "When I reached a certain stage, I wanted to smash every high hat that came to my notice."

One night he inaugurated a smasheroo that lasted for hours, and left some bashed heads as well as flattened lids. The next day he bought a new eight-dollar opera hat for every man in the crowd.

Readers weary of the war swallowed accounts of these escapades like comic strips, before they turned to the news of the day: General Sherman, already on his march south, had tried to cut off the Confederate's masterful strategist Johnston, "whom the Rebels describe as exceeding even Bragg in a retreat, but Johnston was too watchful of his rear to be so readily entrapped. . . . The few prisoners taken asserted that Johnston's force numbered from forty-five to fifty thousand men, from eight to ten thousand of whom were new troops; many of them unfit for duty because of ill health, which is no excuse from the sweeping Rebel conscription."

Northern recruiting was still lenient and loop-holed; the Conscription Act of 1863 required all men between the ages of twenty to forty-five to report for service, unless they paid $300 or hired a substitute. The firm of Turner, Dougherty & Wroe, on Dock Street in Philadelphia, advertised:

> We beg leave to call the attention of those who are liable to military duty . . . to our office for procuring either substitutes or volunteers. We are prepared to furnish men either for the Army or Navy, at short notice and reasonable prices.

The Philadelphia *Sunday Dispatch* reported, "General Grant was lately rallied about the persistent and preposterous use, by a New York paper, of his name for the Presidency. The General replied: 'I aspire to only one political office. When this war is over, I mean to run for Mayor of Galena (his place of residence). And if elected, I intend to have the sidewalk fixed up between my house and the depot.' "

Editorials pointed out crossly that the French had finished the Suez Canal while our country was using its manpower and money on fighting. Several writers asked fretfully "Can we continue to afford this war?" But they went on running stories on the most notorious spender of all, Coal Oil Johnny.

By now, his hotel suite was crowded day and night with hangers-on, fawners and leeches. A relative of Eleanor's who came to try to talk sense to the spendthrift heir and got nowhere, viewed this throng in disgust, and afterward sent Johnny a clipping from the *Inquirer,* giving a cure for "Slobbering in Horses caused by eating clover. A teaspoonful of alum salt mixed with a spoonful of Macassar horse-powders cures slobbering at once." The relative thought it might be a good idea to try alum salt and Macassar horse powder on the human slobberers.

But what they got was more champagne and tureens of pickled oysters.

When other guests in the hotel complained of the noise, Johnny bought a cornet and tooted "Hail Columbia" all night long, till even the obsequious manager complained. Several of the guests threatened to horsewhip the tooter. Johnny, already punchy, now conceived the brilliant notion of taking boxing lessons. His friend Wickham had once taken him in New York to the gymnasium of a retired fighter, Joe Coburn, for a drink at the saloon there. Escaping even Seth Slocum, Johnny got to Coburn's and announced he had learned how to fight in the oil country, where teamsters were tough, and wanted a workout. Coburn knocked him out in the first practice round. Johnny came to, reared up groggily, and said, "Drinks for everybody here on me." Having established this sporting precedent, he spent the rest of the day being knocked out at staggered intervals; by nightfall, he was a mass of bruises and the customers were full of free booze.

It was during this New York visit that the *Sun* commented: "A young man, formerly of humble circumstances, has an income of $7,000 per day paid him as his share of certain oil lands in Pennsylvania. This amounts to $2,548,060, per annum. He may be able to live on it."

The *Herald,* as if wanting to make clear that one wastrel heir wasn't typical of the hard-working, responsible men on Oil Creek, mentioned Will Phillips, the ex-river pilot who had become wealthy from one well: "He attends to the largest amount of business of any man in Oil City without the slightest confusion. He has great coolness and decision of character. All trust in him and are willing to pay somewhat higher for the oil they purchase from him because his representations are so perfectly reliable."

Toward the end of the piece, there was one oblique reference to

Johnny; after remarking on the oil royalties that came so fast the recipients couldn't keep count, it went on:

> Already some of the evil effects of the sudden acquisition of wealth are noticeable. Youths, whose income are said to be in the neighborhood of one thousand dollars per day, without proper education become the prey of the designing, and are sometimes led into temptations far worse than those of poverty. These need educational arrangements for the youth of a section of the country that must rapidly rise to great wealth, to train them properly for their present and future responsibility.

The *Sun* ran another story, about a "Mr. Oilygammon" who had held a séance which the reporter claimed to have attended. When the medium went into a trance and announced that spirits were present, Oilygammon roared, "I'll take Bourbon straight." Next, there was unearthly music, "a cross between a Chinese war gong and that emitted by a brace of cats suspended over a clothes line," and as a further manifestation, the "spirits" produced, for Oilygammon, a decanter and glasses.

> A streak of blue lightning began to trickle from the neck of the decanter into the goblets, each of which as it filled came temptingly to the lips of those assembled. Oilygammon swallowed at a draught the blue wine before him, and sank back overcome by the spirits' manifestations. A loud rap upon the table announced the departure of the ghosts who had thus displayed their wonderful power over poor human nature. The gas having been lighted, our reporter says the sight that met his gaze satisfied him that spiritual science as practised at Oilygammon's was a great improvement over the "spirit" mills upon which Uncle Sam collects his "internal revenue tax." The mediums were lying promiscuous like, muddled completely by a single charge. As this reporter grasped his hat, Oilygammon seized his hand and asked him to "hic, hic, call again."

During Johnny's New York sprees, the most popular dispenser of spirits was Robert Heller, who claimed to have "second sight and hypernatural vision." He was said to have come over from England with the actress Laura Keene, and was known as her "protector." (His touted second sight evidently didn't see far enough ahead to warn her against playing at Ford's Theater in Washington the next spring.) In the murky-with-incense atmosphere of Heller's Salle Diabolique, the owner performed his would-be black magic nightly. Spirit hands gyrated from nowhere; a small boy was suspended in mid-air, appearing and disappearing. There were acts billed as The Witches' Pole, Heller's Goblin Drum, and Lucifer's Punch Bowl.

At a guess, I'd say it was Lucifer's Punch Bowl that must have appealed most to the bewitched, bedeviled boy from Oil Creek. At the Winter Garden, *Nabob for an Hour* was playing, but there is no record that Johnny saw it; he was too busy living it. (A year later there were two plays based on him: *The Amateur Millionaire* and *Struck Oil.*)

Theatres were booming that summer and early fall. A reporter noted:

> The ladies are out on Broadway in full force again, and the display of silks, satins, velvets, in short, everything but *calicoes,* is, as George Francis Train would say, immense. We shall soon have to build new theatres if this war goes on. Last night, people were turned away from every place of public amusement in the city, some houses not having even standing room for them. Below I give you a memorandum of the receipts at the doors of the leading establishments:
>
> | | |
> |---|---|
> | Wallachs | $1100. |
> | Olympic | $1200. |
> | Broadway | $ 950. |
> | Niblo's | $1300. |
> | Winter Garden | $1000. |
> | Bowery | $ 900. |
> | Barnum's | $ 850. |
> | Total, | $7300. |
>
> If Heller's and other places of the kind are taken into consideration, the expenditures for the night will probably not be less, if they are not in excess of, ten thousand dollars. That will do, for one night!

Another account, on the opening of the opera, said more pointedly, "If shoddy will have music, shoddy must pay for it. Accordingly, the admission is placed at $1.50 and $2 for secured seats. This is rather steep, as the boys say, but the profits from Petroleum are such as should induce the MacFlimseys to accept them without a protest."

Coal Oil Johnny was not only accepting the price of seats, but helping to subsidize chorus girls. At Fox's Casino in Philadelphia, he and Seth lolled in a box, smoking cigars and drinking (none of this nonsense about waiting till intermission) while they eyed the shapely dancers to decide which ones were most deserving of a little diamond memento. A favorite undergarment for females was the Patent Shoulder-brace Corset with Elastic Steel Puff Springs, but the chorus at Fox's Casino was less restrained, in form and deed.

Restraints seemed to be loosening among tragediennes, too. The *Sunday Dispatch* noted, "Ada Menken is considerably more undressed than any actress yet tolerated on the American stage. Her costume in 'Mazeppa' may be described as consisting of a flesh-fitting suit with the little end of a dimity nothing fastened to the wrist. . . . Prudery is obsolete. A number of ladies were present, determined to know if the performance was proper for them to behold."

At the Chestnut Street Theatre, where *Aladia* was playing, ladies in nude-colored tights cavorted under a fountain of oily rainbow colors. Johnny also enjoyed a dancing horse named Mayfly.

But of all the shows in Philadelphia, his favorite was Carncross and Dixey's Minstrels, where a singer did a feeling rendition of the great new hit, "Oil on the Brain":

> "The Yankees boast that they make Clocks
> Which just beat all creation.
> With our great Speculation.
> Our stocks like clocks
> They never made one could keep time
> Wind up—run down again
> But all our strikes are sure to cause
> Oil on the Brain.
> Stocks par—Stocks up, then on the wane
> Everybody's troubled with Oil on the Brain.
>
> "There's neighbor Smith, a poor young man
> Who couldn't raise a dime;
> Had clothes which boasted many rents,
> And took his 'nip' on time.
> But now he's clad in Dandy style,
> Sports diamonds, kids and cane;
> And his success was owing to
> Oil on the Brain."

At the end of the song, Coal Oil Johnny would wave from his box to the gaping audience, like a king acknowledging tribute.

But gradually, that fall, the climate began to change. A month or so earlier, a *Ledger* columnist had written, "Nobody thinks or talks of the 'war,' which is now become, in the eyes of the butterflies, simply a means for enabling the old man (that is, pa) to add to his bankbook by pocketing the profits of a Government contract."

Now he complained that men were "at present so immersed in politics that the ordinary elegancies of life and even life's commonest recreations are quite neglected."

The Democrats had nominated General McClellan—little Mac—to run against Lincoln in the 1864 election. Sherman had taken Atlanta, and there was a buoyant new hope, an upsurge of popularity for the President.

"The Political excitement on all hands is running very high. Ordinary business affairs are much interfered with by the various and it might be said incessant mass meetings. The theatres and other places of public amusement, all last week, for the same reason, did a very poor business. The people who usually crowd the pit and the upper tiers being absent. Merchants complain that calls from country customers are few and far between, rustics as well as metropolitans being all alike engaged in saving the country."

Instead of the sweetly sad war ballads that had been popular all over the North—"Aura Lea," "Lorena" and "Just before the Battle, Mother"—the newest rousing favorite was "Hold on, Abraham!"

While a gaunt President was holding on against his enemies north and south, Johnny was looking more frantically than ever for new distractions. He and Seth finally hit on the gaudiest stunt of all: they bought a half interest in a bankrupt minstrel show, Skiff and Gaylord, and dove in head first. Seth ordered $5,000 worth of posters, with a picture of Coal Oil Johnny in the upper right corner, and an advance agent rushed these over to New Jersey, to pave the way for a tour. The company, which included a double clog team, a female impersonator, Skiff as Interlocutor, Gaylord as Bones, and a small, double-jointed comedian as Tambo, followed along. Johnny, according to the accounts, bought every member of the cast, male and female, a diamond ring, a gold watch, and a complete new wardrobe. When he and Seth marched at the front of the parade held in each town before a performance, he added a few more diamonds to his customary high-hat regalia. Then he stood out in front of the theatre, taking tickets and bows.

Gaylord told a reporter, "Reaching Utica, New York, Johnny treated to a supper for the company which cost one thousand dollars. He then conceived the idea of traveling by his own train and purchased an engine, a sleeper, and a baggage car. Dates for two weeks were canceled and we went junketing, Johnny footing the bill. . . . Our dates being canceled, Johnny insisted upon indemnifying us for the loss of time. He paid all salaries, estimated the probable business receipts upon the basis of packed houses, and paid that also to our treasurer."

Steele in later years countered crossly that he never bought a whole train; all he did, when he jumped off for a drink at a way stop and got left behind, was to hire an engine, for $50, and ride with the engineer while the station agent had the train flagged and held for him farther down the line. Hiring a locomotive for an hour for a mere $50 must have seemed very minor, like flicking a toothpick.

At the end of two weeks with the troupe, when he and Seth went back to Philadelphia, offers from circuses and medicine shows poured in. Barnum was too busy with Tom Thumb to pursue Coal Oil Johnny, but lesser impresarios competed noisily. Johnny turned them all down. The idea of being paid to be a freak, instead of paying to be one, insulted him.

He also turned down at least a hundred proposals of marriage, or rather, ignored the letters. His begging mail was now astronomical. One female wrote him demanding money for a trousseau so she could catch a husband; another wanted a piano and music lessons. He was asked to pay for operations, lift mortgages, and even provide new homes. Promoters of fake gold mines haunted him.

Seth screened applicants for loans, and let only his friends profit. One of these ran up enormous bills in Johnny's name, for furnishings for a billiard parlor. No matter who spent the money it was Johnny who continued to collect the notoriety. A rival of Pears Soap put out a soap called Coal Oil Johnny, and enclosed, with each package, a circular giving spicy highlights, true or false, of his career.

At Christmas time, the evergreens piled on the city sidewalks for sale thrust into Johnny's consciousness. They reminded him of the hemlocks that had stood sentinel outside the meeting house, and the cool green forests where he'd hunted, and the Christmas before when he and Eleanor had strung cranberries to trim a tree. What was she thinking now? What was he doing, in the stale litter of an endless binge? Seth reminded him heartily that he was almost due for his million. (Culbertson McClintock's brothers hadn't succeeded in breaking the will, and Johnny had clear title to the farm.) In the meantime, Seth pointed out, there were plenty of pretty creatures at Fox's Casino who needed a few Christmas baubles. The charge account at the jeweler's zoomed up. Life was gay again.

Several old friends arrived from Oil Creek, and did their best to warn Johnny that he mustn't put faith in Wickham's promises. They said the New Yorker had been getting whatever he could out of the two-hundred-acre farm in a hurry, during his six months' rental. Johnny told them to stop being spoil-sports, and threw parties in their honor, complete with dancing girls, to show what a great man he was.

In January, all the bubbles burst in frightening succession.

Wickham didn't pay the million-plus and buy the farm; instead, he entered a judgment for the amount he'd already advanced. The hotel manager, no longer suavely salaaming, presented a bill for $19,824. (He had already collected about $7,000, or over a thousand a month.) Two jewelers and a tailor entered judgments for a total of more than the hotel's. The hat-maker, Warburton, presented a new bill for $300. A cigar-maker wanted $562. Another creditor demanded $2,200 for an oil painting. The billiard tables charged to Johnny by Seth's friend came to $1,500.

The ciphers kept rolling in. Two lawyers claimed $22,500. A man who had leased a small piece of the farm for drilling, and got only a dry hole, even sued for $5,000 to repay him for his trouble.

It was a field day for vultures, as well as the bona-fide, justly angry creditors.

The hangers-on went off in a flap; charioteers turned back into rats. Seth Slocum was the only one who hung on, in a desperate blend of hope and habit. Johnny, completely sober for the first time in months, told him to get out. Seth whined he had to have money to go with, and Johnny, open-handed even in bankruptcy, gave him two notes of $2,500 each, which Seth sold for a few hundred dollars to a Meadville man. Then these too were entered in judgment against the farm.

Dapper Dan Fowler, the ex-barrel salesman, now appeared in the guise of a friend in need. For two loans amounting to about $4,000, plus $3,000 more paid to Johnny's bewildered under-age wife on the farm in exchange for her signature, Dan took over Meadville property for which Johnny's agent had kept up payments totaling $67,000. (This is Steele's own estimate, and I don't pretend to know whether it's exact or not, but I've never seen any figures contradicting it.)

And for the first time, there was an Internal Revenue agent to be reckoned with. To help pay war costs, the government had put through a temporary 10 per cent tax on income, and a luxury tax on various possessions. The 1865 tax form listed, for instance: "Gold watches composed wholly or in part of gold or gilt, kept for use, valued at above one hundred dollars. . . . Carriage, gig, rockaway, buggy wagon. . . . Billiard tables kept for use."

There was no question that Johnny had bought more gold watches than anyone else in the country, but he hadn't kept them for use, or at least not more than half a dozen. He had never known what time it was, until now.

Most of his farm on Oil Creek was sold by the county sheriff for government taxes, then resold to private companies to satisfy some small portion of creditors. The new daily of the oil region, the Titusville *Herald,* reported on Dec. 21, 1866, "Wine, women, horses, faro and general debauchery soon made a wreck of that princely fortune. . . . [Coal Oil Johnny] is now filling the honorable position of doorkeeper for Skiff and Gaylord's Minstrels."

"Mister Bones" and his partner were the only friends who repaid past favors, by giving Johnny a job with their show on the road.

Seth Slocum, the *Herald* said, had "captured" $100,000 from Johnny Steele and squandered it. "At last accounts Slocum was in jail in a neighboring county, for various breaches of the peace, and unable to obtain bail in the sum of $500."

When Seth Slocum was dying two years later, he sent a message begging Johnny to come, but Johnny refused: "If he wants my forgiveness, he has it. I will not say I was not as much to blame."

By then, Steele was back with his wife, and he said long afterward that Eleanor and her parents never once reproached him. "The fatted calf was killed for the returning and foolish prodigal. My welcome was true and hearty. I was 'returned and no questions asked.' "

He repaid this loving faith by going on the wagon, in every sense of the phrase. He stayed sober, his in-laws bought him a team, and he moved his family to Franklin and earned a living hauling freight. After a year of this, he was offered the job of baggage agent on the Oil Creek railroad at Rouseville, at $60 a month. He rented out his team, bought a house there, worked from 6 A.M. till 11 P.M. at the depot, and got a $20 raise. "I kept myself in a comparatively happy frame of mind," he wrote later, "happy because I was winning my way in the world, regaining the respect of my former neighbors and friends, and that too, in sight of the old farm across the creek that had been such a factor in my life."

An old man who had known Steele in those years told me, "Folks around here never paid him too much mind. In the city, he got a lot of gawkin', but around here on Oil Creek, too much was happening. Anyway, we thought he was kind of silly."

But because of all that was happening on Oil Creek, reporters were still there in droves; they soon discovered that the baggage agent was Coal Oil Johnny, and rushed to send stories to their papers. A publisher offered him a $5,000 advance and a ghost writer for his memoirs. Steele refused. (Thirty years later he collaborated with a Franklin man, in writing *Coal Oil Johnny, His Book,* which was brought out by a vanity press, with the author or his friends footing the bill.)

He also refused an offer later to go on exhibition at the Centennial Exposition in Philadelphia. Of all the places he never wanted to see again, the City of Brotherly Love headed the list.

But he soon had to face up to the fact that the rowdy, roistering Oil Creek was no place for him. "The invitations to drink became too frequent. So I concluded to seek pastures new, and felt a deeper longing than ever to find some place where no one knew of my past career."

He found the place in Denison, Iowa, where he settled his family and worked for a Quaker grain and feed merchant whose motto Johnny quoted with pride: "When buying grain, pay all you can for it; but do not pay so much that you will have to cheat your customer in weight."

Only his employer knew of his past. The Steeles became happily involved in church work; life seemed completely reborn. It was a Franklin man who let the mischief loose again; he came to Iowa on business, and in a tongue-wag with acquaintances there, mentioned that Steele was Coal Oil Johnny. Once more the stories and offers started up. Chicago wanted him for an exhibit in a dime museum; reporters surrounded the house; a Burlington newsman got into the house through a ruse, and Johnny pitched him out the door, yelling, "If I'd killed a half-dozen like you during my career, I'd have been better off."

About this time, his kind Quaker employer retired and the Steeles moved to Kearney, Nebraska, where Johnny was in charge of a freight yard.

In his sober, church-going years in Kearney, he used to watch tolerantly as the cowboys rode into town, waving their guns and shooting at the sky. Many of them rode their broncos right into a saloon and up to the bar. "Their fun was of a kind to scare a tenderfoot," Johnny reported. He himself was no tenderfoot when it came to sprees.

One of the recurring stories that annoyed him was that he had given away dozens of teams and carriages, to friendly drivers. Steele said he only gave one away. When he left Philadelphia for good, the only creditor who hadn't dunned him was the driver-groom who had carried him to bed so many dawns. Johnny went to the man's stable to say good-bye, and in lieu of cash, gave him the carriage with the crimson coat of arms. It was his last large gesture as Coal Oil Johnny.

In his memoirs, he wrote, "If someone were to ask me to pen a sentiment for the benefit of young men who have to face the temptations of the world, I do not know of anything better to say than, 'Tell the boys to drink water.' "

---◆◆◆---

From Petroleum Centre to Paris

WHEN Jim Farrel got so mad he spent $200 to go to court and get possession of a mean, rocky thirty acres, early in 1859, his neighbors said it was a sinful waste of money. They clucked more about that $200 than they ever fussed over Coal Oil Johnny's loose-handed craziness later. Farrel's wife and four children weren't exactly delighted either, but the head of the house was roaring like a gored bull, and better he should roar in court than in their cabin.

Farrel, a farmer himself on a well-worked few acres, had felt sorry for a newly arrived Irishman who was trying to farm the miserably barren land next to his, fronting the creek. The man whined that if he just had a yoke of oxen, he might clear away enough rocks to raise some crops. Farrel was so hard up that he had to haul timber every spring and fall to shoe his children and horses, but he did have a yoke of oxen, and in a flush of neighborliness he sold this to the man on credit. The first payment was due after harvesting, but that was the summer of the terrible black frost, and the man simply vamoosed. He hitched up Farrel's oxen to a wagon, loaded a wife and other chattels aboard in the night, and made a slow getaway. All he left behind was thirty acres of the worst farm land in the state. Nobody

wanted it as a gift, and the truth is Farrel didn't want it as a gift
either—he just wanted revenge for his oxen. But it cost him two hundred including court costs to get clear title to the property. His wife's
sister was so exasperated she said Farrel was a big ox who ought to
be hitched up himself, for plowing. People referred to the land as
Rocky Revenge.

After Drake's hit, there were a lot of red faces talking out of the
other side of their mouths; two Crawford County men, Orange Noble
and George Delamater, had paid three times the "sinful waste of
money" for half the acreage of Rocky Revenge. Their lease gave Jim
Farrel one-fourth royalty on any oil found there, and for a while all
the clackers held their breath, afraid they'd have to eat their words
in even nastier doses, but the well, drilled down to 130 feet, seemed
to be a dry hole. That gave the carpers back their self-respect; you'd
think if a man was going to throw money away, he'd throw it on land
that had oil.

Jim Farrel was making good money as a teamster, hauling other
men's oil, and he was satisfied. He'd had his revenge, and a pleasant
profit. His lessees, Orange Noble, an ex-cattle dealer, and George
Delamater, an ex-lawyer, should have been satisfied too. They had a
successful store at Townville, and were also doing a brisk business
manufacturing "shooks." (This term intrigues me so much I don't
even want to know what *shooks* are; in my lexicon, *shooks* are the
tense past tense of "shakes," and I am happily mystified as to why
anybody wanted to manufacture them around Oil Creek, like heaping
coals on Newcastle.* But the dry hole they'd drilled on Rocky Revenge still bothered the partners. Delamater, who looked like a Roman senator, was a drivingly ambitious man. His partner Noble,
although he was only half as big around, had a strong-beaked face
and the kind of eyes my grandmother described as "looking like
burnt holes in a blanket." When an excited sightseer had returned
from Drake's well the day after the strike and told what he'd seen,
Noble had said scornfully, "You sound as if you believe what you're
saying." Now that Noble had been converted to a faith in the new
phenomenon, he wanted phenomena produced as regularly as shooks.

* Editor's note: *Shooks* are staves; authors are willfully ignorant.

Other wells leased by the partners lived up to this brisk production norm (a writer said of ex-lawyer Delamater, "He found it more profitable boring wells than boring juries") but there was still that one nagging failure. When Noble heard that Captain Andy Funk's well, just below Rocky Revenge, had been drilled through the rosy second sand-rock clear down to the third, and had spouted, he decided that maybe the land leased from Farrel wasn't so dry as they'd thought.

Early in 1863, a Pittsburgh firm, Caldwell & Company, brought in a gusher on the other half of the Rocky Revenge, and Noble and Delamater rushed back to retry their luck. This time, they hired a top Titusville driller who took a one-sixteenth working interest in the well as part fee, and provided a ten-horsepower engine and boiler. While he was drilling, Orange Noble chased all over the countryside looking for a particular kind of artesian tubing. None in Cleveland, only a few lengths left in Pittsburgh. He finally got a quantity made in Philadelphia and sent on to a machine shop in Pittsburgh to be fitted with a new kind of stopcock. After it was completed and shipped, it vanished from ken and was located weeks later in a freight car switched onto a siding. Noble buttonholed a director of the Oil Creek railroad, and wangled permission to take his freight on a passenger car from Corry to Oil Creek. He then tipped a trainman ten dollars (a fact Noble never forgot), to find him a space in the already jammed train, and finally landed with his precious stopcocks at Rocky Revenge.

High time, too. The driller was already down 450 feet, and jubilantly expectant. Noble was too tired after his hectic travels to sit on the well, watching. He went to a nearby shanty restaurant, and was wearily chewing some stringy meat when a boy standing at the door looking out said, "That well throws up bully."

Noble ignored this queasy sounding remark. The boy said it again, with even more enthusiastic delivery: "Yup, that well throws up bully."

This time, the words penetrated, and Noble got up calmly. Another well, another dollar. But this wasn't just another well, it was a monstrously crazy rip-snorter. Oil and water were shooting a hundred feet into the air, coating the trees with spray, while the ground heaved like an earthquake. The driller shouted above the roar at his employer, "Bigger than the Empire."

Now to attach the new stopcocks. But how? Nobody could get through the powerful, blinding jets of oil. Noble, babbling with excitement, offered $50 to any man who would do it, but even with that inducement, he got no takers for a while. After the first wild outpouring was spent, three men stripped to the buff, put on tight, heavy goggles, threw rubber blankets over their heads, and waded in. They nearly strangled in oil, but they got the stopcocks attached, and the huge flow was directed into tanks. When the naked, oil-dripping men staggered back out, Noble, delirious with relief, gave them two hundred apiece. It's doubtful if he had to economize to make up for this gesture; the income from the well was $12,000 to $45,000 a day.

As one reporter burbled, "Sinbad's fabled valley of the diamonds was a small side show compared with this, and all the Spanish gold of the Incas looked like a stack of nickels."

Jim Farrel did all right too, with his royalty on the Rocky Revenge leases. Twelve more wells were drilled there, including the generous-yielding Mulligan. When Farrel's daughter Sadie was married ten years later, her wedding was the most stupendous social event Titusville had ever seen. (We'll get to the reception later, and look over the menu and presents, including "a boudoir clock with exposed ruby palette.")

Orange Noble prudently took his earnings to Erie, where he built a business block and opened a bank. Interestingly enough, George Delamater did exactly the same, in Meadville, but the man who looked like a Roman senator still wasn't content. He ran for the State Senate against another oil man, George Anderson of Titusville, and even in the primary both men spent money like drunken landlubbers. Delamater won. Years later his son became a State Senator, then ran for Governor and was defeated. An oil historian said, "Ruined by politics, unable longer to stand the drain that had been sapping its resources, the Delamater Bank suspended two weeks after the gubernatorial election. The brick block, the homes of the parents and the sons, the assets of the concern—mere drops in the bucket—met a trifling percentage of the liabilities. Property was sacrificed, suits were entered and dismissed, savings of depositors were swept away. . . . The senior Delamater went to Ohio to start life anew at seventy-one. George W. [son] located in Chicago and quickly gathered a law practice. That he will regain wealth and honor, pay off every creditor and some day represent his district in Congress those who know him best are not unwilling to believe. The fall of the Delamaters—the beggary of the aged father—the crushing of the son's honorable ambition— the exile from home and friends—the suffering of innocent victims— all these illustrate the sad reverses which, in the oil region, have 'come, not as single spies, but in battalions.' "

Coal Oil Johnny remarked, less floridly, that other men had made a lot more money than he had, and some of them lost it too.

As a reformed character, it must have given him an especially virtuous glow to see that the wildest, wooziest, booziest town in the oil region, Petroleum Centre, had spawned on the farm of the Widow McClintock's brother-in-law, George Washington McClintock.

Most of the 207-acre farm, halfway between Oil City and Titusville, had been sold to George Bissell, who still had a fist in every pie. Bissell, with Ohio lumberman Frederic ("Go dig your own") Prentice, formed the Central Petroleum Company to sublease the creekside land in half-acre lots, with half the oil reserved for the company. Soon the stream that had mirrored soaring trees reflected derricks as thick as masts. Meadows where cattle had grazed placidly were so crowded with shacks, tanks and honky-tonks, all mish-mashed together in the mud, that no cow could be seen for miles around.

A high-voltage railroad contractor, Edward Fox, who blew in with a wad to spend on leases, told Bissell, "Quit calling this Wash McClintock's farm—it doesn't sound right. Call it Petroleum Centre."

Operators who couldn't afford to lease in the town went into the deeply wooded circular ravine beyond, Wildcat Hollow, and soon it was perforated like a sieve, by drillers. It was there that the term was born for the free-lancing, daring oil men who risk their luck in untested fields: wildcatters. One of these men shot a wildcat there (even the wildcats had to give way before the wild rush of humans) and had the beast stuffed and put up on top of his derrick as a mascot. Newcomers who happened to look up suddenly would let out a nervous screech, expecting the beast to spring any second. But there were livelier dangers awaiting them in town: "Petroleum Centre could have given Sodom and Gomorrah points in wrecking weak mortals and sending them to the devil by the shortest cut."

Coal Oil Johnny, a connoisseur in short cuts to the devil, said, "For pure unadulterated wickedness it eclipsed any town I had ever favored with my presence. The scenes enacted caused even a 'rounder' to blush."

Wives who stayed with their oil-men husbands in the midst of this bawdy violence blushed even redder than Coal Oil Johnny. "Ladies picked their way along a plank sidewalk and would draw their skirts in close around them as if fearful of contamination."

The mud-slough main thoroughfare, Washington Street, had dance halls, stores, company offices, brothels and saloons strung along like the set for a Western movie. One New Yorker complained, "Rough-looking men with slouch hats are constantly galloping by on horseback. . . . Frequently two horsemen will halt and do business over the saddlebow, hundreds of thousands of dollars in options, leases and forfeits."

Even by boomtown standards, the setting was slapdash; Bissell's company had refused to sell any land outright, so that every plot was on a five-year lease at exorbitant rentals, with all buildings to revert to the company at the end of that time, and a thirty-day eviction clause in case the owners decided to drill on any spot suddenly. Partly because of this, the buildings were strips and slabs thrown together every which way, unweathered, unplastered, "like dry-goods boxes."

In the makeshift hotels and boarding houses, prices were so high that again there were squawks at the outrageous charges of $2 to $4 per *day,* and most of the workers slept in "cribs" attached to the engine houses, and cooked their own meals.

Toolies who finished the morning tour (midnight to noon shift) had a casually immodest approach to cleanliness, in keeping with the spirit of the place: they'd stroll down from the well to the creek bank, shed their slimy clothes, and bathe in the nude. Wives whose narrow vistas overlooked this public bath protested loudly, but their yelps were muffled in the twenty-four-hour-a-day din.

Dolly Varden's Saloon on Washington Street was a noisy favorite, but with curled-little-finger niceties such as "Choice wines, native and foreign." Patrons of Smith's Lager Beer Saloon thought wine was for invalids. Petroleum House, down the street, had "Billiard and Bath Rooms connected with this hotel." In front of Jimmy Linden's free-

and-easy, there was an astonishingly high flag pole where waved the only flag on display in Petroleum Centre during the Civil War. Inside, the pretty girl-waiters wore flouncy short skirts and red boots with jingly bells, modeled after those in Allen's "fast house" in New York. And like Allen's, the girls here "weren't slaves or servants, but companions." Their companionable costumes exposed bare knees, the mere thought of which caused respectable Venango County women, still cocooned to the ankles, to shudder.

In the dance halls, the so-called square dances bore no family resemblance to the wholesome variety still favored at barn dances, where men and girls lined up facing each other, and the caller shouted:

> "Rats in the buttermilk
> Two by two
> Skip to my Lou"

or to the neatly paced dance, the Needle's Eye:

> First couple leads up to the right
> And four hands round
> Chasse right, chasse left,
> Swing opposite partner once around
> Take care of yourself that you don't fall down.

In the Petroleum Centre dance halls, falling down, or being knocked down, was part of the fun. For females, there was also the chance of being tossed playfully into the air and caught on the downtake. To vary this, a girl would hold up her glass and her partner would kick it to the ceiling, then he'd hold it while she took a turn, displaying her ruffled cambric knickers. In kick-the-glass frolics, contestants and bystanders were showered with everything from beer to champagne.

Dances, carried on with the verve of jitter-bugging, included the Racket (a rowdy, bastardized schottische), Chase the Squirrel, the Galop, and the Crooked *S*. There was a new step called the American Petroleum Stomp, but boomtowners left this sort of trumped-up foolishness to Easterners. In Petroleum Centre, every dance was a stomp-romp, and women stepped lively to avoid having their toes trampled to mush by their partners' heavy boots.

Like cowboys', oil men's boots were a matter of sartorial pride. Stolz the bootmaker, whose shop on Washington Street was about the size and build of an outhouse, had a handsome cowhide pair hung up outside the door as a sample of his craft, and strips of other choice leathers flapping like streamers.

Prices of boots, which ranged from $2 to $12, weren't as flexible as those of two other establishments on the street: Madame Wood's and Miss Lucy Hart's, both of which did a roaring business (perhaps in the spirit of "It's Better with Your Boots Off"). Payday at the wells, usually Saturday, was especially brisk for trade:

> Oh, the toolie he fiddled
> And the driller he drilled
> Fiddlin' and drillin' their pockets they filled.
> But one fine night they met a whore
> And they're back in the rig a-drillin' some more.

At least once a client must have felt cheated, or perhaps it was a case of unrequited love demanding mob revenge. At any rate, the Titusville *Herald* reported an occasion when ex-customers (I assume) approached these recreation centers in a less than amorous spirit:

FEARFUL RIOT AT PETROLEUM CENTRE!

A RAID ON THE BAGNIOS!

TWO OF THE RIOTERS SHOT!

HOUSES DEMOLISHED!

WOMEN STRIPPED AND STAMPEDED!

It appears that about 10:42 o'clock Monday night a gang of bullies and bruisers collected in front of the house of Madame Wood, an establishment of Washington Street. . . . The ball was opened with a discharge of vulgar and profane expletives. [I don't know if one of Madame's girls was sassy enough to remind the bullies, "Sticks and stones may break my bones, but names can never hurt me"; anyway, the stone-throwing came next.] A missile thrown through one of the windows struck a lamp which fell to the floor and set the interior in a blaze.

Fires were so common in Petroleum Centre that the *Herald* neglects to add whether Madame Wood and her girls were singed, or saved for the flames of the Hereafter. "The house was little injured."

After retiring from the premises, the mob, as if by a common impulse, or by preconcerted arrangement, made their way to the residence of Miss Lucy Hart, also on Washington Street. It was a handsome, conspicuous dwelling, two stories in height and 20 feet front by 50 feet deep. [It takes a highly conscientious reporter to find out even the dimensions of a brothel.] It was newly and luxuriously furnished, for a house of the kind, the proprietress having paid $3,000 for the outfit before "opening shop."

On reaching their destination, several of the mob demanded that everybody should leave the house. The woman [Miss Lucy] was called to the door and asked how much time she required to get ready to leave town. She replied 24 hours. After some consultation among the leaders, there seemed to be a disposition to retire, when some party in the house, (supposed to be the bartender), discharged a pistol at the crowd from one of the windows. Shots were also fired from the second story by parties unknown.

Two men in the crowd were wounded by the shots, James Leonard receiving a bullet in his right arm and Peter Cosgrove a similar token in his right thigh. The wounded men were removed to a drug store for surgical treatment, and the crowd, greatly exasperated, stormed the building en masse. The windows and doors were shivered in every part of the house, and the raiders entered at every aperture in front, flank and rear.

Once within the walls, the rioters proceeded to commit every imaginable extravagance. Some of them rushed upstairs and commenced to ransack and pillage. Trunks and closets were broken open and their contents thrown about the floor, or stuffed into sacks and pillow cases and carried off. If the building had been on fire, and the multitude were intent on emptying it in the quickest time on record, they could not have evinced greater energy and determination.

One spectator counted seven hair sofas which were taken or thrown out of the house and instantly carried off. Four or five marble-topped tables were thrown out of the windows. [A favorite accessory in better-class sporting-houses was a gilded harp for the inmates to pluck. It would be interesting to know if a large gilded harp hurtled out of Miss Lucy's window that night, after the marble-topped tables.] Trunks, Brussels carpets, mattresses, bed clothes, chairs and every species of furniture and crockery shared the same fate. There were a dozen casks of lager beer in the house, which were carried away by the crowd. The rioters walked off deliberately with their plunder in every direction and seemed to enjoy the havoc and depredations as the most innocent of pastimes. Wanton destruction and pillage seemed to be the main object of the demonstration. The partitions were all demolished. Some of the women were stripped of their clothing and brutally outraged. There were six in the house, and after their escape they sought shelter in every direction. Wherever they were found by the rioters the house was threatened and they were compelled to seek other hiding places. Our reporter found three of them in a negro shanty who informed him that they stayed all night in a stable, the hotels having refused to accommodate them for fear of being mobbed.

Many of the rioters became intoxicated and paraded the streets in the women's clothing stolen from the house. Scarcely anything of value, excepting stair carpets, was left in the house. It was the property of Einstein Addler. He had given the occupants notice to quit but had been unable to eject them.

Lucy Hart, the proprietress of the establishment, is a resident of Washington, D. C., where she maintains a similar institution on a much grander scale. She is reputed to be worth $150,000 which was accumulated in this profession. Besides the loss of her household furniture on this occasion, her entire wardrobe and diamond jewelry shared the same calamity.

She started for Franklin yesterday morning, alleging that she had the names of the ring leaders, and several of the parties who stole her furniture, and she would bring them to time.

I haven't found evidence that Miss Lucy got anywhere in pushing her claims, although other, friendlier customers may have avenged her honor by taking a few more pot shots. But as the *Herald* pointed out, being shot at *exasperated* the bullies.

A Titusville man remembered that as a small boy, his father took him along in the buggy to Petroleum Centre, where he had business. Just outside town, the body of an ugly-looking man was propped up neatly beside the road, against a boulder. Pinned to his dirty shirt, over a bullet hole, was a scrawled note: "This damfool tried to hold me up."

When the child and his father drove back home late that afternoon, the body had vanished, probably tactfully buried to forestall any awkward questions.

Murder was still a rarity in the oil regions, but lesser crimes flourished like roaches. Sandbagging was so common that men carrying
any real amounts of money tried to walk in pairs if they left the main
street at night.

Often the robberies had the jolly inefficiency of a Mack Sennett
comedy. Two thieves held up the cashier at Bissell's Central Petroleum Company office but he refused to open the safe, so they sat him
down with his back pushed hard against the combination lock and
trussed him up. Then they took off with the few dollars he had in his
pocket. The company being kingpin in the town, this was impudent
enough so that the county sheriff came over from Franklin and with
galvanized energy succeeded in finding the culprits among the hundreds of petty criminals in town. The thieves were tried and con-
victed, and a constable was assigned to take them to the State Prison.
During the train ride, one of the prisoners wriggled out a window,
rolled down among the cinders, and nobody ever had the gumption
to find him again. For all I know, he went right back to Petroleum
Centre and started fresh.

Even after the town became a borough, with its own police force,
two of its three constables were arrested one night by the third, for
being drunk and disturbing the peace. While he was hauling them to
jail, the Petroleum *Daily Record* reported, "The recalcitrant wielders
of the mace made tracks and disappeared." One was found and fined.
Another time, when an obstreperous drunk was jailed, his friends
threatened to tear down the lockup unless he was let out at once.
The *Record* explained gravely, "The man was set free upon
promising to behave himself."

Bounty jumpers who had come to the oil fields plied a fast trade
in stealing machinery. A toolie once went from his own well to a
nearby derrick, hardly a stone's throw away, and stayed about twenty
minutes. He came back to find his engine and boiler had vanished.
After his first shock, he recovered enough to realize no supernatural
spirits would leave fresh wagon tracks. He got on a horse, followed
the tracks to the nearest freight depot, a few miles away, and found
his machinery already loaded on a flatcar, neatly ticketed and ready
for shipment. I don't know its destination, but the chances are it was
either West Virginia or Canada. Canadians had started drilling almost

as soon as Drake (they now claim sooner), in Lambton County, Ontario, and at one time it was a popular outlet for machinery stolen in Venango County.

Gambling was such a passion in Petroleum Centre that the toolie who left his machinery unguarded may well have gone off for a friendly poker game at the next well. Workers played cards on a board put across an upended barrel. Old-timers have recalled the poker games on a board slapped down in the oozing mud, on a street or around the wells, with the players squatting on their haunches. One visitor reported that at any time of the day or night, you could hear "the slap of cards on whiskey-stained tables of groggeries."

What Western gamblers called jawbone money—big talk and bluff unsupported by cash—was considered lower than counterfeit greenbacks, on Oil Creek. Faro was the high-stakes favorite; there were sweat tables in almost every saloon. Small-timers hung out in Schuylet's, armed with nasty tempers and worse. The night Gus Reil won $5 throwing dice, several players insisted the dice were loaded, and as a mark of displeasure, one of the men slashed Reil with a knife. (A nervous bystander said, "I hid behind the piano and could hear the blood gurgling from his wounds. The dancing girls came running back, dodging behind the piano, crying out, 'They will shoot! They will shoot!' " Reil shot and wounded two men, and one of them, Tait, died a few hours later.

The oil men who gambled didn't play for peanuts, and they didn't go in for gurgling blood. Probably the most legendary player was Sam Woods, a debonair bachelor who "was as full of fun as he was of business, well dressed, wearing daily diamonds worth from $5,000 to $8,000." (This conjures up a nice picture of a reporter thoughtfully assessing Sam's rings and stickpin, to decide whether this was an economy-size $5,000 assortment or the full-rayed $8,000 diamond day.) One evening at Rochester House, Sam and a Colonel Brady, referred to by the *Herald* as "another rich producer," started out tossing dice for $50 a throw. Woods was a steady loser:

> When one of the morning hours was ushered in, Woods had lost $32,000 and Brady held his check for that sum. At this juncture Woods said to the Colonel, "Now I'm willing to double the amount

and let each of us take one throw and the highest takes the stakes."

"All right," replied the Colonel, "I accept."

The interest of the bystanders was now worked up to the highest notch. The dice were produced and Woods had the first throw. Eleven spots turned up as his count. Colonel Brady then threw and but nine black spots turned up to be counted. Woods therefore saved a good-sized fortune on the throw, for had he lost, that $64,000 would have been paid with as much promptness as though it had been part of a legitimate business transaction.

According to the *Herald,* Woods then proceeded to clean the Colonel out of his petty cash, $200. At the end of the game, he said genially, "Here, Colonel, is twenty dollars. I can't see a man go away dead broke."

One visitor wrote enthusiastically, "The orgies in Petroleum Centre sometimes eclipsed Monte Carlo and the Latin Quarter combined."

When news of the orgies and gambling got around the country, it was no wonder that women worried about their men. A young lady named Jenny whose fiancé had gone to Oil Creek to seek their fortune wrote him from New Jersey, "I have heard such discomforting things connected with residence in an oil town. Write me a little about the churches and ministers there. . . . I am embroidering a sofa pillow on which you may sometimes rest your weary head." In a touching attempt to remind him of wholesome pleasures, she wrote flowing pages about "sociables" she'd attended where guests played charades or vented their talents in elocution. As a final charm to ward off Oildorado evil from her betrothed, Jenny enclosed a printed lecture of Reverend Henry Ward Beecher's, a denunciation of lying: "Ask oneself when tempted to tell a white lie whether the Lord Jesus Christ would have done it. This is the only safe rule." (It was a rule the Reverend Beecher must have gagged on later. When he got caught in a scandalous triangle, and the lady's irate husband sued, thousands of Beecher's admirers were rocked to their churchly foundations.) Jenny couldn't have picked a naughtier elocutionist, "a dunghill covered with flowers," to quote as an uplifting influence. At least in Petroleum Centre they didn't go in for the sanctimonious seduction which Beecher had coyly described to an inamorata as "nest-hiding." Very little was hidden, on Washington Street.

Occasionally a pathetic notice appeared in a Venango County paper: "Mrs. Bridget Lewis of Buffalo wants to know the whereabouts of her husband, James Lewis, last seen in Petroleum Centre."

Wives devoted enough or watchful enough to stay with their husbands in the boomtown must have been left sitting alone, or with each other, most of the time. They may have smiled a bit wryly at the joke that appeared: "Why is a married man like a candle? Because he sometimes goes out at night when he ought not to."

Saloons were of course out of bounds for ladies. Except for stores, almost the only place they could visit was Loziers, for "Pure Ice Cream Soda Water." Most of them boarded at the Central House; a Mather photograph shows elaborately dressed women and even a few children posed on the veranda and upstairs porches. There's a wistful feminine touch in the three or four potted plants, and straggling vines coaxed up the rickety railing.

The warped, unpainted walls of their bed-sitting rooms often had a cherished print brought from home, Rosa Bonheur horses or a Currier and Ives. Some of the women had pieces of Pennsylvania chalkware modeled after English porcelain: sad-mouthed dogs or monogamous lovebirds. Another proud possession was an oil lamp with the base made in a figurine of Jenny Lind, the globed wick sitting on her head.

By the light of Jenny Lind, they read Mrs. Harriet Beecher Stowe's *Chimney Papers,* and Oliver Wendell Holmes' *Autocrat of the Breakfast Table.* And perhaps some of them leaped at the little advertisement in the Petroleum *Daily Record,* headlined simply:

LOVE AND MATRIMONY

The affections may be gained by simple rules, and all may marry and live happily without regard to wealth, age or beauty. Address with stamp to Madame Lucille De Marre.

To augment Madame De Marre's simple magic, there was "Virgin Wax of Antilles for Whitening & Preserving the Complexion, 25¢."

For tips on clothes, women relied mostly on two magazines, Mme. Demorest's *Journal du Grand Mode,* and *Godey's Lady's Book.* *Godey's* was featuring a dress for "an Afternoon Stroll" built in tiers from the ground up, like a wedding cake, and with Irish lace rosettes stuck on like icing decorations. For an afternoon stroll in Petroleum Centre, through the sticky clay constantly remuddied by water pumped from the wells, this attire may have been a bit fussy. As for "a Home Toilette of Chene Silk with a train of Corinth poplin and a polannaise of the same material trimmed with narrow bands of chinchilla"—perhaps Madame Wood wore this in her establishment, to give her male clients the cozy feeling of a home away from home.

It's also a bit hard to imagine anyone but Madame Wood or Miss Lucy Hart wearing another gown: pink satin with large entwined bottle-green vipers embroidered all down the front, and a coiling snake necklace to set off the low décolleté. With this, the smartest possible coiffure was the new Cleopatra style: "The hair should be brushed high off the forehead and braided low on the neck, coiled around the head like a large imitation snake."

Petroleum Centre women, like those everywhere else, curled their front friz with heavy iron tongs thrust into the coal fire or heated over a spirit lamp. For diversion, they trimmed and retrimmed hats the size of serving trays, heaped with flowers, dead birds and glassy fruits.

Each lady had in her trunk at least one treasured fan, with curlicued ostrich feathers, or Chantilly lace cobwebby over silk; the fanciest had mother-of-pearl bases, and some unfurled to show hand-painted verses:

> Lightly lift the breeze, o' fan.
> Light on Letty let it fall.
> Echo back her charm and scan
> Why she does so soon enthrall.
> Nestle on her cheek awhile
> Gathering there her winning art
> And apprenticed to her smile
> Claim requital from her heart.

Their everyday paper fans stirred the oil-polluted air, and went with them everywhere in a reticule. They wore stout, high-buttoned shoes, partly as a concession to the oozing slime, but their parasols were flirty and flounced. This reminds me that the editor of the Titusville *Herald,* Henry Bloss, a moon-faced man with a large black mustache, always carried a yellow parasol when he had to go out in the sun. Once he forgot it, and nearly died of sunstroke.

If he came around the wells with his yellow parasol, he wouldn't have looked too eccentric. Wives who went to watch when a strike was expected soon learned to hoist their parasols to protect them from sudden geysers; this seemed like such a sensible custom that quite a few city men borrowed it, and unfurled a parasol or umbrella when they too sat on a well. Male visitors with their longish hair and sideburns, their low-flounced coat jackets that ended just above the knees of their tapered trousers, looked very elegant indeed, under this oil-shade.

The uniform for real oil men was still flannel shirts and heavy pants tucked into their high boots. But already at least one of these Petroleumites had bought his wife a Worth gown. This was young Dr. Milton Egbert.

Milton and his brother Albert had studied medicine at Cleveland College (now Western Reserve) and paid part of their tuition in crops from their father's farm. The two doctors had barely hung out their shingle at Cherry Tree village when they caught that contagious disease, oil on the brain. Neither of them had a spare dime, but they scraped up $200, part of it by selling Albert's horse to Drake, for a down payment on the Alex Davidson farm of thirty-eight acres, just across the creek from what was to be Petroleum Centre. After "the squire" drew up a water-tight, or oil-tight, contract, they rushed down to their father in Mercer, to borrow the rest of the $2,600 purchase price. Alex Davidson accepted this money with every show of satisfaction, but within a few days, he realized what he'd lost, and went slamming into the young doctors' office yelling, "You damn land sharks!"

The elated land sharks couldn't quite digest what they'd swallowed. They had no money for drilling, they were already overborrowed, and their consciences hurt. Milton Egbert said later that they called Davidson in and had the contract rewritten to give the farmer a fair royalty. "Alex said, 'Well, all right, then, I take back the names I called you.'" The good-humored, easy-mannered Milton added, "And some of the names he took back were a lot worse than land shark."

Davidson died soon after this, and his wife said *she'd* never signed any papers, and contested the sale. In the end, she got a one-twelfth royalty, but while the stewing and stalling was going on, the fledgling doctors were getting harder up all the time. Dr. Albert Egbert, who looked like a philosopher, with a high-domed forehead and gentle, sensitive face, asked his friend Isaac Phillips of New Castle if he wouldn't like to buy a share of the farm. Isaac said he wanted a few days to think it over, and to consult his three brothers. (The four Phillipses pop up at Petroleum Centre later, looking like the Smith Brothers of cough-drop fame.) While Isaac and the rest of the quartet were still debating, presumably in close harmony, Dr. Albert, who was getting more and more impatient, met Charles Hyde, the store-keeper who had sold Drake his first pick. Hyde was older than the doctors, and solidly heeled. His store had expanded to handle a large volume of drilling equipment and he already owned shares in several paying wells. At forty, his rather bad-tempered, heavy-browed face was so surrounded by sideburns and whiskers that he seemed to be scowling through a hair wreath. He wasn't the man to jump into things rashly (people referred to his cautious nature as Hyde-and-seek) but when he learned that the Egberts wanted a man they knew and trusted as a partner, and that Isaac Phillips was still undecided on the proposition, Hyde didn't diddle. For a half share of the farm, he paid the Egberts $2,625.

The thirty-eight acres turned out to be the most fabulously fertile oil land of any on the creek; at one time, there were twenty-three lush-flowing wells. (Most of them were developed by companies, with the Egberts retaining a 50 per cent royalty.) The mammoth Jersey spouter, in the spring of 1863, and the Maple Shade that summer, made fortunes for both the doctors, with the gushing Coquette still to come a year later. The Olive Branch, Swamp Angel, Tigress and Weasel wells poured out their riches for export profits.

To celebrate this good fortune, Dr. Milton Egbert took his beauti-ful twenty-year-old wife, who looked like a Raphael Madonna, and six of their friends for a European jaunt. They sailed on the American Collins Line's SS *Atlantic*—the crossing took eleven days—and went first to Ireland, which seems to have been a must-stop for travelers from Venango County. According to an Oil City reporter, they met "shoals of titled folks all over Europe." In Paris, the great couturier Worth made the lovely Mrs. Egbert a garnet velvet gown in the pinch-waisted, full-belling style of the period. (He hadn't yet dreamed up that daring new feature, the bustle.)

Although Worth might have been flabbergasted to see where the gown got to—the mud of Petroleum Centre—I must add, as a proud Venango-ite, that he probably never had a more beautiful customer. Looking at a yellowed daguerreotype of the young oil man's wife in her Paris creation, it's the wearer, and not her Worth, that enchants a beholder.

The Egberts and their trunks of new finery came back to settle into a house built in their absence, a trim two-story clapboard with green shutters, and a bush-hammered stone foundation as the one real luxury touch. Enclosed in a white picket fence that looked primly New England, it sat on the slope facing the most violently lawless, wide-open boomtown the East had ever known.

Perhaps the Egberts had thought that by building on the hill, they'd be removed from the uproar around the wells, because the oil-runs-downhill theory confined all drilling to the flatlands. But by the end of 1864, this idea had been stood on its head, and producers were climbing uphill as eagerly as salmon swimming upstream. The four Phillips brothers of New Castle—Tom, Samuel, John and Isaac—had finally made their minds up, too late to buy into the Egberts' property, so they'd leased the Stevenson farm high above Petroleum Centre. With the help of their lawyer-Congressman friend James Garfield, they formed the Ocean Oil Company. In 1865, Garfield wrote a former staff officer, "I have conversed on the general question of oil with a number of members who are in the business, for you must know the fever has assailed Congress in no mild form. . . . Oil, not cotton, is King now, in the world of Commerce, and it is a beautiful thought that oil is found only in the free states, and in the mountains of slave states where freedom loves to dwell."

When he was helping the Phillipses organize a second company, he explained raptly, "It is a work almost as great as a military campaign, but if we succeed it will go far toward settling one of the important and difficult problems in my life which relates to our means of living."

He soon got impatient and disgusted. After a visit to the creek, he wrote his wife, "I feel a little like a slave working in the mines for his freedom, and have just a little touch of the feeling that the pursuit of wealth is not the noblest thing in the world."

It's nice to know he felt that way long before he moved to the White House.

Garfield sold his own stock for a profit of $6,000, but he continued as legal adviser to the Phillips brothers. Their Ocean well had flowed so lavishly that it sparked a rush to other farms in the hills around Petroleum Centre. One of these was owned by Jim McCray, a mercurial, outspoken, fiercely natural Scotsman, "one of the good Christians surrounded by a wicked population."

When Jim McCray and the Egberts decided they must have a Presbyterian church in the town, as one way of holding their own against the sinners, Jim set about this with typical forthrightness, and made himself chairman of a fund-raising committee. Dr. Albert Egbert handed him a thousand dollars in greenbacks that same morning. Jim added a thousand of his own, and by evening had raised the $6,500 they'd set as their goal. He decided that rather than risk taking the money to his farm, he'd leave it with his brother-in-law overnight for safety. His brother-in-law, uneasily remembering several robberies in which the safe had been blown open or carted away, slept with the greenbacks under his pillow, in a locked bedroom. During the night, thieves jimmied a window, slapped an ether rag over the sleeping man's face, and escaped with the church funds. Their victim woke up sick as a dog, and sicker still when he thought how the tempestuous McCray would bellow. But Jim only grumbled mildly that it was too dang bad to have good Presbyterian money spent in the dens of sin. That bothered him more than the actual loss, which he made up out of his own pocket.

The contractor he hired to build the church, George Brown, remembered the first time the warm-hearted McCray took him up to his farmhouse for the night, to get a decent meal and a good sleep. As they hiked up the steep hill in the blackness, a shot sounded almost in their ears. Four men appeared menacingly on the path, peered at McCray, and then marched right past. McCray said bitterly to his companion, "I wish there had never been a drop of oil found on the creek. I can't sleep nights. My dog makes a fearful fuss, as if there were prowlers around. I can't come up through this brush without expecting a club over my head, handled by some of these wretches who would murder me for my money."

When the two men were safely inside the farmhouse, Brown, to cheer up his host, mentioned the high price of oil and how it would boost McCray's royalties. Jim took out a pencil and pad, scribbled busily for a minute, and then said in a surprised tone, "Why, my income is five dollars a minute. If I'd figured this out before we left town, I'd have hired a livery rig to bring us up here."

Five dollars a minute—"nights and Sundays included"—comes to $7,200 a day.

The morning after McCray figured this out, his guest was wakened at sunrise by a bustle in the meadow below. He went to the window in time to see Five-dollar-a-minute McCray, with a pitchfork over his shoulder like a musket, following a wagon load of hay toward the barn. Jim explained at breakfast he had noticed clouds gathering and hustled to help his hired man get in the hay before it was spoiled by rain.

His plump merry wife Martha, "a willing helpmeet in adversity and wise counselor in prosperity," finally persuaded him to buy a rig of his own, because of the outlandish livery stable charges. When out-of-towners hired a horse in Petroleum Centre, they had to pay one-tenth the value of the animal, usually around $10, an hour. McCray, being a native who drove a Scotch bargain, only paid eighty seconds' worth of his income to rent a rig, but that was bad enough by Presbyterian standards. After he bought his own carriage, Jim went on hiking up and down the hill, but he humored Martha by driving her to church in style.

Two other churches, Methodist and Catholic, went up in Petroleum Centre. A Methodist minister once preached such a powerful sermon against greed and materialism that an oil man in his congregation was so impressed he gave the good reverend a block of oil stock as a token of esteem. The minister promptly sold the stock for a fat sum and retired from preaching. A visitor to Oil Creek wrote, "The church universally believed in is an engine house, with a derrick for its tower, a well for its Bible, and a two-inch tube for its preacher, with mouth rotund, 'bringing forth things new and old.' "

It was true that Petroleum Centre's three churches never seemed to have much effect on the drifters and thieves. But in a place where millions were dumped in men's laps, it must have seemed a reasonable law of the wild that God helps those who help themselves to some of the booty.

The exuberant, gregarious top reporter of the oil region, John McLaurin, a Canadian who was at that time a toolie near Petroleum Centre and doing free-lance stories on the side, later wrote in his *Sketches in Crude Oil* that the Davidson farm alone had earned for the Egberts, Hyde, and their lessees, eight to ten million dollars. He mentioned with respectful glee that Dr. Milton Egbert's safe had once held, "by tight squeezing, eighteen hundred thousand dollars in currency and a pile of government bonds. . . . In silver dollars, it would load a freight train. Fused into a lump of gold, a dozen mules might decline the task of drawing it a mile."

Thieves were less fussy than mules, about lugging away whatever they could lift. A favorite trick was to set fire to some building, and while all the responsible men in the community were out fighting the fire, the thugs would break into their homes or offices and loot in a hurry. Eliza Egbert, Dr. Albert's wife, found one way to outwit the looters, a device she'd learned from a popular, if deplorably dissolute, writer, Mr. Edgar Allan Poe. She put silver, jewels and any loose cash in an old burlap bag, draped it over with rags, and propped it against the kitchen wall, as boldly in sight as the Purloined Letter.

She was a small, soft-spoken, charmingly feminine woman with enough spunk and spirit to charge a dynamo, and she needed every ounce of it in Petroleum Centre. The night the Maple Shade well blazed up, her husband grabbed packets of thousand-dollar bills out of his safe and threw them into a saddlebag before he went off to his well. He handed the bulging bag to his tiny wife: "Take this to bed with you and if the fire gets out of control, saddle a horse and leave in a hurry."

Even the wives of very wealthy men seldom had money of their own, a hundred years ago, and it was with delicate irony that Eliza Egbert told a relative, in recounting her night guarding the saddlebag, "You know, that was the only time I had a whole million dollars."

The only time during those years when the money-making frenzy came to a full halt on the creek, was when Lee invaded Pennsylvania in the summer of 1863. As the battle of Gettysburg raged on, most wells shut down, although only for a few sobering days. Now that the war was being fought close to home, the impact hit even Oildorado. Governor Curtin issued a moving proclamation on June 26th:

> The enemy is advancing in force into Pennsylvania. He has a strong column within twenty three miles of Harrisburg . . . and it can no longer be doubted that a formidable invasion of our State is in actual progress. I, therefore, now issue this my proclamation calling for SIXTY THOUSAND MEN to come promptly forward to defend the State. . . . I will not insult you by inflammatory appeals. A people who want the heart to defend their soil, their families and their firesides are not worthy to be accounted men. Heed not the counsel of evil disposed persons. Show yourselves what you are— a free, loyal, spirited, brave, vigorous race.

He got his volunteers.

The oil region had surprisingly few Copperhead Democrats of the sort who plotted the Draft Riots in New York, in which twelve hundred people were killed. A new version of the "Star Spangled Banner" circulated by Southern sympathizers got small shrift in our area:

> Oh say can you see, through the gloom and the storm
> More bright for the darkness that pure constellation?
> Like the symbol of love and redemption its form,
> As it points to the haven of hope for the nation.
> How radiant each star as the beacon afar
> Giving promise of peace, or assurance in war!
> 'Tis the Cross of the South, which shall ever remain
> To light us to freedom and glory again!
>
> How peaceful and blest was America's soil
> 'Til betrayed by the guile of the puritan demon,
> Which lurks under virtue, and springs from its coil
> To fasten its fangs in the life blood of freemen.
> Then boldly appeal to each heart that can feel
> And crush the foul viper 'neath Liberty's heel!
> And the Cross of the South shall in triumph remain
> To light us to freedom and glory again!

Personal loyalties crisscrossed staunch support of the Union; for instance, the Egberts sent money to women cousins in the South destituted by war, with their men off fighting and their cotton burned or blockaded. Yet it was Dr. Albert Egbert who planned the building of a memorial to Venango County war dead, in Franklin's park; he donated the largest sum and raised the rest of the money himself. (Coal Oil Johnny contributed a day's royalties. He was still flush then.) Eliza Egbert was one of the women who rolled bandages, collected clothes for soldiers' families, sent tobacco to the troops, and gave a leather-bound Bible to each member of the Pennsylvania Fourth Cavalry Company. Mrs. Milton Egbert sent the government a check for $5,000, asking that it be used to provide Christmas dinners for all the wounded in fifteen hospitals. Lincoln himself wrote her a grateful letter:

> Executive Mansion
> Washington Jan. 9, 1865
>
> Mrs. Milton C. Egbert
> Col. Forney assures me that you will not be displeased if I tender, as I most heartily do, my sincere thanks for your munificient Christmas donation of five thousand dollars to the sick and wounded soldiers in the Philadelphia hospitals.
>
> Your Obe. Servt.
> A. Lincoln

But many Democrats loyal to the Northern cause were still fuming against Mr. Lincoln. After he made a little speech at the dedication of the Gettysburg cemetery, the Harrisburg *Patriot and Union* announced, "We pass over the silly remarks of the President; for the credit of the nation we are willing that the veil of oblivion shall be dropped over them, and that they shall no more be repeated or thought of."

The Gettysburg Address wasn't wiped out quite that easily. Our Venango *Spectator* didn't drop any veils over it, but just tore them furiously to shreds:

> We hope that we have no reader who will be able to read the official dispatches sent from Gettysburg without a blush of shame. The Governor, it seems, did not reach there in time to participate in the proceedings of Tuesday evening, which were of "a lively character." Mr. Lincoln made a joke or two; Mr. Seward, who has become nervously anxious as to his fame as a prophet, vindicated

his pretensions by the assertion that forty years ago he had anticipated that the battle of freedom would be fought upon the field of Gettysburg, and Mr. Forney referred to the political aspect of the campaign. It is thus that the President of the United States and his confidential advisers disport themselves in the presence of the historic field where two hundred thousand of their countrymen, four months ago, met in deadly conflict.—It is thus that they render homage to the heroic dead. With the groans of the wounded still resounding in the air—the corpses of the slain still unburied—the bereaved still clad in the emblems of mourning, and their tears still flowing—these men met to laugh and joke and electioneer.

During the 1864 Presidential campaign, an anonymous pamphleteer described Lincoln: "His anatomy is composed mostly of bones, and when walking he resembles the offspring of a happy marriage between a derrick and a windmill."

The editor of the *Spectator* thought this comparison was a slur on derricks. On November 16th he wrote: "The election is over and the result is disastrous to the Democratic party. . . . The same appliances of military power were brought to bear to secure the re-election of Lincoln that were used by Napoleon to overthrow the French Republic."

Right next to this doom-laden pronouncement was a cheery editorial commenting on *Prosperity of Oil Lands:* "One fifth of the real estate in this county is now in the process of changing hands. . . . A few years ago, the timid stood amazed at the apparent recklessness of Oil men, whose investments were fully as far from appearing prudent as in many cases now: but time has shown that those who risked their money were wise."

One of the men who had risked their money on oil land that year, a too-handsome actor who spent several months in Franklin, was John Wilkes Booth.

EIGHT

——◆◆◆——

John Wilkes Booth
wants a gusher

IF A GOD had dropped down from Olympus to spend a few months in our town and registered under his own name, he couldn't have created more of a furor than John Wilkes Booth did in 1864.

I caught an echo of the romantic turmoil he caused when I was a child in Franklin and heard a redoubtable old lady talking to my mother about Booth: "After the assassination, we prayed he wouldn't come back here to hide out, because we couldn't face the thought of turning him in. A scoundrel, I grant you, but oh, such a charming man."

What's odd is that men and children were as taken by him as the ladies were. And when I piece together the small, uneven fragments of that summer, I can't help thinking our town gave Booth a kind of life he responded to with almost touching eagerness. It wasn't just a case of his being a big frog in a little puddle, although the uncomplicated, unquestioning admiration he had in Franklin must have been like a herbal poultice for his sick, twitching vanity. But more than that, he was an active member of a small-town community for the only time in his life. It would be ridiculous to claim he wanted to change into a villager who was kind even to old ladies and headed amateur theatricals, but I do think he loved the role and lived the part and was happier and more peaceful than he might have been anywhere else just then.

I'm so ignorant of history all I knew about Booth was that he was an actor, brother of the much more famous Edwin, and that he killed Lincoln, so I've been reading up on his past before I drop him down in my hometown. It started in England when Booth's father, already a well-known actor, saw a beautiful, bosomy, eighteen-year-old London flower girl whose name was not Eliza Doolittle but Mary Ann, and left his wife to elope with the lovely creature to America. They settled on a big farm north of Baltimore, and conceived eleven children between the elder Booth's theatrical tours. John Wilkes was the next to youngest, and if the Baltimore courthouse record is correct, his parents were finally married on his thirteenth birthday, May 10, 1851. His father, great actor though he was, was a dipsomaniac by then, and died the year after. John Wilkes was his mother's favoite. She called him Pet and spoiled him as fondly as women were to spoil him all his short, wild life long.

When her older son Edwin, already a success on the stage, wanted to use some of his father's costumes, Mrs. Booth said, Oh, no, Pet must have the lot, because he would be the greatest Booth of them all. Her son-in-law, John Sleeper Clarke, the manager of Philadelphia's Arch Street Theatre, was one of the first to give the ravishingly handsome John Wilkes a small part. The boy was still so raw, "so uncooked a ham," that the audience booed him. In flowery contrast, the South adored him from the start. Richmond feted him not only as a brilliant new star but as a social lion, and in return, John Wilkes never got over his love of the city that became the capital of the Confederacy. To him, it was the symbol of chivalry and honor, of the only real aristocracy. After Jefferson Davis was installed there as president of the Confederacy, Clarke, riding with his young brother-in-law on a train, made a scornful remark about Davis, and John Wilkes knocked him down and nearly strangled him.

He'd always had an uncertain temper, riding his moods like a seesaw, but this seemed to make him even more fascinating to women. Senators' daughters, actresses, debutantes, and at least one handsome redhead in a Washington sporting-house turned somersaults for him. Waitresses fought over which one would serve him. One writer has said that chambermaids kept tearing Booth's bed apart and remaking

it, for the delicious thrill it gave them. His brother Edwin was idolized, but apparently Edwin's cosmic rays weren't as strong off-stage
as John Wilkes' animal magnetism.

He was only five feet, eight inches tall, but so beautifully co-ordi-
nated and intensified that he carried the authority of height. Who
stops to measure a god? He had silky black wavy hair, deep dark eyes
with startlingly white irises, and a profile he displayed with knowing
grace. Franklinites said his most typical pose, sitting down, was with
his head turned just enough sideways, and one arm thrown casually
across the back of a chair, showing the tattooed initials J.W.B. on
his wrist.

Fellow actors said he was so terrified of having his good looks
spoiled that was why he didn't join the Rebel army. John Wilkes'
own explanation was that he'd promised his mother he wouldn't fight.
Yet he dueled with such fierceness, in the battle scene in *Richard III,*
that the press reported gloatingly his body was black and blue all
over, and he had to sleep covered in raw oysters to heal the bruises.
He was so determined to be the greatest Booth, and so infuriated to
be billed as "Son of the Great Junius" or "Brother of Edwin Booth,"
that when he played in home territory, in Baltimore, his posters
screamed in black letters: "I AM MYSELF ALONE."

One of his heartiest admirers was the manager of the Cleveland
Academy of Music, John Ellsler. He was a florid, benevolent, in-the-
grand-tradition theatre man who once said, "Johnny has more of the
old man's power in one performance than Edwin can show in a year.
He has the fire, the dash, the touch of strangeness."

Ellsler may have been trying to pour oil on troubled waters almost
literally, when he suggested to the actor that they drill a well in Venango County. Booth had been so enraged over Lincoln's Emancipa-
tion Proclamation he had ranted publicly that he wished the whole
damn Union government in hell. He was charged with treasonable
utterances, in St. Louis, and had to pay a fifty-dollar fine and take
the oath of allegiance. The $50 didn't pinch—he was earning around
twenty thousand a year as an actor—but the oath of allegiance stuck
in his arrogant craw. He had to go back to St. Louis for a second engagement the next winter, and this time he throttled his temper in

public, but when he stopped to see Ellsler in Cleveland afterward, he was still fuming. Cleveland, only a hundred miles from the main oil excitement, was already perfumed with young Rockefeller's and other refineries, and Ellsler's rich talk of the fortune he and Booth would make was exactly the kind of lavish scheme to appeal to his listener. At that point, I doubt if Booth wanted to finance a specific conspiracy so much as he wanted to be powerfully wealthy and contribute Yankee dollars to the hard-pushed Confederacy. You can sniff his mood of bravado in the name he chose for their new venture: The Dramatic Oil Company.

Early in 1864, he and Ellsler came to Franklin with another Clevelander, Thomas Mears, an ex-gambler townspeople described as "medium-tough," and they immediately bought three and a half acres of the Fuller farm on the Allegheny River a mile below town. Booth paid half the $4,000 purchase price, and another $3,000 for drilling expenses. Mears was to stay and oversee the work, and he took Booth over to introduce him to the driller they wanted, Henry Sires, who was working on a well near their property. Booth, impressively handsome in an overcoat with astrakhan collar and flowing overcape, genially thrust out his hand, but Sires, rather abashed before such resplendence, hesitated, and apologized for his oily hand. Booth, shaking it, said gaily, "Never mind, Mr. Sires, that's what we're here for." It was his first conquest by charm, in Franklin.

He went right off to fill several engagements, and he might never have come back for a real stay if an odd blight hadn't struck his acting career that spring, in New Orleans. The city had gone into paroxysms over his genius, with critics scattering adjectives like Mardi Gras confetti: "In physique Mr. Booth is greatly the superior of his brother Edward, being a much handsomer and larger man, and in no other particular . . . is he at all inferior." Thus appreciated, John Wilkes outdid himself nightly, and soon the New Orleans *Times* remarked worriedly, "He is at present laboring under a severe hoarseness . . . [but] he has certainly created a furor here, which will continue through his engagement."

Even the adoring South couldn't put up with the hoarse croaks for long. His engagement was cut short, and the doctor advised him to give his voice a rest. Instead, Booth went to play in Boston, where a critic had predicted two years before that if the young actor didn't learn to use his chest register, he was asking for trouble. On this visit, no reviewer said right out "We told you so," but they implied it: "Mr. Booth played the part of 'Evelyn' at the Museum last evening with a tact, grace, and appreciation of the character such as few but himself can exhibit upon the stage, the only drawback being the cold which restrains his voice."

The hoarseness, which kept getting worse, may have been partly emotional hysteria, but whatever the cause, it blocked off income and career, at least temporarily. Now the idea of making a fortune in oil was no longer a side fling, but the main chance. Booth talked constantly about it to his Boston friend Joseph Simonds, a teller in the Mechanics Bank. Jo Simonds was thirty-three, seven years older than Booth, a dapper, precise, sandy-haired little man with one untidy obsession splashed across his neat accountant's mind: he was stage-struck. He had admired John Wilkes extravagantly in each role, and the two had become friends. There was a basic steadiness and business shrewdness in Simonds that Booth respected. The teller had handled some Boston real estate investments for him, and Booth had been so pleased with the results that now he insisted Simonds throw over his bank job and come along with him to the oil fields, to be his business agent there. It wasn't just fondness for Booth, his stage idol, that made the cautious Simonds take the leap. Like almost every other young or youngish man, he yearned to get to Oildorado. Booth was his passport there.

The actor finished his run at the Boston Museum in May, and two days later they were in Franklin. Liveryman Ralph Brigham wrote in his account book on May 30th: "For hire to Mr. John Wilkes Booth, the chestnut mare and saddle."

From then on, the sight of the beautiful young man cantering down muddy Liberty Street was enough to set hoop skirts whirling and tilting like tops. All the best-dressed young ladies were sporting a new contraption, a duplex steel spring that fitted under hoop skirts and made them easier to tilt and manipulate "in crowded assemblies, carriages, or church pews." One oil region reporter complained amiably:

> Tilting, as practised by the belles of this place, renders it posi-
> tively unsafe for a young man to appear upon the street unattended.
> Some of the tilters are so expert they can break a man's heart at
> eighty rods. One little divinity whose father owns a derrick on the
> V——— farm can bring down her man (on his knees) with the
> accuracy of one of Berdan's sharp shooters; besides being a good
> judge of distance, she knows just what elevation to give in order
> to wound or kill.

I don't know if that particular little divinity was out to get John
Wilkes Booth, but my guess is that most of the hoop skirts in Franklin must have been tilting in a tournament to capture him, if for only
ten minutes.

The manager of the United States Hotel couldn't bear to put so
elegant and gracious a newcomer on a cot in the corridor. He persuaded two regular guests, young Alfred Smiley and Harry Smith,
to share their double room with Booth and Jo Simonds. In the two
weeks the men stayed at the hotel in this dormitory arrangement,
before rooms were vacant at Mrs. Sarah Webber's, Booth flung his
charm like one of his flowing capes over the bright, lively, twenty-
one-year-old Smiley. He insisted on paying for all their drinks and
games of billiards. According to Smiley, Booth made this sound like
a favor to himself: "I have plenty of money and I enjoy your company so please let me pay for our fun."

He gave Smiley an autographed picture, and later, his silver-
headed cane. He had another stick, a gold-headed one with a horse
engraved on it, that he sometimes carried as a riding crop. For rides
around the oil fields, he wore a black, tight-fitting coat, sleek black
pants (tailored to hide his bowlegs) with gleaming cavalry boots,
and a broad-brimmed soft black hat worn at a rakishly cocked angle.
"When riding horseback through the streets he would frequently stop
to gently greet some child or perhaps drop them a piece of scrip, so
much used in those days," Smiley wrote later. "In walking along the
sidewalks, this fondness for children was even more noticeable; his
stops were more frequent and his greetings and caresses of the heartiest nature. Stories of the magnetism and fascination in the man's face
are strictly true no matter how strongly drawn."

After Booth moved into the big second-floor front bedroom at Sarah Webber's, with Jo Simonds in the rear room below, the two went on having their meals at the hotel, and they often joined Smiley for dinner there. On the short walk from Mrs. Webber's to the hotel, Booth always stopped to greet his youngest and most single-minded admirer, two-year-old Joey Watson, who had cheeks like cherry blossoms, and thistledown for hair. Joey was the child of the harness-maker, and the Watsons lived over the harness shop. Almost his first day in town, Booth stopped to ask Mrs. Watson the baby's name, and when she said Joseph, told her he loved that name and that his youngest brother was Joseph. (He didn't add that Joseph Booth had been a medical aide in the Confederate Army.) He bounced the child in a fast game of Ride a Cock Horse, and warmed the mother even more by saying "He's as pretty as he is healthy-looking." After that, on his daily stops, he often brought little presents. Mrs. Watson once explained proudly, "Mr. Booth would even leave his pocketknife here for Joey to play with." Booth used to whistle as he came near the harness shop, to signal his small friend, and Joey would come galloping.

As far as I can make out, almost anyone in town would have come galloping if Booth whistled. One of the most sought-after local belles of that time, Martha Vincent Bridges, remarked nostalgically to her family on her hundred and fourth birthday that Mr. Booth had been an unusually attractive young man, and so well thought of by both young men and young women.

When he called on young ladies in Franklin—or on a beautiful Oil City girl who afterward became Mrs. Gaskill—he was as dazzling as a Gay Cavalier, even *sans* plume. Sometimes he wore a claret broadcloth coat with matching velvet lapels, a fawn-colored suede waistcoat, tapered fawn trousers, and fawn gauntlets. His sky-blue waistcoat with silver buttons was much admired too. When you consider that he rode and danced superbly, kissed hands with a gallantry and grace never before or since seen in Franklin, and "recited" at parties —scenes from his most famous roles—you can understand that other men must have seemed rather lumpish in comparison. Besides, the other men worked, and Booth had endless time to be charming, or to be pensive and sad-eyed in the way women found even more melting.

He was never what Venango-ites would have called a real oil man, but he went through the gestures. He often rode down to inspect the driller's progress on his well, which was named the Wilhelmina after Medium-tough Mears' wife, and he made some tours of Oil Creek, but his only other buy was a one-thirtieth interest, for $1,000, in a lease owned by the Boston Oil Company on undeveloped woodland at Pithole Creek. As part of his summer role, he stopped almost every morning at the real estate office where oil men congregated to pick up the latest gossip on leases and read the city papers. Both the *New York Times* and *Tribune* carried daily market quotations and complete figures on oil exports. The week after Booth arrived in town, the *Times* said, "The market has continued active and prices have further advanced. Refined Petroleum 71¢ and 73¢ gallon."

Obviously, an ideal time to have a well going down. And to add to Booth's good humor, the editor of the Venango *Spectator* was howling in full voice over Lincoln's "double dealings" and "disunion schemes" while the Republicans were holding their Presidential convention in Baltimore.

Just the same, Booth was shrewd enough to tell his new pro-Union friends that he only disliked Lincoln for personal reasons. His story, as his young billiards-partner Alf Smiley got it, was that a Confederate spy named Beall had been captured on the Canadian border while carrying dispatches to the nest of Confederates in Montreal, and was sentenced to be hanged. John Wilkes told Smiley emotionally that he had appealed personally to the President for his gallant friend and that Lincoln had promised to spare Beall's life and then had gone back on his word.

I doubt if Booth had even met Beall, and the rest is a complete lie. The story got around Franklin quickly, and friends excused Booth's bitterness (although they never knew the depth and blackness of it) as a personal feeling of betrayal, which is exactly what Booth wanted them to think. When he remarked, "I'd rather cut off my right arm than see Lincoln renominated," they thought they understood the reason. And they tactfully refrained from crowing over the results reported in the *Times:*

**UNANIMOUS RENOMINATION OF
PRESIDENT LINCOLN
GOVERNOR ANDY JOHNSON, OF
TENNESSEE, FOR VICE-PRESIDENT**

. . . It is, withal, peculiarly meet that Andrew Johnson should receive this nomination, as among all the Southern Senators he alone
at the outbreak of the rebellion remained faithful. . . . [The *Times*
went on to remind readers of the speech Johnson had made after
the Southern states seceded in 1861:] "Traitors are getting to be so
numerous now that I suppose treason has got to be respectable;
but God being willing, whether traitors be many or few, as I have
hitherto waged war against traitors and treason, and in behalf of the
Government which was constructed by our fathers, I intend to continue it to the end."

Two days after the convention ended, Booth made an overnight
trip which may tie in with an odd little incident historians have never
made much of. As a writer sharpened on murder mysteries and inflamed by feminine intuition, I like to think it has some connection.
On June 10th (and again later that month) Booth went up to Meadville and registered at the McHenry Hotel there. Meadville was outside the oil region, and it was no longer necessary to go there to get
a train east, so Booth must have wanted to meet somebody in secrecy,
but whether a lady or a conspirator I can't say. At any rate, now comes
the part that intrigues me: sometime later that summer of 1864 the
hotel housekeeper noticed that a windowpane of Room 22 was
scratched up, and when she examined the scratched words, she was
startled to read: "Abe Lincoln departed this life August 13, 1864,
by the effects of poison."

She brought the manager up to take a look, and they agreed it
must be the work of some practical joker "while partially intoxicated."
It wasn't until after the assassination that the pane was removed, together with Booth's signatures on the hotel register, and eventually
turned over to the government.

There were other, longer unexplained absences of Booth's from
Franklin that summer. By then, he may have been meeting his
shabby lot of accomplices at Mrs. Surratt's boarding house in Washington. It's interesting that Mrs. Surratt insisted at her trial that when

she asked her son John what the meetings were about, John told her he and the other men were involved in "oil speculation" with Booth.

Their plot at this time was to kidnap Lincoln and take him to Richmond as a hostage. Booth must have been in a frantic hurry to get money to finance this involved operation. Here again I'm guessing about what happened, because there are no substantiating dates; all I know is that the Wilhelmina well was shot (dynamited) to increase production, and instead this wrecked it for good. I think Booth must have been the one who insisted on this, at a time when shooting a well was still a crude, dangerously uncertain method, in his impatience to get a gusher.

He was also drinking more noticeably, mostly "the strongest brandy," sometimes rum. Yet he still fitted his behavior to his company; for instance, when he called at the Plumer McCalmonts', Plumer, a teetotaler, insisted that Booth never seemed to have had a drop to drink. Two of the McCalmont clan were colonels with the Union Army, so it's also certain that Booth never talked "secesh" there.

To sit on a porch drinking lemonade, and watching the young girls flower under his look as innocently and sweetly as morning glories, must have been quite a change from his usual hotel-room amours, but I doubt if he even tried to pluck one of our prettily flowering maidens that summer. I think he saw himself reflected in Frank-linites' eyes as the most chivalrous, kindest, and most beautiful of men, and couldn't bring himself to deface that image.

There was another side of his small-town life I find downright appealing, although the Presbyterian in me hesitates to use such a soft word as *appealing* for a monstrous man. He and a dozen of his new friends, all men, formed a club to get together to give readings and discuss poetry and plays. They rented a room above a saloon on Doe Street, and met there several nights a week, as eagerly as twelve-year-olds who dream up a secret password. Two young brothers, the Robisons, who had a tailor shop, were in the group. Frank Bailey, an oil man from Pittsburgh, was the club member who knew Shakespeare almost as well as Booth. He and John Wilkes spouted passages from the plays, or leaped up to act out a scene, and all the men agreed that Booth never treated Bailey or any of the others as amateurs. He did impromptu comedy skits with John Garmiley and a Mr. Barton, also from Pittsburgh, and a beaming butter-tub of a man, Fatty Patterson. Booth himself never laughed out loud, although he was unmistakably enjoying himself.

Once or twice, the men got on the subject of religion. Booth said frankly he had no particular creed, that he believed in a Master of the Universe, but felt he must live according to the teachings of the Bible and of nature as he himself interpreted them. In one of these talks, he said, "There's a part of the Bible that seems to me the most beautiful of all," and he began to recite the Sermon on the Mount: " 'But he that heareth, and doeth not, is like a man that without a foundation built an house upon the earth; against which the stream did beat vehemently, and immediately it fell; and the ruin of that house was great.' "

His listeners said it was the most moving performance they'd ever heard. The fact that Booth must have been applying the words twistedly to justify his own terrible plan for action—"he that heareth, and doeth not"—would have given a passion of conviction his audience felt without understanding.

When Booth went to the Methodist Sunday School with his business-agent friend Jo Simonds, he joined in the Bible discussions and gave his opinions modestly, but the part Methodists remembered was that he put a ten-dollar bill in the collection plate.

Perhaps in exchange or retaliation for being taken to Sunday School, he dragged Jo Simonds along on his walks in the woods around Franklin. Simonds was so fastidious that if he got a speck of mud or a burr on his jacket, he was miserable. Frankliners had already noted with amusement that he wrote down every cent in a little book the minute he spent it, "couldn't even bear a crooked line," and was as fussy as an old hen about his possessions. Robert Brigham, the liveryman's brother, loved walking in the woods as much as Booth, and he mentioned that Simonds, "reluctantly accompanied us on these rambles. Booth was a good fast pedestrian and a great lover of nature and pure air and freedom of the country and hills. Used to talk on all sorts of subjects on these walks; poetry, theatrical profession, literature. . . . Nothing was said on politics."

Booth would cut himself a walking stick from a low-hanging

branch, and away they'd go. Once he held his stick threateningly over a teamster, when they came across the man beating his horse to prod it out of a mud hole. Booth snatched away the man's blacksnake whip, fondled the exhausted beast's ears, and blasted its driver with a fury of rhetoric. It's probably one of the few times an oil-country teamster was too dumbfounded to talk back.

Booth told Brigham about how his own father had loved animals. When a pony named Peacock died on their farm, the elder Booth wrapped it in a sheet for a shroud, and invited all the neighbors to its funeral. Booth didn't mention that his erratic, drunken father had once called in a Baltimore clergyman and asked the astonished minister to deliver the funeral oration for a basketful of dead pigeons.

John Wilkes talked affectionately about his brother Edwin, and told about the time Edwin had played with the red-haired, husky-voiced prima donna Laura Keene, in *The Love Chase*. She was furious over the lukewarm reception she got, and blamed it on her leading man's acting. Edwin, grinning, had remarked that he "felt it Keenely."

There was one role John Wilkes thought he outshone even Edwin in, Richard III. One night when he was drunk (and friends said it took a staggering amount of liquor to make him show it) he began declaiming a scene from the play at 2 A.M., on the corner of Doe Street near their club room. He brandished his cane like a sword, and the few night owls who caught the performance were so carried away by the acting they completely forgot he was drunk.

Another night, a brawl started in front of the saloon below their club, and Booth, leaning out the window to watch it, exclaimed, "My God, how I would love to be in a fight!"

But his first fight in Franklin was thrust upon him. He and Alf Smiley, after a game of billiards one evening, decided to go slumming to a dance hall down at the end of Catfish Street on the river. They went in and stood quietly on the sidelines watching the dancers, mostly raftsmen and steamboat deckhands, with their girls. The rivermen resented Booth's la-de-da clothes and looks, and they began to mutter about "damn dudes" nosing in where they weren't wanted. A half-dozen of the biggest and toughest charged like irritated bulls at

Booth and Smiley, and there were bloody noses on both sides before
the rivermen picked up Booth, tossed him out the door, and told
him not to come back. Smiley, who was ejected too, reported that he
and John Wilkes tried to keep the incident secret, but the news
leaked out, and Booth took their friends' ragging good-naturedly.

Jo Simonds must have realized by now that Booth was too unpredictable to hitch his future to. I assume Simonds had been living
on his own savings, because he stated under oath later that he'd
never even received a fee as Booth's agent in the oil business, and
they hadn't made any money from the well. In midsummer, he decided to open a land-agent office of his own, next door to the
U.S. Hotel opposite the courthouse.

> Maps and plans of the entire Oil District kept open for inspection.
> Directories of all the large cities can be consulted, and Leading
> Newspapers of the Country kept on file at this Office.
> Agents for the Purchase and Sale of Petroleum Lands, Leases,
> Interests in Oil Wells.
> Lands and Interests on all the Streams in this region for sale
> strictly on Commission.

This office became one of Booth's regular daytime stops, to chat
or write letters, and now it was Simonds' city papers he read. Most
of the war dispatches were bad news for a Confederate sympathizer.
General Wilson's cavalry raiders had ripped up and twisted like
taffy twenty miles of track on the Danville-Richmond railroad. The
Rebels' General Johnston had been so outmaneuvered by Sherman
at Kennesaw he was being relieved of that command and sent to
wait passively in Richmond.

Several Frankliners talked indignantly about reports that Confederates in Charleston had deliberately placed Yank prisoners in
the line of fire from Northern mortars. Booth said it was a lie, and
he showed them the *Times* article quoting a letter which had originally appeared in the Richmond *Examiner,* from the South's Major
General Gillmore to the North's Major General Foster, denying this
charge and saying bitterly that the Charlestonians never knew *where*
the Yanks might aim next:

The shells have been thrown at random, at any and all hours, day and night, falling promiscuously in the heart of the city . . . indicating no purpose or expectation, on the part of those directing the fire, of accomplishing any military result, but rather the design of destroying private property and killing some persons, no matter whom—most probably women and children quietly asleep in their accustomed beds. A few weeks since, between 1 and 2 o'clock at night, one of your shells passed within a foot of the bed occupied by a man and his wife. They were of the class whom your people denominate "American citizens of African descent" and were more than half a mile from the nearest naval or military work. . . . On another occasion, [the Yanks had] opened and continued a very slow fire. It was apparent that the fire was especially directed at churches during the hours for public worship.

Booth believed every word of this, and expected the good Methodists, Presbyterians and Catholics of Franklin to be equally shocked. After the first accounts appeared of the burning of Atlanta, he became so openly bitter about the war that his friends avoided the subject as much as possible. One warning signal they learned to recognize was that when Booth was working up a temper, he'd lash at his boots with his riding crop.

He idolized Robert E. Lee, and one odd thing came out in Franklin; when he found that John Brown had lived near Meadville, Booth told about the few hours he'd served under Lee, when Brown was hanged. The actor had borrowed a uniform and gone with the Richmond Grays under then-Colonel Lee to stand guard at the foot of the scaffold. It drove Booth wild to have anybody criticize Lee.

Old Mr. McAmirch, the ferryman who had run passengers back and forth across the river ever since the Franklin bridge burned, was devoted to the actor, who always tipped him lavishly, "and treated me with the greatest respect," but he announced with Scotch logic that it was a waste to argue with such a hothead. Another of his passengers, a tough-talking carpenter, Titus Ridgway, was on the ferry on several crossings with Booth and tried to goad him on, which was the equivalent of shaking a rattle at a rattlesnake. One afternoon he reeled off a string of foul names for General Lee, and Booth was so enraged he began screeching terrible things about Lincoln. Ridgway grabbed a spiked river pole and advanced on Booth, yelling that he was a liar. Booth drew a gun, and said he'd "shoot any man who calls me a liar." McAmirch forced the pole out of Ridgway's hand and jumped in front of him. He stood there bravely and quietly as a shield, until "Booth slowly put his revolver back in his pocket."

The actor must have known by now that the Confederates couldn't win, and he began talking about the need for a negotiated peace that would be fair to both sides. Lincoln had already answered the peace-at-any-price howlers earlier that summer:

> War, at its best, is terrible, and this war of ours, in its magnitude and its duration, is one of the most terrible. . . . It has destroyed property, and ruined homes; it has produced a national debt and taxation unprecedented. . . . It has carried mourning to almost every home, until it can almost be said that the "heavens are hung in black.". . . We accepted this war for an object, a worthy object, and the war will end when the object is attained. Under God, I hope it never will end until that time.

The peacemonger most after Booth's heart was Copperhead Governor Seymour, who made the opening speech at the Democratic convention late in August:

> There are reasons why the Democratic party should be restored to power, and they are great reasons.
> The Democratic party will restore the Union because it longs for its restoration; it will bring peace because it loves peace; it will bring back liberty to the land because it loves liberty; it will put down despotism because it hates the ignoble tyranny which now degrades the American people.

There had been some talk of nominating the virulent Seymour for President, and Booth had exaggerated the Copperhead's chances wishfully, but the newspapers jumped angrily on his irresponsible speech, and too many people remembered how carefully the Governor had absented himself from his state when the murderous Draft Riots were going on in New York. General McClellan was the odds-on favorite anyway, and he got the nomination.

Booth disappeared from Franklin right after this, on his longest absence yet, and when he came back in September, he told Simonds he was through with the oil business. Ironically, the newspapers were fuller than ever of oil companies declaring fat monthly dividends, among them the Maple Shade at Petroleum Centre, the Noble ("throws up bully") well, and several at Rouseville. Booth asked his agent to draw up papers arranging for a transfer of his property: two-thirds of his share of the Fuller farm lease to his brother Junius, and a third to Simonds in payment for his services. The one-thirtieth interest in the still-undeveloped Pithole Creek land went to his sister Rosalie. Altogether, Booth had put $6,000 into his oil ventures, and hadn't made a cent.

He must not have wanted townspeople to know he was leaving for good, because months later several citizens testified innocently that the assassin still owned property in the area, and the *Spectator* said the same thing in print.

The week before John Wilkes left Franklin, he was in the barber shop run by a popular local Negro, Jim Lawson, when another colored man, Cale Marshall, came in talking happily about the Union victory at Harpers Ferry, where five thousand Rebels had been taken prisoner.

Booth said to him furiously, "Is that the way you come among gentlemen, and with your hat on too?"

The Negro said, with dignity, "When I go into a parlor among ladies, I take my hat off. But when I go into a barber shop or any other public place, I keep my hat on."

Booth, trembling and white-faced, reached for his gun. (Six months later, the big discussion in the barber shop was whether this was the same gun that killed Lincoln.) Booth's companion, the "medium-tough" Tom Mears, grabbed the actor from behind and pinioned his arms. Another customer leaped up, with lather still on his face, and took Cale Marshall away to safety. Mears finally persuaded the still-distrait Booth to leave with him.

Booth had already told the barber that he was going off to play an engagement in Washington. It wasn't true. He left town on September 28, 1864, about the same time another man with oil connections headed, as Booth did, for the Canadian border. The difference was that John D. Rockefeller was going to Niagara Falls on his honeymoon, and John Wilkes Booth was meeting a Confederate ring. He stayed in a boarding house near Montreal's St. Lawrence Hotel, the headquarters for Rebels in Canada. I have no idea what part this

short visit had in his conspiracy, but it certainly wasn't a pleasure
jaunt to talk over old times in the South.

By the end of October, Booth was in New York, and went to the
out-of-state commissioner with the deed transferring his property to
Junius:

> Be it remembered that on this 29th day of October 1864 before
> me Charles Nettleton as Commissioner of the State of Pennsylvania
> duly appointed and qualified according to the laws thereof to take
> acknowledgements and to be used and recorded therein, personally
> appeared the foregoing named J. Wilkes Booth who in due form of
> law acknowledged the foregoing Indenture to be his act and di-
> rected that the same might be recorded as such.
>
> In witness thereof I have hereunto set my hand and official seal
> this 29th day of October 1864.

It seems to me that Booth was behaving like a man who is determined to get his affairs in order because he knows he hasn't much
longer. The next month, he stopped in Philadelphia and left with
his sister Asia a bulky sealed envelope, which he told her was only
to be opened in case of his death. He returned to New York to appear with Edwin and Junius at the Winter Garden on November 25th, in a one-night performance of *Julius Caesar,* a benefit to
raise funds for a statue of Shakespeare in Central Park. It was the
first time the three brothers had played together; the friends and
fans of John Wilkes in Franklin, who read the city papers' dramatic
columns as never before for any word of their hero, and fretted because he hadn't been appearing, must have been enchanted to learn
from reviews that his Mark Antony was the hit of the evening. Older
women who had been warmed by his graceful attentions read with
tearful vicarious pride that his mother had sat in a box and that the
three sons, in the midst of a cheering ovation, had turned and bowed
to her. They also read that the performance had been interrupted,
briefly, by screeching fire sirens and firemen bursting into the theatre.
There had been a fire next door at Lefarge House which threatened
the Winter Garden, and the papers reported it was one of a dozen
fires that had broken out in large gathering places all over New York,
part of a Rebel plot to harass the city.

Edwin had calmed the audience, and the play went on, but he

couldn't quench the furious family argument over it at breakfast the next morning. Junius said the Rebel arsonists ought to be strung up. John Wilkes promptly started one of his tirades, and Edwin told him bluntly he had voted for Lincoln's re-election earlier that month. At this, John Wilkes ranted and screeched, and left in a headlong rage.

Five hundred miles away, in the oil region, at least one of his friends sensed the upheaval in the actor that winter. (His two amateurish, abortive attempts to kidnap Lincoln had failed; Richmond was doomed, and Booth, already cracking up within the tightening vise of inner and outer pressures, must have revealed his mental state, if not the reasons for it, in letters.) Jo Simonds, in his excruciatingly neat, small script, wrote Booth worriedly in February of 1865:

> Your strange note of the 16th rec'd. I hardly know what to make of you this winter—so different from your usual self. Have you lost all your ambition or what is the matter. Don't get offended with me John but I cannot but think you are wasting your time spending the entire season in Washington doing nothing where it must be expensive to live and all for no other purpose beyond pleasure.
>
> If you had taken 5 or 10,000 dollars and come out here and spent the season living here with us, traveling off over the country hunting up property I believe we both could have made considerable money by it. It is not too late yet for I believe the great rush for property is to be this Spring and if you are not going to act this season come out here John where at least you can live prudently and where I really believe you can make money. Come John immediately. We have plenty of room at our house [Mrs. Sarah Webber's] now.
>
> You must not tell such extravagant stories John about me. We work very hard and from the office derive so far a very comfortable income but nothing even compared to what you used to make acting, large indeed though compared to what we formerly rec'd. We have not got rich yet John and when I do you will be the first one to know of it. But I do wish you had come out here and staid this winter and still wish you would come now.

At the Presidential inauguration on March 4th, the boy who was to become our town's most honored Civil War veteran saw Booth on the platform with Lincoln. Eighteen-year-old Corporal Roe Reisinger had been with the Bucktails Regiment at Gettysburg, and during the fight at McPherson's barn he'd been wounded three times and wouldn't give up until he'd almost bled to death. During his long convalescence in a Washington hospital, he'd been invited to the White House to be personally commended by the President, some time before he received the Congressional Medal of Honor. At the time of the inauguration, he was on duty with the 14th Veterans Reserve Corps in the capital, a limping, still-valiant little gamecock. Whether because of his lameness, or his heroism, or both, he was given a special vantage place to watch the inauguration. Booth got *his* special consideration, and his spot among notables on the stand, through an infatuated daughter of a New England senator, plump, foolishly loving Bessie Hale, who thought she was engaged to the actor. (He must have wangled for the ticket long ahead, because a letter found in his trunk later, from an accomplice, implied that the kidnapping had been re-scheduled for Inauguration Day but finally postponed "until Richmond could be heard from.") With his murderer-to-be watching him, Lincoln said:

> "Both parties deprecated war; but one of them would make war rather than let the nation survive; and the other would accept war rather than let it perish. . . .
>
> "Both read the same Bible, and pray to the same God; and each invoked His aid against the other. . . . The prayers of both could not be answered; that of neither has been answered fully. . . . With malice toward none; with charity for all; with firmness in the right, as God gives us to see the right, let us strive on to finish the work we are in; to bind up the nation's wounds; to care for him who shall have borne the battle, and for his widow, and his orphan— to do all which may achieve and cherish a just, and a lasting peace, among ourselves, and with all nations."

Young Corporal Reisinger reported next that he and a comrade had been given tickets by a kind Washington gentleman to see Booth play Romeo in a benefit at Grover's Theatre, on March 18th, and that it was soppy enough to make all the ladies swoon.

It was John Wilkes' next-to-last appearance on a stage. He was on his way to see Edwin in Boston on April 3rd when the headlines waved joyous banners:

GRAND HOLIDAY AND JUBILEE OF VICTORY
SALUTES, PARADES, & ILLUMINATIONS

Jubilations—jubilations—jubilations! Richmond is captured—not evacuated but absolutely captured. . . . Washington is ablaze with enthusiasm. . . . Stalworth men embraced and kissed each other upon the streets, friends who had been estranged for years shook hands and renewed their vows of friendship. By one common impulse, the storekeepers closed their places of business, flags were everywhere displayed, the people turned out en masse, and joined in one solid universal expression of enthusiastic joy.

Both our Corporal Reisinger and Booth were on the White House lawn the evening of April 12th for the official after-surrender jubilee, when Lincoln gave his short, troubled, uncrowing speech on the problems of reconstruction. The corporal didn't see Booth this time, because the actor had already moved into the shadows; he was standing behind a tree with the accomplice who was to stab Secretary of State Seward.

Two nights later, Booth made his last and most sensational appearance on stage, at Ford's Theater, when he leaped from the box of a dying President.

At about eight o'clock the next morning, Booth's silver-headed cane came swinging into the Valley railroad depot in Franklin. His ex-billiard partner Alf Smiley was going to Union City to visit friends for the week end, and he was carrying his dearest possession, the cane Booth had given him. Alf's roommate, Harry Smith, was the railroad telegrapher there, doubling as ticket-taker. He waved to Smiley, and went on making change for a woman customer, while he listened absently to the clatter, click-clack of the telegraph keys. Suddenly he left the ticket window and crouched over the machine as if to shake it. Then he said in a choked voice: "Alf—my God, Alf —Lincoln was shot last night in a theatre and they're looking for John Wilkes Booth."

The twenty-one-year-old who had loved a gay, high-spirited actor sat clutching the silver-headed cane while his train for Union City came and went, without him. Several days later a United States deputy arrived to search his possessions and question him. All Booth's friends in Franklin were questioned, but only Jo Simonds was hauled down to Washington under arrest, by an embarrassed Venango County constable, McAlevy. He liked the conscientious little Simonds, thought his grief and horror were genuine, and was convinced he'd never had a notion of Booth's conspiracy, let alone been a part of it. The constable argued this so sturdily with Washington officials that he soon persuaded them not to jail Simonds, but simply let him remain on call in the capital to testify.

One reason the authorities suspected Simonds was that he'd known Laura Keene during his stage-struck days in Boston, and they saw a sinister tie-up there. Although the actress was the first to say, the night of the killing, that she had recognized the assassin when he ran past her as "Edwin Booth's younger brother Johnny," she was taken to prison anyway, with her leading man Hawk. She was released in a hurry, partly because of pressure brought to bear by her current lover, a gambler named Lutz, and partly because cooler heads had decided she couldn't be implicated. Perhaps they reasoned that an accomplice would hardly have rushed from the stage to the State Box and cradled the President's bloody head in her lap, as Laura Keene did.

In connection with this, I must slip in one Franklinite's story which experts jeer at because they can't find any documented proof. Well, I can't offer *proof,* either, but why must a story be labeled One Hundred Proof, like whiskey, to be savored? Our old family friend Miss Katherine Officer says her mother told her that she came to Franklin as a bride soon after the shooting. A year or so later, Laura Keene was playing somewhere in western Pennsylvania, and became ill and in need of money. To help her out, Jo Simonds bought a trunkful of her costumes, which he later sold when he left Franklin for the Bradford oil fields. Among the costumes was the billowing pink brocade Laura Keene had worn the night Lincoln was shot. Katherine Officer asked her mother reproachfully why she hadn't grabbed at the chance to get so historic a memento, and her mother said, "Well, you must remember I was young then, and more interested in spending money on new clothes. After all, dear, that dress was *ruined* with blood stains."

Another old friend, Miss Mary Hancock, said she'd been told that the week after the assassination, "all the gayest young bucks in town were being yanked off to Washington to tell what they knew about Booth."

I think the gay young bucks in their gouty old age must have indulged in wishful exaggeration, wanting to be linked to history even with handcuffs, but at the time it was the last thing they wanted. All Booth's friends in Franklin were afraid, with that nerveless unreasoning terror of the innocent, that they might be held guilty by association. The Robison brothers who had belonged to Booth's club hurriedly draped the front of their tailoring shop in black crepe, and closed it for several weeks.

Nobody in town got much business done. All over Franklin, people huddled in agitated clumps, discussing the crime. All the men wore black arm bands, and many of the ladies carried mourning handkerchiefs with two-inch-wide black borders. I suspect, though, that some of them mourned as much for their fallen Apollo as for the fallen President.

Booth had given some of his pretty admirers there autographed pictures of himself, and several of the local belles had reciprocated, blushing, with tintypes of themselves. They must have shivered with dread when the newspapers reported that Booth was known to carry pictures of five girls in his wallet. (It turned out to be four actresses, and the senator's daughter, Bessie Hale.) Remembering the debonair gallant who had danced with them, who had recited poetry romantically in parlors and on moonlit carriage rides to Oil City, and kissed their hands so exquisitely, they must have cringed even more, reading the purple press accounts of Booth's amours. His red-haired occasional mistress Ella Turner, who lived in a Washington brothel run by her sister, swallowed chloroform while bloodhounds hunted her lover, and lay down to die with Booth's picture under her pillow. Her suicide try wasn't a success, but it made a sensational story. Some of the papers said Booth was a drug addict, but most of the emphasis was on his Don Juan activities. A Philadelphia reporter described with relish how a pure young society girl had been so infatuated she had chased John Wilkes from one city to another. Booth, so the story claimed omnisciently, told her to go home and beware of actors, but the poor, bewitched virgin insisted on being seduced.

The editor of the Venango *Spectator* didn't run any seduction-scene stories, and in fact, he hardly mentioned Booth. Having ranted against Lincoln in print almost as virulently as John Wilkes, he now brought out an issue with columns ruled off by the same somber, heavy black lines appearing in newspapers everywhere that week. An editorial said:

> So horrible an affair has shocked the nation to a degree hereto-fore unknown, and caused universal sorrow. The supposed assassin, J. Wilkes Booth, spent several months in this place last summer and fall, and is well known to many of our citizens. He was engaged in the Oil business, and we understand has large interests here now. Those who knew him best, say he was mild and retiring in his disposition, and displayed none of the qualities of the desperado he has shown himself to be.

Privately, the editor announced he'd always thought Booth was a perfect gentleman, and that he'd never been so flabbergasted in his life. Several bewildered Franklinites tried to explain the crime by thinking up signs that Booth had been going insane. The man who had just gone into partnership with Jo Simonds, Moses Coleman, must have felt especially determined to prove this, and I have always thought his theory was the most fascinating of all. He said he had met Booth on the Atlantic & Great Western Railroad the summer before, returning from one of his unexplained trips, and that Booth had complained of a terrible bursting pain in his head. He told Moses he'd been hit on the head by a dumbbell in a gymnasium, and Moses now brandished this dumbbell as the blunt instrument that had cracked Booth's sanity and made him a killer.

From the start, there were constant rumors that the assassin was hiding in Pennsylvania, which was certainly more plausible than the report that he'd been seen skulking around Ford's Theater in disguise, and must have a hidey-hole right there at the scene of the crime. It sounded all the likelier because almost every newspaper mentioned the actor's oil investments. One of the dozens of stories was that the desk clerk at the National Hotel, where Booth was staying, asked him on the day of the killing why he was so gay: "Have you just made another thousand in oil?" Booth's alleged reply was, "No, but I worked hard enough today to deserve it." Several accounts claimed Booth had juicy gushers in Venango County, and all this fed the rumors that he was heading for our state.

Governor Curtin of Pennsylvania issued a special proclamation:

WHEREAS IT IS RUMORED THAT J. WILKES BOOTH, THE ASSASSIN OF PRESIDENT LINCOLN, HAS WITHIN A DAY OR TWO, BEEN SEEN IN PENNSYLVANIA—

NOW, THEREFORE, I ANDREW G. CURTIN, GOVERNOR, DO OFFER

A REWARD OF TEN THOUSAND DOLLARS

TO BE PAID TO THE PERSON OR PERSONS WHO SHALL CAPTURE HIM

The War Department's handbill included a description of the killer, with one item that was to lead to the wildest contretemps in our town:

THE MURDERER

of our beloved President, Abraham Lincoln

IS STILL AT LARGE

$50,000 REWARD

Will be paid by this Department for his apprehension

Booth is Five Feet 7 or 8 inches high, slender build, high forehead, black hair, black eyes, and wore a heavy black moustache which there is some reason to believe has been shaved off.

Although the War Department concentrated its search in Virginia and Maryland all along, police were distracted by the phantom Booth being seen all over Pennsylvania. The New York *Herald* announced, "A man has been arrested in Pittsburgh as Booth, but it wasn't him." The next day, headlines proclaimed:

BOOTH DISCOVERED
Seen on A Train
Near Reading [Pa.]
But Escapes

The *Sun* soon reported rather crossly under a Reading, Pennsylvania, dateline: "The man said to have recognized the individual arrested as Booth denies having any knowledge of him. . . . He is anybody *but* Booth."

In Franklin, we had the most spectacular capture of all. One after-noon the week after the assassination, a handsome, black-haired stranger got off the train from Pittsburgh. He had been working as a teller there when he had been approached by the president of Franklin's new International Bank, James Bleakley, about coming to our town as head cashier. The young man was delighted at the chance to better himself, and had bought an elegant suit of clothes to wear for his grand entrance into his new life. He had been invited to stay at the Bleakleys' until he found a room, but his first stop that day was at the post office, to leave word he'd be receiving mail in care of General Delivery.

The postmistress' sister was helping out there, because the post-mistress, Mrs. Sarah Webber, had her hands full running the rooming house. The sister had seen Booth several times, from a respectful distance, during his stay at Mrs. Webber's. Now when the handsome, black-haired, elegantly dressed man came to the post-office window, she thought uneasily he looked familiar. Suddenly she realized why: the reward posters had mentioned that the killer had shaved off his mustache! *This was Booth disguised by a clean upper lip.* (As a matter of record, it wasn't too hysterical reasoning. There was quite a definite resemblance.) When the newcomer told her his name was Cain, that clinched it. What more natural alias for a killer? When he added that his first name was John, his terrified listener didn't wait to ask, "And is your middle name Wilkes?"

She let out a squeak of terror, and ran back to tell the workers sorting packages and letters what she'd got hold of.

At this point, poor Cain must have thought the stories he'd heard of the crazy goings-on in the oil country were an understatement. People swarmed at him from all sides and backed him into a corner. A young constable who had been chasing a runaway pig through the park was hurriedly summoned indoors to do his duty. He too thought the face was familiar, and he couldn't help remembering the enor-mous rewards. In a quavering voice, he said, "Mr. Booth, sir, you'll have to come with m-m-m-me."

His capturee now understood what it was about, and he said crossly, "There's been a ridiculous mistake. My name is Cain. John Cain." The crowd began muttering ominously, and nobody really listened to

the man's next words, which were, "Get Bleakley. He knows me."
The constable took the insistent "My name is Cain" as final proof of
the insanity all Frankliners had been talking about. He said more
nervously than ever, "Come with me, sir." Looking at the glowering
faces closing in around him, the victim went quietly.

When the word got around town that John Wilkes Booth was
locked in a cell at the prison, and mad as a hatter, all the people
who had known and loved him were too horrified and unhappy to
go near the place. Bleakley, the bank president, had a new well going down, and he was somewhere back on Hill Point. The sheriff was
in Meadville talking to a provost marshal about taking Jo Simonds
into custody. It was several hours before Bleakley got back and heard
the news, and a confused, fifth-hand gabble about "He says he wants
to see you." What did Booth want to see him about? He hurried to
the jail, peered through the bars, and said in a surprised tone, "Why,
it's Cain."

For the members of Booth's own family who were thrown into jail,
there was no comedy-of-errors ending. Deputies reading through the
papers in John Wilkes' trunks, for clues to accomplices or escape
routes, found a letter from Junius to his brother advising him to
"give up the oil business." As the *Sun* said, "It was suspected by
some that the 'oil business' mentioned in the letter was but a cover
for the more desperate enterprise Booth had in hand." (This seems
especially far-fetched in view of the papers' constant mention of
Booth's oil investments, still magnified to millionaire proportions.)
Under the headline, THE ARREST OF JUNIUS BRUTUS BOOTH, the *Sun*
reported:

> The officer told Booth he would dispense with the irons, where-
> upon the prisoner thanked him in much agitation, and the twain
> proceeded to the station-house in 13th Street. Here Booth was kept
> for some hours, during which time he occupied himself in copying
> passages from the Bible—some from the 49th Psalm, etc. At 11
> o'clock Tuesday night he left for Washington, where he arrived at
> 8 1/2 Wednesday morning, having conversed little on the way,
> merely remarking that "he wished John had been killed before he
> had done that deed." [Some papers reported that Junius had said,
> "I wish he'd been killed for the sake of the family."] At 9 1/2

o'clock he was taken before the Judge-Advocate, where he stated that the published accounts of the contents of the letter alluding to the oil business contained a different phraseology from what he had written, and he desired to have the whole letter published. After the interview at the War Department he was taken to the Old Capital Prison and locked up. . . . Booth frequently spoke of the oil letter. Speaking of the name of "Alice" mentioned in it, he said he merely added a postscript in his letter to the assassin, requesting him to give his love to her, as the lady in question had frequently sent him such tokens in her correspondence. "Alice" is believed to be an actress employed in one of the theatres in Washington. There does not appear to have been anything unusual in the manner or demeanor of Junius during his stay in Philadelphia, but he seems at times concerned about what he calls the false construction put upon the letter in question.

Already there had been a far more sensational letter published, written by John Wilkes himself. Asia Booth Clarke had remembered the bulky envelope her brother had left with her, and she and her husband had opened it, apprehensively. They found a letter to their mother absolving the family of any knowledge of the "kidnapping." There were also deeds for the Venango oil shares transferred to Junius and Rosalie. The remaining contents were a packet of U.S. savings bonds and a ranting, tortured paranoiac letter: "To Whom It May Concern."

They turned this over to the provost marshal at once, and the papers had a black-letter day reprinting the document:

To Whom It May Concern
   Right or wrong, God judge me, not man. For be my motive good, or bad, of one thing I am sure, the lasting condemnation of the North. . . .
   In a *foreign war,* I, too, could say, "country, right or wrong." But in a struggle *such as ours,* (where the brother tries to pierce the brother's heart) for God's sake, choose the right. When a country like this spurns *justice* from her side she forfeits the allegiance of every honest freeman, and should leave him, untrammeled by any fealty soever, to act as his conscience may approve. . . .
   This country was formed for the *white,* not for the black man. And looking upon *African Slavery* from the same standpoint held by the noble framers of our Constitution, I for one, have ever considered it one of the greatest blessings, (both for themselves and us)

that God ever bestowed upon a favored nation. . . . Yet Heaven knows, *no one* would be willing to do *more* for the negro race than I, could I but see a way to *still better their* condition.

When I aided in the capture and execution of John Brown . . . I was proud of my little share in the transaction, for I deemed it my duty and that I was helping our common country, to perform an act of justice. But what was a crime in poor John Brown is now considered (by themselves) as the greatest and only virtue of the whole Republican party. Strange transmigration! *Vice* to become a *virtue,* simply because *more* indulge in it. . . .

But there is no time for words. I write in haste. I know how foolish I shall be deemed for taking such a step as this, where, on the one side, I have many friends and everything to make me happy, where my profession *alone* has gained me an income of *more than* $20,000 a year, and where my great personal ambition in my profession has such a great field for labor. On the other hand, the South have never bestowed upon me one kind word [This is, to me, the most paranoiac of all, but it also makes me think perhaps he'd once approached the heads of the Confederacy with his kidnapping plot, and that they'd told him off], a place now where I have no friends, except beneath the sod; a place where I must either become a private soldier or a beggar. To give up all the *former* for the *latter,* besides my mother and sisters whom I love so dearly (although they so widely differ from me in opinion) seems insane; but God is my judge, I love justice more than I do a country that disowns it, more than fame and wealth, more (Heaven pardon me if I'm wrong) than a happy home. . . .

My love (as things stand today) is for the South alone. Nor do I deem it a dishonor in attempting to make for her a prisoner of this man, to whom she owes so much of misery. . . .

A Confederate, doing duty upon his own responsibility,

J. Wilkes Booth

He was a man who had wrapped himself in the banner of his own self-made kingdom, and he must never have faced the hideous reality of what it would do to his family—of the shame and grief that would shroud them as long as they lived. In the first weeks, hatred for any relative of the missing assassin was so menacing they hardly dared go out of their houses. The whole family, even Edwin and their mother, were flooded with threatening letters, many of them anonymous and filthy. Public hysteria, as well as the deep-flowing sorrow, was prolonged almost unbearably, as bells tolled on and on, day after day, and muffled drums sounded a primitive dirge. Lincoln's body was being taken from city to city, and even his one-time vilifiers came to pay their last respects who had never shown respect before. It was the longest wake in our history. Songwriters were busily turning out laments to fit the occasion: "A Gloom Is Cast o'er All the Land" . . ."A Nation in Tears". . ."Oh, Send Me One Flower from His Grave."

Every day that the search for the assassin went on only heightened public feeling. A brigadier general announced that after Booth was caught and executed, they should take the body, ram it into a mortar and point the muzzle seaward toward Great Britain. "Then explode the charge of powder, breaking the damned assassin's carcase into ten thousand fragments, none of which should be allowed to fall upon the soil of a country the foul murderer and his confederates sought to ruin." A New York butcher offered a $500 reward if Booth were brought to him alive, because he wanted "to stick tacks in every square inch of his body."

Booth had evaded capture for eleven frantically suspenseful days when the cashier of the McHenry Hotel in Meadville wrote the Secretary of War about the scratched windowpane:

Sir:
Recent dispatches, referring to a former and futile attempt upon the life of the late Abraham Lincoln by poison, have induced me to write you regarding a circumstance occurring at this hotel, where I have been cashier for a year and a half. Sometime ago the following words were observed to have been scratched upon a pane of glass in room No. 22 of this house, evidently done with a diamond: "Abe Lincoln departed this life August 13, 1864, by the effects of poison." I give this just as it appears upon the glass. In view of recent events, it was deemed best to take the pane of glass out and preserve it, and we have it safe. It was noticed some months ago by the housekeeper, but was not thought particularly of until after the assassination. . . .
My theory now is, that the words were written in prophecy or bravado by some villain who was in the plot, and that they were written before the date mentioned, August 13. As to who was the writer, we can, of course, give no definite information. J. Wilkes Booth was here several times during last summer and fall [here he

gave dates of the visits]. He does not appear to have been assigned that room, still he may have been in it in company with
others who did occupy it. . . .

Should you consider the matter of sufficient importance to desire
it, I will give you a list of the persons occupying the room in question for a long time preceding the above date, as you may request.

With a hearty desire to do all in my power to bring to light and
to punishment the author of this terrible crime,

> I remain, very respectfully,
> Your obedient servant
> S. D. Page

On the same day, Jo Simonds, who had been allowed to return to
Franklin but was still sending depositions on Booth's oil shares, wrote
a pages-long account detailing all the transactions for the provost
marshal. He ended on a moving personal note:

> You will excuse my writing more concerning this terrible affair.
> There is a private war, which his relatives and friends suffer in ad-
> dition to the grief that all are sharers in, which is none the less
> poignant that it can have no sympathy. Sudden, sharp and terrible
> was the blow upon all his *true* friends (and he had many) and it was
> one which at first could not be believed, cannot yet be realized and is
> a sorrow which time can never heal.
>
> God bless our whole country and bring her safely through every
> peril to peace and prosperity—again a happy and united nation;
> and, may we not without a thought detrimental to her highest in-
> terests, pray that He in His infinite love and goodness will forgive the
> unhappy author of this his last and greatest calamity, though man
> never can.

The friend Jo Simonds wanted God to forgive was hiding in a
Maryland swamp, and writing in his small red-leather notebook: "I
do not repent the blow I struck. . . . Though I am abandoned, with
the curse of Cain upon me, when, if the world knew my heart, that
one blow would have made me great, though I did desire no great-
ness. Tonight I try to escape the bloodhounds once more. Who, who
can read his fate? God's will be done. I have too great a soul to die
like a criminal. O, may He, may He spare me that, and let me die
bravely."

It was early the next week that Franklinites sat in Jo Simonds' office

reading the bitter end. Booth and his moronic accomplice Dave Herold
had been hiding in a tobacco barn near Port Royal, Virginia, when
detectives and cavalry men surrounded the place. Herold had come
sidling out to surrender, and told his captors he "had always liked
Mr. Lincoln and was very fond of his jokes."

"Booth on the contrary was impudently defiant," the *Tribune*
said, "offering at first to fight the whole squad at 100 yards, and sub-
sequently 20 yards." It went on:

> He was hobbling on crutches, apparently lame. He swore he would
> die like a man, etc. . . .
>
> As soon as the burning lighted the interior of the barn sufficiently
> to render the scowling face of Booth, the assassin, visible, Sergeant
> Boston Corbett fired upon him, and he fell. [Franklin never believed
> this—the whole town preferred to think Booth killed himself.] He
> was pulled out of the barn with one of his crutches and carbine and
> revolver.
>
> The wretch lived about two hours, whispering blasphemies against
> the Government and messages to his mother. . . . "Tell mother I
> died for my country. You, gentlemen, have spoiled my fun in
> Mexico."
>
> His body was fully identified by his initials on his hand in India
> ink, his memorandum books and other papers, and by the personal
> recognition before and after death of the detective officers who knew
> him.
>
> He had his moustache shaved off, and had a uniform beard of four
> or five days.
>
> He wore a gray woolen shirt; had on dark cassimere pants; one
> cavalry, or theater, top boot, which drew up above the knees but
> was turned down when captured. On the other foot, he had an old
> shoe. His leg was bandaged where it was broken. . . .
>
> The smaller bone of his left leg was badly fractured, one of the
> smaller arteries ruptured, and the leg badly swollen. . . .
>
> He had $105 in greenbacks and sundry Canadian bills of Exchange
> dated last October.
>
> His hair was badly matted; his clothing soiled, and the body
> looked more like that of some dirt bearer than of the whilom fop. It
> has not yet been disposed of.

Six weeks after the body had been dumped in "an ordinary gray
army blanket and sewed up" and hastily buried under the dirt floor
of the Arsenal, the well Booth had owned a share of, on Pithole

Creek, came in a gusher. The Titusville *Herald* reported it as "Probably the most productive well in the oil region of Pennsylvania." It mentioned Booth's transferring his share. "He was very particular about the assignment in due form of law, and carried the assignment to the Registry office himself."

If there's a hell-after-death, then the shabby, crippled ghost of Booth watched his family destroy the oil stock, as they did all his other ex-possessions.

But if the strike had happened a year earlier, when the actor was first in Franklin, then it might have swerved the course of history. Diverted by a brand-new, high-flowing gusher, Booth might have stayed in Pennsylvania.

Anyway, it's fitting that John Wilkes Booth once owned a piece of what became the most brilliant, unbelievable boomtown of all— Pithole.

N I N E

Pithole, where seeing's not believing

IN MAY, 1865, there were four log-cabin farmhouses; that summer, the city of Pithole shot up like a gusher, a wild, wonderful outpouring of money and men and exuberant hopes released by the end of the war. A reporter from the *Spectator* rode over on horseback for a look at the new wells and he was so mesmerized he stayed three whole weeks, probably nibbling lotus leaves to keep calm. "This once benighted but now flourishing region is the Mecca of the Oil World or the 8th Wonder, I don't know which," he reported. "Even while I write, buildings are going up and some are put up and have groceries in them in six hours. . . . There are many commodious buildings that are a credit to any place."

By September you had your choice of fifty hotels, ranging from slap-ups just a cut better than field beds (less mice, more men) to the elaborately furnished $100,000 Chase House with its real, live, starchy French chef. Murphy's Theatre on First Street was a wooden gingerbread with casual chinks between the wall boards, but dazzlingly lighted by crystal chandeliers from Tiffany's. Its eleven hundred seats were occupied night after night by the most gallant lot of dramalovers who ever hoisted a star.

177

Toolies and roustabouts sat upstairs—fifty cents a perch—and the balcony shook with the boots thumping out applause. Oil men in greasy army khaki or claw-hammer dress suits crowded into the boxes—$10 for a close uninhibited view of a four-hour show. In one evening, for instance, you got a "Sublime Tragedy" by William Shakespeare, plus a "Grand Dance" by Mlle. Brignoli, and a "Song" written expressly for Mademoiselle, "Fenian Brotherhood." It didn't take an Irish rebel to savor a combination package of the Bard, Mlle. Brignoli, and the Fenian Brotherhood.

Every box was a cheering claque for some favorite, and the occupants had forthright ways of showing appreciation. When Imogene Teasome, a heady bundle of blond corkscrew curls and firm ingénue curves played there in *Love's Sacrifice,* a group of oil men marched up to the stage and presented her with a gold watch "in a costly hunting case with brooch." The note with this token read:

> May each tick be an echo of the warm, palpitating hearts of
> Your Friends in Pithole

Their testimonial of appreciation to another actress was more direct; in fact, it nearly gave *her* heart palpitations. She was a plumply pretty girl known as Miss Eloise, who played Lady Macbeth with a sunny disposition and friendly gestures. Strolling in a nightie, in the sleepwalker scene, the effect she gave off was really quite cozy, and her audience responded to a man, and conferred among themselves at intermission. When she came out for a curtain call, what she took to be a note was flung on the stage at her feet. You must admit that normally Lady Macbeth is not a character to send mash notes to, or an invitation to share a cold bird and a bottle, but this Lady Macbeth was a lovable murderess. Beaming, she bent low to retrieve the paper, and discovered it was a five-hundred-dollar bill wrapped around a silver dollar. She was so startled she let out a girlish squawk, as if she'd just been whacked on the fanny by Banquo's ghost. This unstudied show of appreciation pleased her admirers even more. Several gentlemen stood up in their seats shouting "Bravo, Lady Macbeth." All the perfumes of Arabia were as nothing, compared to the oil-perfumed gestures of Pithole.

It was more than a city; it was a state of postwar euphoria. At least half of the twelve thousand people in Pithole were veterans, ranging from a general down to army muleteers with tattered slouch cavalry hats and curses like cannon blasts. They were all hungry for luxury, for fancy furnishings and good food, for pretty faces and social graces. Some of the gayest blades formed the Swordsman's Club and met in elegant rooms at the Metropolitan Hotel, which boasted truthfully that it had wallpaper and "Fresh oysters brought in daily." A note preserved by one of the dashing ex-Swordsmen says in heel-clicking prose: "It will afford me great pleasure to take oysters with you Saturday evening. With my kindest regards to each of the gentlemen interested, I subscribe myself with much respect . . ."

Invitations to the Swordsmen's Grand Social Hops featuring Tompkins Opera Organ Band were the most sought-after in all Venango County. On the night of one of these soirées, a landslide blocked off the road into Pithole, but guests from Oil City slogged and slithered eagerly for miles on foot, around the blockage, and arrived in time "to thread their way through the intricacies of the mazy dance."

As far as I can make out, membership requirements had nothing to do with swords, but any applicant was foiled if he was found to lack "the attributes of a gentleman and good fellow." Swordsmen who passed this test included future governors of two states, several congressmen, and a brace of oil tycoons. When one of the prettiest and most popular girls in a Pithole sporting-house died of pneumonia, the Swordsman's Club attended her funeral in a body, soberly garbed in black, and linen snowy as angel wings. A gentleman and good fellow could do no less. The one fiercely upheld Swordsman's taboo was "No word of talk in the club rooms about politics."

It was a sensible rule, considering how many ex-Confederates were mixed in with the Northerners at Pithole. Most of the Yanks had army pay in their pockets—and their guns. The War Department had announced: "All the honorably discharged soldiers have been granted the privilege of retaining their arms at the following rates: muskets, $10, all other carbines and revolvers, $8." Confederates, if they'd surrendered their arms, still had their fierce, raw pride and humiliation, and a need to blot out the grim years past by making a fortune or at least a try at it, in a place where anything was possible: "Money circulated like wastepaper, and for weeks the scene recalled the wildest fiction of the South Sea Bubble."

The ghosts of Holland Land Company agents must have joined Booth's in wry contemplation, watching the wild stampede. Early pioneers had been so loath to go there that around 1800 the Holland company, trying to get rid of a dud, had offered one hundred extra acres with each purchase, as bonus-bait. The settlers who accepted were mad as hops when they found where they'd landed: on a puny little stream running a desolate course parallel to Oil Creek, but far from any roads or connecting waterway. It got its name—Pithole Creek—from the fissures torn open by ancient rock upheavals, that gave off a strange, warm sulphurous gust. One hunter who had sat on the edge of a pit dangling his buckskinned legs over to get warm was so overcome by the fumes his companions had to carry him home. They spread the word about "sulphur and brimstone pits inhabited by the Evil One," and this made settlers even more disenchanted with their lonely lot. Only a few hardy souls stuck it out, among them a Baptist preacher, the Reverend Walter Holmden. It was on his land, inherited by his son Thomas, that a diviner went feeling for oil in 1864.

The diviner had been hired by a shrewd, lanky ex-refiner turned wildcatter, Ian Frazier, who had already made a quarter-million with a share of the whopping Reed well at Cherry Run. Now he'd organized the U.S. Petroleum Company, and the land he leased for his firm included sixty-five acres of the Holmden farm. Frazier chose the most godforsaken spot of all, a few miles above the spooky pits, for his diviner to test first.

I say *test,* although Professor Silliman of Yale, who had been accepted as the top scientific authority ever since he'd analyzed the first flask of Seneca Oil, was insisting loudly that to locate a well by divining was "A cheat, an Art abhorrent to Nature." But wildcatters have always had a cheerful disregard for scientists; like horseplayers, they prefer a nice, solid bit of abracadabra. As the old diviner walked along holding a witch-hazel twig stretched out before him like a sleepwalker's hands, Frazier followed respectfully, and on the spot where the forked twig dipped and pointed down, he promptly installed his driller. The Art abhorrent to Nature paid off with a well that spouted in January, rising to 1,200 barrels a day.

Frazier commandeered teamsters with sleighs and rushed the oil off to market over the frozen woodland paths. Spring floods isolated the territory for two months, and the East was preoccupied with the end of the Civil War. Frazier's sudden death (I think a heart attack) left his company rudderless, and while they were hiring a new superintendent, two oil-country men, Duncan and Prather, stole a fast march by talking Farmer Holmden into selling them all his land outright. They paid him $25,000, then quadrupled the price to keep him from going to court yelling "Foul." As the original lessees, the U.S. Company still retained three fourths of the oil; Duncan and Prather got the other quarter, but they made a fortune by chopping up the farm into lots, laying out streets for a town, and renting building plots, on a three-year lease, for as high as $14,000.

Unlike Petroleum Centre, where derricks, boarding houses and brothels were all mish-mashed together in the grease, Pithole City rose handsomely on the higher slopes, and most of its great wells were down on the flats by the creek. The two-story Astor House, the first hotel up, was finished in a day, and at the end of a week, Holmden Street was a teeming, built-up business center. A broker who still couldn't find space advertised in the Titusville *Herald,* "Office in the tent at the foot of the hill, Pithole City."

Bona-fide companies rubbed elbows with sidewalk con men like the ex-soldier named Pierce, who claimed he could locate new oil territory because he was "the only man now living that was wounded by a magnetic instrument. He possesses magnetic polarities and electric shocks pass off daily. His condition and peculiar feelings give him great confidence in discovering the important openings containing Petroleum."

Newcomers got a more peculiar shock on discovering Pithole had a female land agent, although one male admitted she was "a persevering expounder of the beauties of her territory." I suspect from that the lady wasn't pretty, but if she held her own in that swarming speculators' paradise, she must have been quite a woman.

One of her most chivalrous business rivals was a young ex-Confed-

erate, Roger Sherman, who arrived when the town was a month old
and set up as an oil-lands agent until he could open his own law
office. This letter from a fatherly relative near Erie reflects the
hurly-burly he landed in:

Lavinia, July 30, 1865

Dear Roger,

Yours from Pithole came to me two days ago and I was extremely
glad to hear from you. From your description of the *hole* it must
be a raw place to live in, I console myself with the reflection that
you have roughed it in Ark. and also when in Dixie, and that you
are not altogether new or green even in Pithole and that you will
get on with less annoyance than most others until things improve as
they must after the first flush of speculation is past and people get
sober. I trust you will get your share of what good things the hole
produces and that you may not be in any way disappointed. [In a
later letter, he wrote "Burns says that 'Fortune is but a bitch' and I
sometimes think he is right."]

There are several persons now in Pithole City from Lavinia and
vicinity. Sam Wymer whom I think you must know is engaged in
getting up teams and wagons which he takes to Oildom with a load
of saleable things and sells the whole and returns to buy again. He
was at Pithole last week and now he's looking up a team and wagons. I will see him before he goes again and ask him to call on
you. . . .

Mr. Brown has recently learned that his nephew Henry M. Brown
is at Pithole and is said to have been a fortunate speculator and is
in funds. Three years ago last fall Henry's wife came here alone and
staid here some months giving birth to a son while here. Her husband was traveling on business it was said. In the spring he came
and took his wife and child away giving Mr. Brown his note for
some $50 of which only a few dollars has been paid. Since that time
he enlisted in the U.S. service and deserted to Canada, and now he
turns up at Pithole. Mr. Brown wishes me to ask you to make en-
quiry about him and if you find that there is a chance to get his
money he will send you the note for collection. Henry Brown is a
scamp of the first water. . . .

By the way, although I have no reason to even allude to political
matters I must say Bully for Emerson Etheridge. How he lets the
light in upon Andy [President Andrew Johnson], the whole letter is
inimitable no other man could have done it. What can Andy do but
let him go and let him severely alone. His arrest is undoubtedly a
political move—will his constituents stand it? I say Go it, Emerson—

In your next tell me all about everything. We are as well as usual. We are getting it dry here and I have to water my plants daily.

Yours as ever,
E. M. Conklin

To a Pitholian, the idea of watering plants every day must already have seemed like something done on another planet. It was much the scarcest liquid in town. The new City Water Works, with pipes laid from a high-up spring and reservoir, networked the town, down the half-mile-long Holmden, Brown, and across the intersecting First and Second streets, providing modest service at splashy prices: "Water for Private Closets, $1 to $5 per week; $1 for Cold Tub; Stables $3 for First Two Stalls." Hotels signed a contract promising "to use the water agreeably to the established rules of the Company." The elegant Chase House had imported a chef and wines from New York, but guests with too strong a compulsion toward cleanliness were urged to patronize Crum's establishment: "Next to Water Tank above Chase House. Bath! Bath! We will give it to you at any degree or temperature you desire."

The reporter from the *Nation,* who came in August, complained:

> A person at Pithole is indeed placed between fire and water. To drink water is to drink a solution of salts. To drink whiskey is to drink poison. Every glass of water I took I forswore water, and every glass of whiskey, I forswore whiskey, and thus lived a life of zigzag perjury. . . . Every other shop is a liquor saloon. It is safe to assert that there is more vile liquor drunk in this town than in any other of its size in the world. Indeed, a bar is almost the invariable appendage to every building. Lawyers have bars appurtenant to their offices— each hotel, dwelling-house, or shop has its separate bar. . . .
>
> Hearing that the great hotel of the town was going to be christened, I went to witness the ceremony. Drinks and billiards free—and a thousand thirsty men to enjoy them. Never before did I know how strong was the love of freedom in the human breast. A wild mass of teamsters, operators, workmen of every kind and costume, drank in the varied liquor of the generous host. I myself, in a private room, imbibed some capital sherry.

Even a *Nation* man had to admit that the Chase wine cellar was pretty good and the brandy-smashes bully.

The stranger who sat near him at dinner described how the proprietor of the Fifth Avenue Hotel (on Holmden Street) had "turned off a servant girl yesterday. She didn't like such treatment and taking a horsewhip, drove him out of the hotel and down the street."

"Business seems to be done in a queer way here," the *Nation* man replied thoughtfully.

As another sample of Pithole upside-downness, his new friend mentioned that the town's circus was to give a benefit to raise money to build a church. The *Nation* man went off to see Thayer and Royer's Great Circus, which was tucked into rather midget quarters beside a livery stable; what fretted him was how the owners had managed to haul in the Fat Lady, "a buxom young maiden of eight hundred pounds. How she was brought over these roads without being reduced to a skeleton, how she held her own against the water and the food, must forever remain awful mysteries."

It's true that even by oil-country standards, Pithole was hard to get to, but already there was a feverish rush to lay better paths to this gilded mousetrap. By fall a hundred and seventy-one workmen had finished laying a double-track oak-plank road from Titusville, twelve miles away. Down this, stagecoaches came rolling like thunder, and pulled up at the Chase House. When the mail sacks were disgorged and carried into the post-office wing of the hotel, such mobs closed in that just-arrived travelers must have thought it was a mass holdup. Six mail clerks sorted letters frantically * while men stood in lines that stretched for two blocks, waiting, and fought over places. Wealthier citizens paid drifters a quarter an hour, to hold their places in line.

The Western Union office, in the opposite wing of the Chase House, was almost as frenzied, with speculators, producers, company agents or Wall Streeters sending out reports of new strikes. The U.S. well had twenty-three tanks around the great spewing giant that had been tapped with a witch-hazel twig. There were six more wells go-

---

* There is an often-printed old wives' tale—or since this is the oil country, an old husbands' tale—that the Pithole post office ranked third largest in the state, next to Philadelphia and Pittsburgh. The records in Washington don't show any such thing.

ing down on the Hyner farm Booth had owned a share of. New gushers roared in that summer—the Grant, Pool, Twin wells, and the mammoth No. 54. Hotels had long outside sinks like watering troughs—street-washers—where guests could scrub off the top layers of oil when they came from a well, and these became the founts for exchanging hot tips and arranging deals.

There was a saying that buyers would grab anything within rifle shot of a gusher. The owner of a barren farm outside Pithole leased it at a staggering figure, and when he came home and told his gaunt, overworked wife, she didn't say a word; she just took all the dishes out of the cupboard and smashed every one, laughing hysterically.

In the midst of this crazy laughing-gas atmosphere, real oil men went on working solidly and shrewdly. Reading a lease signed that year, I was surprised and impressed by the meticulous, matter-of-fact attention to details:

> . . . The second party, in consideration of one half of the Working Interest in said Lot, agrees to sink two wells for the discovery of Oil thereon and . . . to place on said Lot two good and suitable engines of not less than ten horse power each, two good engine houses and two serviceable derricks, together with the necessary complement of tools, walking beams, band wheels &c, all of which shall be inspected and accepted by the first party before operations are commended. . . .
>
> The said second party further agrees to sink each of the said wells to the depth of six hundred and fifty feet, if necessary, to obtain oil in paying quantities, to guarantee that each well shall have a round hole at least four and one half inches in diameter, and further agrees to properly tube, seed-bag and test each well for the space of two days after its completion without expense to the first party. . . .
>
> Said second party agrees to commence each of the said wells within ten days from the date hereof, to furnish good and experienced drillers for sinking the same, to prosecute the work day and night with the exception of Sunday. . . .

And next comes the bit that impressed me most of all:

> Said second party further agrees to keep an accurate record of all rocks passed through in drilling said wells, which record shall show the kind of rocks found, their thickness and depth from the surface, and the location of water and oil veins. . . .

To combat the flood of boomers' worthless leases, some of the town's most responsible citizens organized, for small investors, what may have been the first Mutual Funds deal in the country: The Working Men's Pithole Creek Oil Association. The *Spectator* noted approvingly: "The society purposes to have a one-sixteenth interest in seven different wells, all in the vicinity of the U.S. and other flowing wells. It is emphatically the project of the people. They secure leases at lower rates in good wells than private individuals could do, that all may be associated together for mutual benefit and protection . . . [and this] leaves the chance for failure very slight. When viewed all around, it is the safest investment in the oil region or any other."

By then, the country was in such a speculators' whirl of inflated dollars and hopes that servant girls who made $3 a week bought fifty-cent and even twenty-five-cent shares of oil stock. One witness reported that chambermaids at Pithole hotels had bulging rolls of bills tucked in their garters, but whether from tips, or sure tips on stocks, he didn't say. Anyway, I'm not sure he's a reliable reporter; he sounds like a snooper and garter-snapper.

I'd be more inclined to believe what ex-whaler Henry James told his son: the day he arrived in Pithole, he saw two filthy, unshaven men squatting on the Flats by a tree stump, using it for a desk. They were concluding a little deal for two hundred and ten thousand dollars.

Another New Englander, a recent Harvard graduate and Back Bay Bostonian, accepted the mad wonders of Pithole so phlegmatically that the old-timers who had been there a month or so decided to play a little joke. One of them brought a pile of government bonds to the hotel where they and the Bostonian were staying, and arranged with the proprietor to seat the newcomer at their table and use the bonds for napkins. As soon as the young man sat down, each of his table companions casually lifted a five-twenty government bond, and tucked it into his vest. Then they chatted pleasantly of the million so-and-so had made, and the astronomical sun that such-and-such well would sell for. The Bostonian listened calmly, picked up his government bond with no sign of surprise, and draped it over his spotless stuffed-shirt front. The practical jokers, rather abashed, decided he hadn't even noticed how valuable a napkin he had. But a minute later, he summoned a waiter imperiously: "See here, this napkin is too small. When you bring my soup, bring me a ten-forty bond."

The joke had snapped back on the jokesters: "A laugh went around the festive board that could have been heard at the Twin Wells, and the matter was explained to the bean-eater."

As a reward for his imperturbable Brahmin calm, the oil men set the visitor on the track of a good buy, and he went home to Beacon Street four weeks later with enough greenbacks to supply napkin-coverage for a lifetime.

He probably never knew how lucky he'd been; hundreds of would-be investors lost their shirts and went home in a barrel. Even cautious business men with a motto of "Look Before You Lease" were hooked by the artful new tricks of the traders. Almost-dry wells were rigged to connect by secret underground pipes with a distant tank, and when a prospective buyer checked on the yield, the oil seemed to be pumped up fresh from the well in a rich, endless flow. Or buyers were urged to inspect a tank holding "the last twenty-four hours' yield," and how should the unwary know that beneath the top few inches of oil was salt water?

Owners of dry holes poured a few gallons of oil on the ground, scattered greasy sand around, and let the excited victim discover these surface indications and buy with greedy haste. A widow who got rid of her land by this trick was furious when the new greenhorn owner actually struck oil on the very spot where she'd scattered the liquid bait. She screamed that he'd cheated a poor lone widow woman.

Pitholians were amused by a new song that satirized the gyp-artists in strokes as broad as an ax:

"FAMOUS OIL FIRMS"
Words by E. PLURIBUS OILUM
Music composed and well greased
so as to run smoothly,
by PETROLEANA

There's "Ketchum & Cheatum," and "Lure um & Beatum"
And "Swindle um" all in a row;
Then "Coax um and Lead um" and "Leech um & Bleed um,"
And "Guzzle um Sink um & Co."

CHORUS: Oh! Oh! Oily firms pay
In Pennsylvania. Just so.

There's "Gull um & Skinner" and "Gammon & Sinner"
"R. Askal & Oily & Son,"
With "Sponge um and Fleece um" and "Strip um & Grease um"
And "Take um in Brothers & Run."

There's "Watch um and Nab um," and "Knock um & Grab um"
And "Lather & Shave um well," too;
There's "Force um & Tie um," and "Pump um & Dry um"
And "Wheedle & Soap um in view."

There's "Pare um & Core um," and "Grind um & Bore um"
And "Pinchum good, Scrape um & Friend,"
With "Done um & Brown um," and "Finish & Drown um"
And thus I might go to the end.

Naïve stockholders were so greedy for the alleged fabulous profits and so suspicious of being swindled they wrote accusing letters and sent abusive wires even to the hard-working managers of wells that paid top dividends, saying in effect, "You crook—you're holding out on me." One of the most efficient well superintendents, Pap Sheakley, later Governor of Alaska, suggested to colleagues that since they were being blamed for large-scale larceny, they ought to form a club called the Forty Thieves. Other citizens were so enchanted they clamored to get in on the act, and the Forty Thieves soon included bankers, merchants, lawyers and just plain little new millionaires. Members assured gullible strangers solemnly that they were banded together to unload phony stock and steal valuable machinery.

It was typical of Pitholians' humor that when they decided to incorporate the borough and introduce law and order in real earnest, they held two elections at once—the Legal and the Illegal. Citizens who hadn't yet been in town the six months' residence required for voting (and that included most of the population) set up Illegal Headquarters at the Chase House and nominated a banker, Harry Kemp, as Illegal candidate for Burgess. The legal polls were set up at the National Hotel on Brown Street, with Alfred Keenan, co-owner of the Twin Wells, running lawfully.

Kemp, Illegal, got eight times as many votes as his rival. The loser was then declared Burgess of Pithole. This seemed to satisfy every-body. James Guffey, later famous as a Democratic politician and oil producer, was another Legal-ran; he was elected Borough Council Clerk.

For Justice, they chose old Charles Highberger, who had lost a leg and whatever patience he'd once possessed. One afternoon, a witness has said, Pithole attorney Ruth "was urging the conviction of a miserable whelp when he noticed Highberger had fallen asleep, as was his custom during long arguments.

"Mr. Ruth aroused him and remarked, 'I wish Your Honor would pay attention to the points which I am about to make, as they have an important bearing on the case.'

"Highberger opened his eyes, glared around the room, and rose on his crutches in great wrath, exclaiming, 'There has been too blamed much chin-whacking in this case; you have been talking two hours and I haven't seen a cent of costs. The prisoner may consider himself discharged.' "

The real wielder of law and order was an ex-cavalry colonel, David Gardner, the new Chief of Police. He was six feet, four inches, built in heroic proportions, and he rode a white horse like a knight's charger. One of the spots he kept a stern eye on, which nestled under the wholesome name of Heenan's Cottage, harbored the worst toughs around, and their camp followers. Heenan's bartender, Simpson, had a yen for the girl of another Cottager, Matt McEntee, and he got her too, or at least got a turn at her. When McEntee surprised them together, Simpson, who had prudently taken his gun to bed along with the lady, fired first. Aiming as he did, from a lying position, he missed and dove hurriedly through the window. McEntee found him in another saloon, and told Simpson to lay off his girl. Simpson settled the argument by shooting his rival through the heart. This was considered so excessively unfriendly—stealing a man's girl and then killing him—that McEntee's Cottager friends rushed to the jail in a vengeful mood, to lynch the murderer. Colonel Gardner stood at the door of the jail and faced the armed mob calmly. "Why, of course you can lynch the b———," he said mildly. His voice rose. "There's just one little stipulation: first, you'll have to lynch me."

The toughs almost blubbered with terror at the thought, and retreated in not very good order. Simpson was tried in Erie and acquitted on the plea of self-defense, but he didn't push his luck; he stayed away from Pithole.

On another occasion, two hot-blooded South Carolinians rode into town to avenge a lady's honor. Their sister, married to a Pithole doctor, had written them that her husband of less than a year was being unfaithful. They stopped to pay a courtesy call on the Chief of Police, and to invite him to come along. The Colonel explained that this wasn't the kind of frontier town where justice was triggered by amateurs. He would investigate and do what was proper. With two aides, the Colonel "descended on the doctor's office after midnight and found him in bed with a young woman whose reputation is not of the best. He politely requested the pair to dress and come with him, but the pair indignantly refused." This didn't faze the Colonel. "He took them off to the Justice's office in an almost Adam state."

These happenings were reported in the newspaper owned by another Civil War colonel, Leander Morton. A small, darting man with mustaches a monkey could swing from, he arrived in town lugging a carpetbag full of job type. First he printed posters and circulars, and then launched the Pithole *Daily Record,* twenty-five cents a week, and now that I've read old copies, I consider it a broth of a bargain. The star reporter, a recklessly brilliant, hard-drinking twenty-year-old named Charles Leonard, had joined the Union Army at the age of sixteen, but he looked more like Pan than an ex-infantryman, with his quick, fey grin and flowing Bohemian tie. He wrote under the byline Crocus, and he gave the *Record* its rollicking Pithole flavor. For instance, the time he heard the rumor of a vice roundup: "We understand that the Burgess is to issue an order for all lewd women to retire across the Mason and Dixon line." The next day, Crocus blandly furnished a fresh bulletin: "We are informed that Colonel Gardner, and the police forces, by direction of Burgess Keenan, are to make a raid this A.M. with the purpose of carrying into effect an order mentioned in yesterday's paper. For a list of the killed and wounded, see the *Record* tomorrow."

The raid, he later recounted, took place around dawn "when honest folk were supposed to be in bed." Mary Shane, the proprietress of a questionable resort at 17 Brown Street, was released on $400 bond. One drunken male customer was fined $10—"for the luxury of a little spree."

Crocus listed the casualties of another fast-house raid as: "Three severely injured, one fined. One gay and festive lady from First Street ran off at five in the morning with the officer in pursuit. One took refuge under her bed until the officer left."

Another time, he reported that the dancing girls at the Old Free and Easy "lowered their necklines to half mast as a mark of respect for departed modesty."

The Old Free and Easy's advertisements in the *Record* blatantly solicited customers for the lowered necklines: "The managers guarantee to citizens at large who wish to pass a jovial evening to do all in their power to please."

Doctors' notices in the same column were almost as bad: "Dr. George Gyles, a graduate of the New York Medical College, with ten years of Medicine & Surgery in New York, has adopted the following fees for Pithole:

> Medicine & Advice in Ordinary cases, 50¢ to $1
> Special Cases, $5 to $15
> Teeth extracted safely, each 50¢
> Teeth extracted without pain, $1
> Midwifery, $5 to $15

When the news of the day seemed dull, at least by Pithole standards, Crocus commented pungently on happenings in nearby communities:

> A scamp named Henry Funk recently ran away with the wife of one Henry Dietrich who was boarding with her six children in Allegheny City, the runaways taking the half dozen babies with them. Mrs. D. and her paramour were arrested at Kittaning and with the children brought back to Pittsburgh where Funk is in jail. He should be put into an insane hospital. Any Lothario who runs off with another man's wife and six children when beef is 25¢ a pound and tenant houses are scarce, is fit for a madman's jacket.

The *Record* gave space to the letter of another Fallen Woman, a favorite performer at Murphy's Theatre, explaining "a Mr. Nichols has circulated a pamphlet on Mlle. Brignoli and advanced charges most detrimental to the character of a lady who had previously been looked upon as virtuous, so we could not refuse her the chance of a public reply":

To the Pithole Public:

It appearing that a man named Nichols claims me as his wife, I wish to state that he is a base falsifier. He has a wife in Comstock. He imposed upon my credulity and got a pretended compact of marriage—but discovering what a low scoundrel he was, justice to my religion as well as the laws on bigamy compelled me to abandon him. . . . If I am the degraded creature he and his old chums *of the varieties* would make me, then he is a mean poltroon in again seeking to live with me.

In either case let Nichols hang his harp on a willow tree and seek some buxom widow who may bring him greenbacks. Brignoli will not come. . . . Her own common sense tells her to shun a reptile who would crawl into her bosom only to suck her life blood. Nichols loves only my poor earnings. Failing to get me to live with him again, he seeks to defame me and destroy my means of obtaining an honest livelihood for myself and poor *fatherless* children.

Mlle. Brignoli

Crocus, a man who appreciated a well-turned phrase even more than a well-turned ankle, should have drunk a toast to that mademoiselle—and probably did.

When he got bored with local material, Crocus made up his own. He wrote a long, impressively detailed story about how Drake happened to drill the first well. According to Crocus, Drake had been conductor on the New Haven Railroad when there was a bad wreck: a passenger car had fallen from an open drawbridge at Norwalk, and fifty people were killed. Drake, fearing he'd be blamed for this, had fled with a nervous breakdown to India, where he observed natives drilling for oil. Then he had come back to the States, and copied the heathens' drilling methods in his first well at Titusville. Crocus ended this fantasy with the solemn statement, "This is the flat, unvarnished truth."

Pitholians adored these *Crocuses,* but even the truth in their city was so preposterous that occasionally they gave Crocus credit for making it up too. One time a fast-talking inventor who said he'd been at Berea College brought in a cumbersome mud-throwing machine, to demonstrate to Pithole's Fire Chief. As I've already mentioned, mud had been used to smother the Rouseville blaze, and it had been a sure but slow method ever since, in fighting oil fires. The inventor said his machine scooped up a great mass of mud in its iron hopper, and threw it onto a blaze lickety-split. He would demonstrate as soon as there was a fire. In Pithole, there were fires almost every day, so this was easily arranged. The inventor arrived with his monster at the next conflagration, and bustled about getting it ready to operate. The next day, Crocus reported solemnly that the machine's inventor had slipped and fallen into the hopper, and had been accidentally thrown on the fire with the mud and burned to death. Pitholians slapped their thighs and roared that nobody could tell a tall tale like Crocus. But this one happened to be true.

What went on at another fire seemed to come right out of Crocus' head too. In fact, when the *Record* brought out an Extra on it, early readers agreed joyously he'd really outdone himself this time. There had been a fire at the Chautauqua Livery Stable, and a Negro worker had rushed to the nearest water well, at Widow Ricket's. He pumped up a few bucketsful quickly and tossed them on the fire, and other volunteers followed suit, but their efforts only made the blaze burn faster. They sniffed, and discovered the should-be water was oil, pure unadulterated *Oil*. Once the fire-fighters had taken in this astounding fact, they forgot the fire entirely and rushed to the Widow Ricket's. She got a score of offers for her sixteen-foot-deep well—and two proposals of marriage that day. Then Pitholians discovered that all over town, oil was suddenly close to the surface. They dug in their cellars and struck oil at three feet down; one eyewitness saw a carpenter take a shingle, scratch idly at the ground, and out oozed oil.

Out-of-town reporters rushed to the telegraph office to send dispatches on the phenomenon to their papers. City editors around the country had outgrown their early distrust of stories from Oil Creek, but this latest tale—that at Pithole they didn't even have to dig, it just bubbled up—this was too much. Back came the indignant, "Refuse print such nonsense. Sober up."

Pitholians themselves were sobering up fast after the first exultant scramble, because they found it was really an awful problem. Spring water was undrinkable; even the coffee and tea reeked of oil. Water had always been scarce in Pithole, but now it sold for as high as a dollar a pail. Women and children ran all over the countryside with kettles and pans, trying to find unpolluted springs: "Dirty shirts could not be washed. Dirt fastened upon the damask cheeks of Pithole damsels and found an abiding place in the whiskers of every bronzed fortune hunter. . . . The editor of the *Record,* a strict temperance man, was obliged to travel fourteen miles every morning by stone boat to get his glass of water. Stocks of oil companies were the only thing in the community thoroughly watered."

This only lasted three weeks, and like Midas, the too-oiled residents were relieved to get back to normal, which was abnormal enough in Pithole.

Distinguished visitors were so commonplace that the *Record* gave most of them short shrift. Sir Morton Peto, a gilt-edge English financier, came to Pithole and later wrote a book, *Resources & Prospects of America, Ascertained During a Visit to the States in the Autumn of 1865.* He had a great deal to say on petroleum's part in helping the North win the war: "It is difficult to find a parallel to such a blessing bestowed upon a nation in the hour of her direst necessity." He was startled by the small-share stock frenzy brought in with Pithole, and marveled that at city brokerages, the favorite oil shares were "two to four shilling each." Sir Morton was the first titled visitor to stop at the Chase House, but the *Record* wasn't impressed.

The Chase was still the most popular first-class hotel, but it had rivals now; some of the celebrities went to the imposing new Bonta House, which opened that winter on the east slope across the creek, a solid, dignified, four-story hostelry that cost $80,000. Horace Greeley registered there, signing himself large and round, but the *Record* gave this famous newspaper colleague no puff. There was only an oblique reference to his presence, a tiny paragraph in the paper that week, undoubtedly inserted by Crocus while his left hand thumbed his nose. It quoted a remark made by Secretary of State Seward: "Horace Greeley is a great man—a man so full of genius and of such power that if he had a particle of common sense we should have to hang him. But he is a d—d fool, and therefore harmless."

Another genius who came to Pithole, Samuel Van Syckel, was

called everything from a harmless fool to a villain. Teamsters called him even worse than that, because he was the first real threat to their fat livelihood. They had become more kingpin than ever in this city that demanded luxuries hauled in load after load—thick carpets, massively framed bad paintings, mahogany four-poster beds, an enormous variety of foods and liquors. With all this and 5,000 barrels of oil a day, teamsters could name their price. Van Syckel had been working as a commission buyer on Oil Creek, and had seen how the full barrels piled up, waiting the drivers' pleasure and weather that made the roads passable. He decided to build a pipeline from Pithole to the nearest stop on the Oil Creek railroad, Miller Farm, six miles away. This involved up-and-down grades and covered a much greater distance then earlier, leaky pipelines—mostly failures. In the late summer of 1865, he came to stay at Pithole's Morey Farm Hotel, which charged $21 a week for board and such touted luxuries as "gas light, steam heat, colored waiters, and 'spring mattresses.' " Easterners said the Morey's food almost equaled Delmonico's, but to the over-wrought, jeered-at Van Syckel, it must have tasted like oily waste. At mealtimes in the big dining hall, fellow diners hooted at his pipe dream: "Do you plan to girdle the earth, Van Syckel? Do you think water runs uphill?"

It got so bad that Van Syckel bounded out of the dining room one day like a frantic fox pursued by hounds, and asked the proprietor, Mr. Morey, if he might have all his meals in his room. Morey, a hearty ex-Western grain merchant, would have liked to get rid of this jinx-guest altogether, because he didn't want teamsters boycotting the hotel and refusing to haul in the daily supplies of fine meats. He agreed to send meals up on a tray, but suggested tactfully that if the inventor came and went by the back door, he'd avoid the kibitzers lying in wait in the front lounge.

So the man who was to contribute one of the most lastingly important ideas to the oil industry snuck in and out the back way like a tramp.

Like most inventor-geniuses, he was single-minded and tense, with no small talk. In the Pithole of the convivial Forty Thieves and Swordsmen, the sophisticated Easterners, the rough-and-ready new rich, and the suave-talking boomers, he was considered daft in the head. But he was shrewd enough to hire one of the most popular, quick-witted Swordsmen, young Alf Smiley, as his timekeeper and paymaster, at $150 a month.

Smiley had come over to Pithole—without Booth's silver-headed cane—soon after War Department detectives had cleared him of any connection with the assassination. At Franklin's U.S. Hotel, he had been pointed out to every newcomer as "Booth's closest friend in town," until he had fled the scene not of the crime but haunted still by the criminal. In Pithole his spirits fizzed high again, and the exuberance that had made Booth say "I enjoy your company," made Smiley an ideal assistant for the unpopular inventor. He helped Van Syckel hire workmen who could lay a pipe with one hand and fight the aroused teamsters with the other, if necessary.

On September 5th, they began laying the two-inch pipe which Van Syckel had had made to order in fifteen-foot sections, lap-welded at the joints, pressure-tested with nine hundred pounds to the inch. From then on, there were broken joints—human or welded—night and day. Van Syckel stationed guards all along the line, but the teamsters roamed in bands at night; they ripped up whole sections of pipe, tied them with log chains hitched to horses, and hauled them off to throw in the pits upcreek. What they couldn't rip up, they pickaxed. Van Syckel armed his watchmen with carbines, and doggedly had new pipe laid to replace every piece stolen or wrecked. He became more and more an outcast; even producers who secretly cheered what he was doing, and resented teamsters' high-handed ways, didn't dare show any friendly feeling. Every night there were brawls in saloons between pipeliners and the worried, enraged drivers, but no brawling or vandalism halted the inevitable. Van Syckel made the first test run in October, using steam pumps that forced 81 barrels of oil an hour through the six miles of pipe—equal to the load carried by 160 teams. It was the start in girdling the earth.

Pipelines multiplied like worms, a strange, rigid new breed, all through the oil region. Van Syckel laid a second line, and the two brought him in over $2,000 a day. (The charge per barrel was $1, much cheaper—and faster—than hauling.) Several other firms built lines fanning out in other directions. The business men of Titusville, seeing their town being by-passed, built a pipeline all the way from there to Pithole, with a 3,000-barrel capacity. The procedure was to haul oil from the wells to dump stations, where the pipeline took over. Alf Smiley persuaded Van Syckel to build auxiliary accommodation pipelines directly to all the big wells.

By now, the teamsters were aroused over a new, stronger adversary, a burly, bustling civil engineer and tycoon-to-be, Henry Harley, who operated his network of pipeline in a large-scale way. The teamsters said bitterly that he was infringing on their rights as public carriers, trying "to take the bread from the mouths of our children." They sent him letters "threatening his certain assassination if he did not abandon his scheme." Next they added arson to their activities, and burned a shipping platform and several tank cars at a storage depot. (The tank cars were the first bulk carriers, built that year by Amos Densmore. They had two huge wooden tanks, one at each end of a flatcar over the wheels.) Even before the fire, Harley had sent to the city for Pinkerton men, and in the meantime, kept watchmen on around-the-clock patrol. At 2 A.M. one night soon after the first fire, a mob of men—nearly a hundred—came whooping out of the woods, firing into the air, yelling to the watchmen, "Run or be shot down." The outnumbered watchmen backed off, the teamsters closed in, screeching like Comanches, and one of the attackers threw a fireball that set five tanks blazing.

Harley was a much more ruthless opponent than the quivering, brilliant Van Syckel. He used the Pinkerton detectives as stoolies; a half-dozen got jobs as teamsters, won the confidence of other drivers, and learned the names of the fireball attackers. Twenty ring-leaders went to jail. Fifteen hundred teamsters left Pithole in one week, licked by the onslaught of progress.

Not that the town calmed down then. There was a new kind of shooting-match around New Year's, when Ben Hogan, an ex-prize fighter, ex-Northern and Confederate spy, ex-smuggler, gambler and pimp (without the *ex*), came to Pithole with a rolling-hipped beauty, French Kate.

TEN

———◆———

The host wore a gun

Coddled Easterners arriving in Pithole often mistook Ben Hogan for a deacon when they saw him walking down First Street. He was a large, solid, deliberate-moving man, always dressed sedately in a black broadcloth suit, white cravat and a tall ministerial hat. Westerners weren't taken in for a second by the unctuous clothes and manner. They recognized him as one of a familiar breed—the Bad Men— even before they took in the small cold deep-set black eyes, the powerful shoulders, the bull-neck hidden by the white stock, and under the churchly topper, the flattened head and slickly pomaded black hair.

The closest Hogan had ever been to a minister was as a boy in Syracuse, New York; a kindly old churchman had befriended him and allowed him to read in his library, and Hogan repaid the favor by stealing several dozen rare books from his benefactor, tearing out the prints that displayed the female form in Grecian statues, and selling them to his neighborhood pals as sexy pictures.

After this promising show of initiative, he went to New York, gave boxing lessons in a gym, and fought in some small bouts. Just before the Civil War, he headed south on a river boat and murdered his first man in New Orleans, "in self defense." He was given a suspended sentence for joining the Confederate Army, but deserted the next day. In Mobile, he killed two more gamblers because they were crookeder than he was, and then left town fast. Both the North and the South paid him handsomely as a spy, or so he said, but he probably made more running drugs through the blockade, with smuggling and a dash of piracy to boot.

When he put a sign over the door of one of his oil-country establishments—"Ben Hogan, the Wickedest Man in the World"—the claim may have been a bit overstretched, say by four continents and west of the Great Divide, but nobody challenged his right to the title locally. To establish himself as the most notorious character in Pithole, a man had to have sins taller than gushers, and Hogan's were.

He started there modestly as the "business manager" at Emma Fenton's sporting-house, with his mistress French Kate doing what came naturally. No newcomer, not even a Harvard boy, would ever have mistaken French Kate for a deacon, or deaconess. She was a startlingly beautiful brunette with dead-white skin, a haughty Romanesque nose, full pouty lips, a bosom made for cleavage, and a voice like a sliding trombone. Two glossy black curls rested on her forehead, a double-barreled version of the nursery rhyme: "And when she was bad, she was horrid." One of her favorite costumes had a cascade of fringe wriggling down over her voluptuous hips like spaghetti.

She was so popular with gentlemen callers that within a few months her lover had opened his own sporting-house on First Street—Hogan's Lager Beer Hall—with French Kate dispensing whatever the boys in the back room wanted. Hogan had fifteen girls, and he boasted that they could converse with customers in six languages, including, no doubt, Kate's French idioms. This multilingual activity earned $1,000 a day for the owner. On Saturday nights, so many patrons crowded in that after the dance hall filled up, Hogan would stand at the door with a gun, to discourage importunate latecomers who wanted to join the party.

Next to French Kate, his most famous girls were Dolly the Swede, Kitty Bowers, a twenty-two-year-old with "pale gold hair, moist lips and violet eyes," Lizzie Toppling, whose breasts toppled over, and Champagne Mamie. (The champagne that customers bought at Ben's to launch Mamie was usually a mixture of Catawba wine and soda.) Lesser staff members, who doubled as dancing girls, wore mid-thigh-high frou-frou skirts, like French maids in burlesque. Ben Hogan stuck to his deacon garb, and he looked the picture of an affable, if conservative, host as he stood by the piano with a glass of brandy and a good cigar, keeping an eye on his guests. The guests numbered twenty men to a girl, so that when, say, nine men decided to dance with the same little dove simultaneously, feathers and fists flew. At such moments, Ben's prize-fighter technique was useful in bouncing the troublemakers out into the mud holes of First Street.

One visitor, a prominent citizen of Titusville, must have wished he too had been bounced while he was still upright. Hogan, according to his own proud admission, got the man to go a few rounds with French Kate in the back room, and then "blackmailed that Pillar of the Church."

There was still no church in Pithole when Hogan arrived, but he made the need seem more acute than ever. The *Record* said there was talk of bringing in Henry Ward Beecher as a moral influence, and of raising $180,000 for a tabernacle high enough to contain him. This plan was as evanescent as Beecher's morality, but Pithole's Reverend Daniel Steadman finally succeeded in raising enough to build a small Methodist church on the hilltop, which was dedicated in April. Until then, he had been holding well-attended services from such impromptu pulpits as the Metropolitan bar or Murphy's Theatre. Steadman never stood on his dignity—he trusted God's—and he befriended hundreds of men down on their luck. If he gave a derelict a pair of khaki pants, he also gave him some self-esteem to carry in the pockets. Wives came for advice and help when their husbands got Pithole fever, and if necessary, the Reverend Daniel would go beard a stray in Hogan's den. The Calvinist doctrine of Total Depravity made him fighting mad; once when he was arguing with a Calvinist, he started out ringingly, "I believe Christians may fall from grace—" His opponent interrupted tartly: "Reverend, your flock proves that convincingly."

As an ex-army chaplain, Steadman had a hell-for-leather style of delivery Pitholians admired enormously. "His sarcasm would skewer a hypocrite." On Sundays, he flayed his listeners for their sins, and they took it and asked for more. The Forty Thieves sent him $150 for Christmas, with a note thanking him for his "true charity and moral teachings." The Swordsman's Club, which had a congenial motto of RCT—Rum, Cards, Tobacco—gave a benefit dance and concert promenade to help furnish his church.

I think it was the Presbyterian minister who once asked a Swordsman what RCT stood for. The Swordsman improvised hurriedly, "Religious Counsel Treasured," and the minister was so gratified he exhorted his congregation to support this worthy group. The poor man wasn't anywhere near so popular as Reverend Steadman. He had to hold services in a makeshift little place in the business section; the Presbyterians had started a church almost next door to the Methodists', but then their rectitude and contributions languished, so the Catholics finished the job and took it over as St. Patrick's. A priest advertised briskly in the *Record:*

> *Rare opportunity to the citizens.* Having been appointed to take charge of the Catholic congregation of Franklin, in conjunction with that of Pithole, and being thus obliged to be absent from Pithole every second Sunday and part of the week, I find that it will be too expensive to keep house in either place. So accordingly I closed the pastoral residence in Franklin and I will do the same here. When in Franklin I will be seen at the Philadelphia House, in about a week from now I will take up quarters at the Chase House in this city; now I come to an interesting point. In consequence of breaking up my house here, I have no use of house furniture and will accordingly dispose of them at auction at the house adjoining the church, next Thursday, May 8 at 4 o'clock P.M. The articles to be disposed of are miscellaneous and useful and appropriate. Let all, young and old, who want great bargains be sure to come. I will not be here next Sunday, but some priest will be here to celebrate the Holy Sacrifice.—Jno. L. Finucane.

He was able to shuttle between flocks because the railroad, a branch of the Oil Creek line, had finally arrived at Pithole. The Bonta House bragged that it had built a footbridge over the creek and a plank walk all the way to the depot. The Duncan House, not to be outdone, promptly laid its own planks down part of First Street, so that guests might walk a straight line to the cars. These sidewalks were rather casual affairs; a Boston journalist said, "I notice one that seems undecided in its mind whether to keep on, retreat, or climb a tree."

Oil men had to flounder down through a last slimy unplanked

stretch to reach the wells, but a lady shopping on Holmden could make her way intrepidly, without muddying her skirts, to MacPherson's Ladies and Gents Furnishings & Variety Store, just beyond the Danforth House. She averted her eyes (and stopped her ears) while passing Birdsell's Free Concert Saloon and the Alhambra Billiard Parlors. Once past, she was in a respectable stretch that contained Kemp's Bank, "dealing with currency from England, Ireland, Scotland and Wales," and irresistible bargains at *"The Original Cheap John of New York*—Beaver Cloths, Doeskins, Mittens and Hoods."

Dutch John's, not to be confused with Cheap John's, was a low, unladylike hangout, and so was the Venango Saloon. And if you were a gentleman making the grand tour of questionable resorts, you continued over First to Brown Street and a den known as Number 18. One victim took space in the *Record* to warn others to watch their step: *"To all whom it may concern:* Having been bitten and swindled by a large dog known by the name of T. P. Burt, I feel it my duty to inform the inhabitants of Pithole to beware of him. . . . Said dog owned and resided at the notorious 18 Brown Street. W. H. Rutter."

It was on these streets, Brown, First and Second, that the famous daily promenade of the soiled doves took place. Each noon, thirty or forty sporting-house females appeared on horseback, but not like Lady Godiva. They were dressed within an inch of their chins, impressively hatted and gloved, and they sat modestly sidesaddle, looking neither right nor left as their mounts moved gracefully in a highstepping procession. Crowds of men gathered every day to watch the spectacle, and perhaps decide on a bit of horseflesh or otherwise for future use, but there were no wolf whistles or other caddish manifestations. The whole thing was quiet and dignified, a tribute to beauties and beasts.

A few of the more high-spirited riders occasionally broke loose and cantered on over to the respectable Holmden Street, to race their mounts pell-mell. Crocus reported in the *Record* that a Miss Frieda Harris was caught and fined $5 for *fast riding* down the main street.

He had small use for fast-house proprietor Ben Hogan, and pelted him with contemptuous nicknames. During one of the periodic raids, French Kate was brought before the irascible Justice Highberger and had to post a $400 bond. Crocus announced snidely, "She put up no resistance, although Bully Ben was present."

Pithole's earliest madam, Emma Fenton, the former employer of Hogan and French Kate, had purplish mattress-stuffing hair, a parrot's beak, and a fiery passion for money. She was enraged at French Kate for taking away good paying customers and monopolizing them in Hogan's establishment. Once she and Kate had a lively reunion with no holds barred, and both contestants retired with a hunk of the other's hair. Bully Ben didn't care for Emma's attitude, and the *Record* reported his chivalrous rebuttal: "Emma Fenton made information before Justice Highberger against one Ben Hogan, a prize-fighter, for assault and battery. She reported that he entered her establishment and knocked her down."

On another occasion, Ben took along an ax and whacked her bar to smithereens with the fury of a Carrie Nation. Once a group of Temperance women marched into Hogan's saloon and exhorted the customers to give up the Demon Rum. Several of the bar patrons made rude noises, and Ben called them down sharply. Rather to the surprise of his customers, he told the women callers that he himself "believed in temperance, although not total abstinence" and that he certainly wouldn't allow ladies to be insulted in his presence. "Men," he said suavely, "remember you too had a mother. Let's drink to the health of these good ladies."

When he was hauled off to the county court, to stand trial for running a house of ill fame, he explained to the judge that the charge was a dreadful mistake. He was, he said, only running "a gymnasium where members of both sexes may enjoy wholesome exercise, using the different parts of the body in such a way as to bring all the muscles into play." He informed His Honor solemnly that if people would spend a few hours each week in Hogan's gym, it would do them more good than all the pills in the world. The judge, who may have been a physical-education fan himself, seemed rather edified by this defense, and he fined Hogan a mere $200.

For wholesome outdoor exercise, Hogan set up wooden hurdles and had his girls, attired in scanty costumes, run races on Sunday mornings, to the tight-lipped fury of respectable citizens on their way to church. Once he dressed ten of these bosomy handmaidens in boys' clothing and took them in a hay wagon for a tour of the oil fields, where they made friends easily, and were warmly repaid for their efforts. As another change in the workday monotony, he enlisted several of his staff as assistants in a local vaudeville act; a Pithole playbill for February 3, 1866, features *"Professor Ben Hagan * and His Dramatic Athlete and Pantomime Troupe.* Professor Hagan will have a stone broke on his breast weighing 800 lbs. . . . Sports by the Gymnasts. . . . Officers will be in attendance to preserve order."

Later that spring, Hogan got out his boxing gloves and put on a match with another prize fighter who'd come to town. The event took place in a grassy ring on the hill where Balltown, an annex of Pithole, sprawled out. At least a thousand spectators crowded around the ring, some of them on horseback. Several dozen were women, among them French Kate, looking as if raw meat wouldn't melt in her mouth. Just before the contest, she pouted her lovely lips and told Ben that if he didn't win the match—and the $500 gold purse—she'd leave him. Considering that Kate was the heart of his business, and games-mistress in his gym, it wasn't entirely loverly sentiment that made Ben fight his bulliest.

The fighters' costumes alone must have been worth the price of admission ($2). They rated a memorable notice in the Titusville *Herald* story "By our special reporter," who was either Crocus or a rapt disciple:

THE FIRST PRIZE FIGHT
IN THE OIL REGIONS

A prize-fight for a purse of $500 and the championship of the Oil Regions came off in the classic suburbs of Pithole City, or rather Balltown, on Wednesday afternoon, between Benny Hogan, alias "Grease-spot". . . and Jack Holliday, alias "The Samson Post," of Pithole City.

We know very little about the antecedents of these bruisers. Hogan is a notorious "rough.". . . Holliday hails from Rochester, N. Y. He first got his name into the papers by trundling a wheelbarrow from Rochester to Buffalo, a distance of about sixty miles, without stopping for food or water, a feat that no locomotive has ever accomplished. He is a lineal descendant of the "Game Chicken," an

---

* He had been born Hagan in Switzerland, changed it to Hogan in this country, and evidently reverted to it as a stage name.

English fighter who flourished about twenty years ago and was immortalized by Charles Dickens in his celebrated novel *Dombey and Son*. . . .

The seconds were supplied with lime juice, tincture of arnica, cork plaster, brandy, lancets, sponges, blankets, etc., and duly appeared and took their places in the ring.

At precisely 2 o'clock, the new bell at Pithole giving the signal [this must have been the just-installed Methodist church bell], Hogan shied his castor into the ring, turned a handspring after it, and then went to his corner amid the cheers of his backers. Holliday followed and was hailed with the same manifestations of delight. The men were then uncovered by their seconds and exposed in their gladiatorial costumes. . . .

Hogan wore white stockings and velvet tights, bands and knee-buckles, and a green sash, signifying that he belonged to the Fenian Brotherhood, and after making war on Holliday intended to challenge the British army.

Holliday was dressed in gray tights, white stockings, and a petroleum-colored sash. He wore a black moustache but his head was bare and smooth as a billiard ball. He is tall, spare and bony, and betting was two to one in his favor.

[In Round One] Hogan, after complacently surveying his antagonist, made a couple of feints with his right bower, and then sent his left duke into the ribs of the "Samson Post" with such force as to lift him clear from the ground and send him onto the back of his head with a thump like the sound of a pile driver. . . .

Third Round. The betting had changed to five-to-one on Hogan, but Holliday's friends cheered him on, telling him to "go in for a big strike on good territory." . . . Hogan hurled a bunch of fives into the center of Holliday's nose, opening a huge crevice, from which there was a sudden gush of claret. (Cries of "First oil for Hogan.") . . .

Fourth Round—Holliday, looking both scared and hurt. He succeeded, however, in making a slight abrasion on Hogan's left cheek, and the latter retaliated with a severe body blow, which sent the Rochesterian to grass in short order. . . .

The sixth and last round was soon over. Holliday came to the scratch very reluctantly and Hogan gave him a square knockdown, and then fell over upon him. Holliday clung to him when down and struck him a "foul" blow. Time one minute.

This ended the fight. The referee decided in favor of Hogan. . . .

Remarks—We have given our special reporter's account of this brutal performance as a matter of local interest, and a record of the first (as we trust it may be the last) prize fight occurring in the Oil Regions. . . . Physical bruising is among the most revolting of vices.

Holliday, descendant of the Game Chicken, wasn't the only one fighting Hogan that day, although the others stayed out of the ring—at gun point. Several months before, a glib crook from Buffalo, Stonehouse Jack Vance, had moved into Pithole with a gang of his toughs, or as Hogan said scornfully, "footpads." He made no secret of his contempt for this would-be rival. Once Stonehouse swaggered into Hogan's saloon with a gaggle of his toughs, and the rumor was that he'd come to kill Bully Ben. French Kate stifled this ambition by whamming Stonehouse over the head with her revolver. The next day, oil men congregated at the Chase House bar had a ringside seat for the spontaneous slaughter on the sidewalk outside. Stonehouse, still emotionally bruised from his encounter with French Kate and her revolver butt, was foolish enough to shoot at Hogan. This time he got a bullet in his right arm, and a promise of more to come. Hogan announced coolly that the burgess had given him permission to shoot to kill. This doesn't sound like the sort of thing a burgess would tell Bully Ben—especially not a Legal Burgess—but it discouraged Stonehouse. He left town the next day for parts known, where we'll follow him in a minute. When Hogan fought the match with Holliday in April, the few of Stonehouse Jack's minions still in Pithole came to the fight in a plug-ugly mood, determined to break it up. But whenever they tried to get into the ring, oil-men spectators drew their guns in good-natured warning. Hogan said later it proved "The business men were on my side," but I think it simply proved that Pitholians were a sporting lot and wanted the fight to go on.

Citizens of Titusville thought the new boomtown was entirely too sporting, and they were incensed at the overflow lot of dubious characters they inherited from Pithole, among them Stonehouse Jack and most of his thugs. Arsonists were more than ever the terror of the oil-soaked settlements, and Titusville had been plagued by a series of these burn-and-loot outrages. The climax came soon after Stonehouse's arrival in town, when arsonists set fire to the office of an oil company on a cold January night, and the blaze spread down an entire business block and left it in rubble. The next morning the parasol-carrying editor of the *Herald,* Henry Bloss, felt understandably inflammatory himself:

> Titusville has suffered enough from incendiaries. The town is full of vagrants, harlots and pimps. Let them be cleaned out en masse. The suspicious characters arrested last night should be first dealt with. If shown that they had any complicity in these acts of incendiarism they should be hanged. We shall have no more incendiary fires after one or two desperate characters have been LYNCHED.

The paper was barely on the streets that morning before two hundred citizens swarmed to a mass meeting—angry as bees whose hive has been overturned.

Ex-lumberman Jonah Watson got up and said boomingly that a hundred volunteers were needed as vigilantes, to clean up the town. One of his listeners said mildly, "Well, they're here." A roar went up: "They are here!"

With that settled, they got down to business. A Committee of Ten was appointed to tell the pimp-proprietors and inmates of fifteen brothels to get out of town within twenty-four hours. A Vigilante Committee of Thirty voted to hold a hearing that day of the arson suspects already rounded up, Stonehouse Jack included.

The hearings were held in Corinthian Hall, while directly across the street a dozen aroused citizens erected a gallows on the still-smoking ruins of one of the burned buildings. As the *Herald* remarked, any suspect being interviewed by the vigilantes had only to glance out the window at the gibbet to feel he might not be long for this world. This must have given a special fervency to the thugs' protestations of innocence, and I'm pleased to report that the vigilantes listened with scrupulous fairness. After deliberating all day on the evidence, they ruled there was not enough to convict Stonehouse Jack and the other suspects of setting the fires, but decided that "On the evidence as to their characters, they were not necessary to the welfare of Titusville or the region." As if the gallows weren't enough of a hint to ensure speedy departure, a procession of three hundred citizens marched Stonehouse and his pals to the depot and saw them off, with a warning to stay away. One reporter insisted that, as the procession went to the train, a band played the "Rogues' March."

A week after this forcible farewell party, the *Herald* published a rather unusual thank-you letter from Stonehouse Jack:

> Buffalo, January 26, 1866
>
> Editors Morning Herald:
>
> I avail myself of this my first leisure moment since my return to Buffalo to convey through the medium of your paper my heartfelt thanks for the very hospitable manner in which I was received and entertained during my late visit to your city. To the committee of Vigilance who so kindly relieved me of every expense during my stay and furnished me with my free passage on the way to Buffalo, and to the citizens generally who joined in the procession which accompanied me to the cars on my departure, my thanks are especially due. As also to those persons (their names I regret to say being unknown to me) who in the goodness of their hearts made arrangements to raise me to a more "elevated" position than I desire to occupy.
>
> In conclusion I wish to say, that should you, Messrs. Editors, or any of the persons referred to visit this precious locality, I assure you they will receive a warm reception on making themselves known to
>
> Yours respectfully,
> Stonehouse Jack

Papers within a hundred-mile radius also published laconic travel bulletins like this one in the Cleveland *Herald:* "A party of about twenty disreputable females banished from Titusville by the Vigilance Committee of that place, passed through here last night en route for different points in the West."

Titusville had got rid of its human sludge, as befitted a town that had become the self-styled Queen City of the oil region. There were now the Queen City Barber Shop, the Queen City Dairy, the Queen City Bakery, the Queen City Saloon and so on *ad commercium.* In this purged, relatively clear air, oil men found a place where they could live with their wives and children, not as transients, but as settled families.

Oil City was still an obstreperous hassle-and-rassle market place, "like a pedlar's cart divided down the center." One observer wrote: "Where no person expects to remain, except for the briefest possible period, who feels interested in giving *tone* to a community. Who cares for its reputation outside, whether it be good or bad? . . . The Spartans made their slaves drunk, in order to exhibit them in that condition to their children, and thereby fill their minds with disgust at the practise. If I wanted to impress on the mind of a youth the debasing effects of *selfishness,* I should transport him for a whole week to Oil City!"

Another visitor commented, "It is bad any time for men to be separated from their homes and families and get together hurrying to get rich. The oil region has demoralized more men proportionately than the army; for here there is no restraining influence whatever, not even discipline or red tape."

But now Titusville was again circumscribed by the family circle; there was the restraining influence of a Good Woman—and a newly strong police force. The town had five new churches and three schools, even a soldiers' orphans' school. Right after the war, public-spirited citizens founded Appleton's Collegiate Institute, which was under the supervision of Episcopal vestrymen.

Titusville had grown from three hundred people to ten thousand, but there's a nostalgic touch of its village past in one advertisement in the *Herald:*

> **HOT AND COLD BATSH***
> **at SIPE'S SHAVING SALOON**
> **OPPOSITE THE GRIST MILL**
> **Shaving, Hair Cutting**
> **CURLING AND DYEING**
> **Done In the Best Style**

Other tonsorial establishments assured readers they could provide "Frizzing in the Latest Fashion," and "Bleaching Done on Short Notice."

The sons of ex-farmers ordered sixty-five-dollar suits made to order in the city, and showed a worldly wariness in dealing with buyers of their properties. This letter was written in 1866:

> Dear Sir:
>   I transmit herewith copy of my contract with Byles and wife. It is a curious document you will think, but it is strong. . . . Morris and I saw Andrews and Potter—they are smooth and oily fellows but we

---

* Maybe it was still too exotic a thought for oil-country typesetters to handle.

could not see any policy in their terms. Andrews offered a bonus of $7500 if we would ratify the lease. . . . I talked $20,000 bonus and finally said I might not stand out about it if the balance of the company were in favor of leasing at $10,000. But I think this too small.

Those fellows are sharp as lightning—don't let them bamboozle you. They talked scare at first but when they found this did not win, they endeavored to excite our sympathy. Morris will write you.

Yours truly,
Fenner

And Morris did write, but in high exasperation. Perhaps he resented the very idea that city slickers might bamboozle local boys.

Friend Lamb:
Yours enclosing Fenner's letter has been received. I regret Fenner should express himself so old maidish. . . . He must have written to you after he had been out all night at some taffy-pulling bee.

L. Morris

In the whirlpools of speculation, oil men made an oasis of their own at Titusville's American Hotel, where Drake had first boarded with his family. The proprietor was now Major Mills, probably the most charming, warm-hearted hotel man in the oil region. On the wide shady porch, and in the taproom where lumberjacks had once wrestled like bear cubs, producers and refiners got together in an informal Oil Exchange. In lieu of ticker tape, they had the market quotations clattering in constantly over the wires of the Atlantic & Pacific Telegraph Company. Buying agents who had formerly ridden like Lone Rangers from well to well, and purchased oil at wildly fluctuating prices, now gravitated to the hotel; most of the real buying and selling went on there. If you look at the "Residence" column of the old hotel register, you get a lively sense of the mud lanes meeting macadam: Walpole Map next to New York; Petroleum Centre nudging Cleveland; Cherry Tree beside Philadelphia, and Sugar Creek meandering above London, with Pithole below.

If Drake had stayed on there, to sink or swim in the cosmopolitan flow, at least he'd have had friends to haul him out of deep water. Jonah Watson and another wealthy oil man, Dr. Atkinson, had tried to ensure Drake's getting some share of the grab-fest by maneuvering him into a tidy profit on a real estate deal. (Townspeople said Jonah swallowed a whale of a profit himself that should have gone to Drake, but the records show only that Jonah sold the land to Drake for $2,500 loaned by Dr. Atkinson, and then bought it right back for $12,-000. At least Drake got almost $10,000 clear.) With this backlog, and his income as justice of the peace, Drake would have been able to afford his two adored luxuries: good cigars and his horse and carriage. Instead, he moved his family to New York, invested every cent in a partnership in an oil brokerage, and went bust when he was already too crippled by arthritis to look for work.

Meanwhile, in Titusville, his rambunctious, off-again-on-again benefactor, Jonah Watson, kept slicing into new enterprises as fast as he'd once cut into western Pennsylvania forests for his mills. The *Herald* suggested drily that there might be a new firm named Jonah's Gourd and Some Pumpkins Oil Company.

Jonah had bought into the first refinery in Titusville, started by ex-shoemaker Barnsdall and William Abbott. Now the town had ten more refineries, machine shops, foundries—and Jonah happily gulping shares all over the place.

The most booming new business in Titusville was the torpedoing of wells. (Pun intended.) The inventor of the device used, Colonel Edward Roberts, was a robust young six-footer so crackling with vitality and ideas that he seemed explosive himself. Before the war, he had been in partnership with his brother Dr. Walter Roberts, manufacturing dental appliances. Probably Edward's most profitable early invention was a set of false teeth, *Continuous Gum Teeth, to Fit Any Size or Age,* that sold for $1.

While he was with the Army of the Potomac under General Burnside, Roberts made sketches of his newest brain storm— "Torpedo for Artesian or Oil Wells with Super Incumbent Fluid Tamping"—a phrase so awesome and yet ambiguous that it later drove contesting patent claimants nearly to drink. In January of 1865, financed by his dentist brother, he came to the American Hotel in Titusville with six gunpowder torpedoes, and went around begging producers to let him blow up a well. Naturally, the idea made them nervous. Several years before, a man they regarded as a Mad Scientist sort had suggested "shooting a charge into the earth to ignite gasses," and the owners of wells were so horrified at the thought they had him put in jail till he promised to stop that dangerous talk. Another inventor had recently dynamited some wells, but the poor results—and the risk—made producers all the more leery of letting Roberts try out his gunpowder gadget.

Proprietor Major Mills of the American Hotel was the kind of host who wanted to see his guests happy, especially a war veteran like Colonel Roberts who was a *bon vivant* after his own mold; if the Major had had a well of his own, he might gladly have offered it as a guinea pig to be blown up. (When he got his own King of the Hills well several years later, he'd collect a carriage-load of hotel guests— gentlemen and their ladies—and drive them out on gay afternoon excursions to watch the King flow.) But a cousin of his, a Captain Mills, owned the Ladies well on Watson Flats, and the Major persuaded the Captain to take a chance on the Colonel, for auld Army lang syne. On January 21, 1865, Roberts' first torpedo—eight pounds of gunpowder—was unloosed on the Ladies. To the surprise of probably everybody but the inventor, the explosion, at a depth of 463 feet, increased production considerably. A Philadelphian said enthusiastically it performed on the earth like a stomach pump. Roberts himself had argued it would shatter rock to free the oil, but what it actually did was to blast away paraffin clogging. A list of the first thirty-eight wells torpedoed that next year shows an increase in daily yield ranging from 2 to 200 barrels per well.

Dr. Walter Roberts sold out his New York dental practice and came to Titusville to join the Colonel in manufacturing an improved kind of torpedo, using nitroglycerin instead of gunpowder. (He had gone to Europe to get instructions on handling this, so he must have consulted Nobel there.) The Robertses made up their first batch with what they thought was extraordinary caution, hieing themselves and their ingredients to Church Run, two miles beyond Titusville. They had the glycerin in a five-gallon crock placed in a huge wooden bucket of crushed ice. When they poured in the nitric acid—wham— windows were blasted out all over town. Citizens urged them nervously to try another location, so they put up a factory shed of green pine slabs, deep down in a valley on Hammond Run. The finished product was stored in a magazine dug in a safely distant hill. Thieves who broke into the factory's safe one night, smashing it open with sledge hammers, must have felt unnerved when they discovered the safe was full of nitric acid.

The men who torpedoed the wells—shooters—loaded their wagons with the nitro in maple-syrup-like cans which fitted into felt padding under the buckboard seat. The sections of torpedo, each about five feet long, were fastened to the sides of the wagon like organ pipes. Shooters used anywhere from five to fifteen nitro-loaded sections on a well. Each section was lowered cautiously, and then a five-pound shell—the go-devil—was sent dropping point downward to detonate the charge. As a mark of honor, like laying a cornerstone, distinguished guests were often invited to drop the go-devil. It's conceivable that the timider among them may have pleaded a pressing headache and stayed away. But if they proceeded bravely to the place of honor, they had headaches in earnest, often lasting three days, from the powerful nitro fumes.

Shooters who sat over this lethal load on the way to a well, driving over the muddy ruts, knew that one sudden jolt might land them in Kingdom Come. Along Oil Creek, they tell about Doc Haggerty, the shooter who was hauling fourteen hundred pounds of nitro in his wagon; after the explosion, not a trace of Haggerty could be found, and the story is that the insurance company said, "How do we *know* he's dead?" and refused to pay a $5,000 policy. Other nitro explosions left grisly traces: a horse cut cleanly in two, and strips of the shooter's face. Old Titusvillians have told me that later in the century small boys used to rush to the scene of an accident to get souvenirs, and the child they all envied most was the boy who found a piece of an ear.

Shooters themselves had an Eat, Drink (especially drink) and Live-it-up bravado, but they were a superstitious lot; for instance, no shooter would say good-bye to his wife in the morning when he went to work—it might be bad luck.

The Oil City *Blizzard* once fired off an ode in their honor:

"A WELL SHOOTER"

Pat Magnew was a shooter bold
Who handled glycerine;
And though he had no printing-shop
He ran a magazine. . . .

He seemed to like his daily toil,
Its dangers did not fear;
He'd help his patrons to find oil
And then he'd disappear.

He always had a great tin shell
Beside him on the seat,
Had horses good and drove like—well,
No moss grew on their feet.

And when he drove along the road
And that was every day,
Wise people all, who knew his load,
Gave him the right of way.

His wife once said: "I greatly fear
That you will yet be blown
To atoms, if you don't, my dear,
Let well enough alone.

"Some day there'll be a thunder-sound
And scattered far and near,
O'er hill and dale and all around
Will be my husband dear."

Replied Magnew: "I call to mind—
His words were nowise sickly—
That Billy Shakespeare once remarked:
' 'Twere well it were done quickly.'

"And I'll be blown," continued Pat
"If I didn't want it known
That I'd rather be by dynamite
Than by a woman blown."

The Roberts price for torpedoing a well was $1,000 on paper, but
if you paid cash, the discount was a lavish 75 per cent. Even $250
was considered too high by some producers; they hired workmen to
mix the nitro illegally at night, making their witches' brew deep in
the woods. The men—called moonlighters—didn't dare risk traveling
to the well in a wagon, so they hauled ten-pound cans of nitro in meal
sacks slung over their shoulders. If a moonlighter stumbled over a root

or ran into a tree in the dark, at least he couldn't be tried for boot-legging in this world, only in the next.

Most of the Roberts brothers' profits went into legal suits. There were five rival claimants for patents, and it took years before the Colonel's torpedo was established once and for all as the legal, Super Incumbent Fluid Tamping winner.

As a gayer way of spending their profits once the legal suits were settled, the Colonel and his brother built "the most sumptuous hostelry" in Titusville, the New Brunswick Hotel. Guests walked ankle-deep in velvety carpets, sat on brocaded upholstery, and in the gold-leafed dining room ate gourmet fare. The hotel's stone front had a cornice frieze of huge gargoyles, *à la* Notre Dame, but what gave it a special oil-country flair was that the Roberts brothers had their faces carved in stone too, by the sculptor, and placed between the gargoyles—for fun.

But to go back to the years just after the war, the fanciest hotel then was Crittenden House, and to judge by one of its menus, Titus-villians had already come a long way from home-cured salt pork. I pick a few items at drooling random:

Entrees

Fillet of Quails
Rum Omelettes a la Paris
Fricassee of Partridge on Toast
Clam Fritters, sauce de vin

Cold	Relishes
Lobster Salad a la Anglaise	Oyster Catsup
Oysters au Natural	Chow Chow

Fine Wines: Piper Heidsieck or Mumm, $5
London Dock Port, $3 qt.
Waiters are provided with Wine Cards and Pencils.

Townspeople lapped up cultural fare on as lavish a scale as the Crittenden's. Visiting lecturers included Mark Twain and Artemus Ward, *Authors au Natural;* or for the equivalent of partridge on toast, that exotic suffragette Kate Field. Most of them spoke under the auspices of the Literary Association. As the *Herald* reported in

1865: "A number of young gentlemen of Titusville, feeling the urgent need of some place of resort in which their leisure moments might be passed, not only harmlessly, but with profit to themselves, resolved to establish a Literary Society. The name assumed was The Culver Literary Association. The dues were fixed at 25¢ a month, and the initiation fee at one dollar. . . . The meetings were very spirited. Ladies and gentlemen, not connected with the institution, were in the habit of attending the readings, lectures and discussions."

I assume they originally called themselves the Culver Literary Association as an admiring gesture to thirty-four-year-old Charles Vernon Culver, who was touted that year as the brilliant boy wonder, financial wizard and gentleman promoter of the oil region. But within a few months, they hastily dropped the name Culver, when their hero's reputation exploded with a bang louder than any torpedo.

ELEVEN

The man who sold the moon

To CALL Charles Vernon Culver a crook would be as wrong as calling the Egyptian kings who built the pyramids a bunch of slave-drivers. Like a Cheops, Culver thought big and boldly, with the very real sincerity of a megalomaniac. One of his sayings was, "Think out your plan—then go and do it." Coming from a young man who in a few years had made himself known as the greatest financial wizard of the oil region, this was quoted with considerable respect. Anybody could see that Culver practiced what he preached; for instance, the time he decided to bring two hundred of the country's top capitalists out to Pithole and environs at his own expense—and did it—with astonishing results.

From the time he came to the oil country as a brilliant, poor-but-honest twenty-nine-year-old banker, he was busily pyramiding the damnedest, biggest financial structure that had ever been piled end to end—toward the moon—in those parts. He had been connected with the Citizens Bank of Logan, Ohio, when he made a profit of about $10,000 as part owner of a well on Oil Creek. Instead of buying more wells, he promptly started in buying up banks. First he went to Meadville and bought the charter of the Bank of Crawford County, which was reputedly shaky. After redeeming the old issue of notes, and putting the bank on a good, solid (it seemed) basis, he moved on to Franklin in 1861 and opened a bank of discount and deposit, then the Venango Bank; next, the Petroleum Bank at Titusville. Within three years he founded thirteen—count 'em, thirteen—banks to handle primarily oil business, from Erie through Crawford and Venango counties down Oil Creek and the Allegheny River to Pittsburgh, and on to Philadelphia. In New York, he founded his last two banks, and the Venango Transportation Company with vast warehouses and docks for oil export. In 1864, admiring friends in Pennsylvania insisted he run for Congress, and he became the youngest congressman in the House—and the most absent. I think he attended three half-days altogether, as was bitterly pointed out later, but at the time he could do no wrong, and besides, he was awfully busy making dollar signs.

Strong-minded millionaires begged him to take their money and invest it. One look at his round, open face, his candid blue eyes, his frank boyish smile and unaffected manner, and everybody knew here was a man to trust. Well, almost everybody. About the time the Pithole boom started, Culver approached Franklin's leading citizens —the Honorable Plumer, lawyers Heydrick and McCalmont, bankers Lamberton and Bleakley—with a splendid plan: he would promote Franklin as a great new land development and boomtown, greater than Pithole. He complained to a friend later that his listeners "weren't responsive as businessmen should have been."

I suspect they told him politely—because one is naturally polite to a charming young man who has thirteen banks in his pocket— that you can't make a big oil boomtown without big wells. The chicken comes before the egg, they said in reasonable language. Charles Vernon Culver was pretty exasperated at such provincial thinking.

I'm not absolutely sure that he put the same plan to the leading citizens of Oil City—the Hassons, Morans, Hannas, Vanausdall, William Lay and so on—but I think he did and got turned down again even more tersely, because the story is that he developed a lordly grudge and decided to build a town that would show them what they'd missed. He bought twelve hundred acres of land overlooking the Allegheny River two miles below Oil City, and christened it Reno after our Venango Civil War hero, General Jesse Reno, who'd been killed at the battle of South Mountain. Then he organized the Reno Oil and Land Company, with the ex-Speaker of the House, Honorable Galusha Grow, as president, at least on paper, and Culver modestly listed as vice-president. Following his precept of *Think out your plan, then go and do it,* he announced that Reno would become the center of the oil industry. (The Titusville *Herald* commented that it was a "magnificent but astounding scheme," as indeed it was.)

As a first step toward wiping Oil City off the map, Culver imported General Ambrose Burnside as head engineer to build a railroad from Reno to Pithole. All Pithole oil, Culver said, would whiz over his railroad-to-be and be shipped from his Reno docks-to-be, instead of shipping from Oil City. This made quite a little engineering headache: in order to lay tracks by-passing Oil City, they had to build trestles in a dizzying curve, over steep ravines, up cliffs and down gullies. A visitor saw General Burnside testing a grade one day, sitting on a pile of ties on a flatcar attached to a shiny new locomotive. Three times the car chugged up the steep hill almost to the top and three times rolled downhill in a hurry, with General Burnside right back where he started from, cursing and stomping. The fourth time, the locomotive made it up over the top of the hill and hurled the General, on his flatcar, down the other side of the precipitous grade, but by then the visitor was so nervous watching that he left in a hurry before he might hear a crash.

Stories about this reached Pithole long before the tracks did, and Crocus wrote blandly about Culver's railroad: "Each car is to be provided with surgeons and undertakers and other luxuries. It was thought that the arrangements would be so perfect and accidents so sure on this railroad that many would have their limbs taken off and get embalmed before starting, to avoid delay while on the cars."

Unfortunately, business men didn't have Crocus' eye for the ridiculous; the new Reno Oil and Land Company was already getting investors before the stock was formally on the market. Culver had 340 men working on the railroad, not counting General Burnside and the weight he carried, and another two hundred workmen drilling and building at Reno. Several wells were completed, mostly of a yield Pithole would have yawned over: 7, 10 and 15 barrels. I think one was 150, but that too was tiddly-winks by real boomtown standards. Then why did so many smart, experienced Venango men go on believing Culver knew what he was doing? For instance, William Raymond, an ex-merchant, had made a nice fortune in oil and retired and moved east to Long Island, where he built a fine mansion. Culver, who commuted all over the lot every week—Pithole to Reno to Pittsburgh to New York and home again—called on the older man on Long Island, and said he'd be happy to help him with investments. He suggested with great thoughtfulness that Mr. Raymond give him power of attorney for accounts and bonds in such-and-such banks. Then Culver wouldn't have to bother him with silly business trifles every other whipstitch. Raymond was delighted, and drew up a power of attorney for most of his assets. Some leftover merchant shrewdness made him hold back an unmentioned nest egg, although he felt an almost irresistible longing to let the brilliant Mr. Culver handle that too.

Certainly nobody else could keep money moving so fast, juggled from one enterprise to another, with Good Works included. Culver donated $35,000 to a new boarding hall for Allegheny College, and contributed a plot of land and a gratifying sum to help build a Methodist church in Meadville. He was reputed to be worth several millions, but it was often remarked, approvingly, how modest and upright he was. He ruled the Reno company with such a firm moral grip that any workman who was seen having so much as a glass of beer *even after hours on his own free time,* would be fired that instant. Which makes Culver's great Pithole-to-Reno excursion of capitalists, plied with enough liquor to drown them (and it very nearly did), all the more interesting

When I look over the list of men who came on what the New York *Tribune* called admiringly "a Monster Excursion," I'm staggered at the array. There was everybody from a Chicago bank president to the U.S. Banking Commissioner of New England; from big industrialists and congressmen (including, of course, Culver) to a representative of the great financier Jay Cooke. Although it wouldn't have occurred to Venango-ites to bring these Mountains of Finance to the Mecca of Oildom—especially as free-loaders—once Culver had unfolded the plan, several of the oil region's most respected citizens signed their names under his, on the invitation sent out that fall of 1865:

October 4, 1865

Dear Sir:

For the purpose of affording the capitalists of the country an opportunity of inspecting personally the Pennsylvania Oil Regions, an Excursion has been arranged in which you are invited to participate.

Two hundred guests will be in attendance including prominent business men from each of the principal cities in the Northern States. Rendezvous at Meadville on Tuesday Evening, October 17th.

Leave Meadville Wednesday 7 A.M. By Special Train . . . [Here followed a time schedule of each stop, including the arrival at Pithole after a six-mile horseback ride from the nearest railroad depot.]

As the equestrian portion of the excursion is absolutely necessary, it is suggested to the guests that their clothing should be adapted to the occasion.

Your expenses during the entire trip and return will be paid by the projectors of the excursion.

I don't know how the guests converging from the west got to Meadville, but Easterners boarded a special train of the Atlantic & Great Western line in New Jersey, and I have seen the traffic superintendent's memo to all hands:

These trains will have the exclusive right to the Road against all other trains of every kind and against all other occupants of the Track.

The Culver-chartered train went so lickety-split from New Jersey to Meadville that some of the valuable passengers clocked it in alarm at a runaway forty-five miles an hour, and sent irate orders to the engineer to slow down at once. He did, too. It would have been pretty embarrassing to derail that many tycoons all at one whack.

One hundred and fifty moneyed personages estimated to be worth a joint two hundred million dollars, plus forty reporters worth possibly a total cash value of $201.47, met their delightful host Culver in Meadville. As a Detroit journalist said, "Even if he hadn't been our host, he would have pleased everyone. . . . Mr. Culver is of an open, candid expression and genial pleasing manner."

A writer for the *Western New Yorker,* whom I picture as a dog-eyed little man running along beside the host, looking up at him with devotion and trying to catch every word, panted in print: "Mr. Culver is keen-eyed, alert, full of an irresistible nervous energy that is stopped by no obstacles, with a mind that comprehends as by intuition financial plans of the greatest magnitude, who talks about and uses thousands as though they were pence, and millions as though they were single dollars."

Of course so large-minded a host wouldn't have begun a sales talk for the Reno Oil and Land Company at the start of this Gargantuan outing. As far as I can learn from reading a couple dozen accounts, his main sales speech came after dinner at Pithole. But by then most of the guests were in no condition to appreciate it—or perhaps that's just when they *would* appreciate it, through a champagne, brandy-smash haze. Just to be on the safe side, I'd better put down a few details of the Culver sales plan right now, because by the time we chase a hundred and ninety capitalists and reporters on horseback cross-country to Pithole, we may never get back to statistics.

Culver's plan was so simple as to be laughable, but nobody laughed. The Reno Oil and Land Company would be capitalized at ten million dollars and no cents. Twelve directors were to be chosen, one from each principal city. These twelve would appoint ten traveling agents, who in turn would each designate twenty local agents: "Then, if each agent sells but *forty shares* of stock, the whole ten million will be sold." And here's the crux, in Culver's own crystal-clear words: "For every share of stock issued, the Par Value (One Hundred Dollars) will be deposited in the *United States Treasury* and may be withdrawn by stockholders at any time. . . . It might be called A Legal Tender Oil Stock."

It might, if Confederate money were still Legal Tender.

Now back to our Financial Wizard and his guests. Starting at 7 A.M. from Meadville, they reached Corry by midmorning and took a whirling tour through Sam Downer's refinery. Sam was the man who'd remarked, "The Lord Almighty doesn't like things done in a small way," and Culver was so much of the same mind that he used the huge Downer plant as his opening salvo to bowl over the party. One visitor wrote:

At Corry we gain the first realizing sense of the magnitude of this trade by an inspection of the large oil refinery of Mr. Samuel Downer, which has a daily refining capacity of 500 barrels. Last year the amount paid for crude oil amounted to $1,200,000. The proportion of refined oil varies from 75 to 90 per cent. About 10 per cent of naptha is profitably distilled from the crude petroleum. The tar, which, in Europe, is converted into rare dye stuffs, is here burned in the shape of coke. One peculiarity of all crude oils is developed here—the presence of paraffine crystals, which, upon condensation and congelation, become visible. Heavy or lubricating oil can be extracted from all oil in various proportions. After the heavy oil is pressed, after the manner of linseed, a white cake of paraffine remains, which resembles pure white wax in color, consistency and taste, and, I am informed, is sold for the same purpose, even to the making of chewing gum!

After this impressive beginning, the party boarded their train again to reach Titusville in time for lunch. The *Herald,* noting that they enjoyed a sumptuous repast, added "The financial leaders of the country were there—men who control stocks and build cities."

But none of them, not even superman Culver, could control the elements; an early drizzle had turned into heavy rain, but the schedule called for a brisk canter cross-country to Pithole. Culver sent minions scurrying off to every store in the area, and they brought back raincoats and ponchos, even some umbrellas, to waterproof the precious guests. Thus attired, the excursionists left the Oil Creek line eight miles below Titusville at Shaffer, where exactly the right number of horses were waiting at the terminus depot. Each gentleman carried a numbered ticket signed by Culver, and each horse was correspondingly numbered. But now came another upset in the hyper-efficiency.

Guests who knew horseflesh, including millionaire huntsmen and ex-cavalry officers, took one look at the odd assortment of horses and made a rush for the best mounts, letting the numbers fall where they might. This left the worst nags for the worst riders. As the New York *Express* man said, "Many of the number were never in saddle before, or not for years . . . and neither Jehu nor John Gilpin ever saw such riders before."

In the driving rain, through mire and muck, forests and stumps, sliding up and down gullies, crossing swollen streams, they proceeded.

Several of the party were slow even in getting off, because the impetuous artist sent by *Harper's Weekly* insisted on making a sketch right there at the depot of a restive, tossing-maned horse. He sat on a stump sketching while a banker who greatly admired *Harper's* stood holding an umbrella over the artist's head and a brave reporter clung to the model's tail, to keep it from bolting.

The *Harper's*-loving financier rode this rolling-eyed beast afterward, and when the party was fording Oil Creek for the ninth or tenth time in an hour, they were startled to see the banker flung headlong into the dirty cold water. His was the only complete dunking, but at the end of a rain-pelted three-hour ride, most of the men looked like drowned rats or "moving bodies of mud." The invitation had mentioned six miles on horseback, but it turned out to be thirteen horrible miles round Robin Hood's barn, or as the Culver crow flew. What happened was that the direct route, as originally planned, included too many abandoned wells, always a morbid sight to show prospective investors, so Culver had persuaded some of the fast riders in the lead to detour down around Petroleum Centre. The procession trailing behind them, down to the last limping horse and rider, had innocently followed the leader, and as a result many of them nearly died a slow death in the saddle. Doc Townley of the *New York Times* must have been one of the lucky ones who'd ridden a horse before in his life, because he had strength left to describe the others rather wickedly:

> Here were heroes of a hundred crises in the stock market, the corners of whose firm-set mouths had never drooped in the worst throes of a financial panic—heroes who had valiantly resisted the bulls and bears of Wall Street and of State Street. . . . Here the millionaires whose gaily painted equipages roll musically through our city parks, along our city boulevards, laden with their rich freight of bedizened beauty. . . . Here the conquerors of time and space, the men whose willing labor has made all mankind akin, spreading their gigantic network of railway and telegraph over continent and sea; . . . Heroes on the Exchange, in the counting-house . . . bringing up the rear of our procession with trembling knees and nervous rein.

By the time this weird-looking assortment of almost two hundred horses and riders slogged single file into Pithole, even the town's oldest inhabitants stared with a certain degree of amazement. They had seen many sights in Pithole's six months of existence, but never one quite like this.

At the Morey Farm Hotel, where the entire party was to stay over-night, most of the riders fell off their steeds and staggered into the bar, "mud to their eyebrows."

A few hardy mudders who still wanted to see the sights slid and slithered down the slope to the Pool well, and that's when they really got excited:

> Climbing over the full and empty barrels that lie between us and the place, we reach the gate where a dozen teams are waiting their turns to load, and rapidly as pass the flying minutes, barrel after barrel goes into the possession of the teamsters. Fifteen hundred barrels per day, more than one per minute, is the yield of this most wonderful fountain. Passing through the gateway and turning to our right, we ascend a stairway leading to a platform which surrounds the largest tank and now for the first time we see a "flowing well." See it! forgetting the slime in which we tread, the gaseous vapors which assail us, and the blasphemy of the teamsters down below. See it! with hearts oppressed with wonder and admiration at this miracle of creation. See, in humility and reverence—this new revela-tion of the untold power and wisdom of Omnipotence.
>
> Rising alongside the tank and above it, about two feet, then arching over it like an upended letter J, is the tube, two and a half inches in diameter, through which comes up from beneath the riven rock seven hundred feet below, this Geyser of flowing wealth.
>
> Gushing out of the mouth of the pipe as if impelled thence by some hidden engine, at the same time escaping with it the gas which ac-companies it and bears it upward. Gush! gush! gush! with regular and convulsive beat as rapidly as you can repeat the word distinctly, and incessant as the living pulse. . . .
>
> What language, used to express our wonder at the mysteries of creation, would suggest to the reader the emotions these miracles excite? None.
>
> We move along from well to well, regardless of the unctuous slime and mephitic odors of the place, till warned thence by the good-natured workmen who remind us that in this region traveling to strangers is unpleasant, if not dangerous after dark, and that "Con-necticut honey" as they call the mud, is uncomfortable bedding.

Millionaires were rather disgruntled at being bedded down ten to a room, at the Morey, but as it turned out they wouldn't have had much time to sleep anyway. They were impressed by the quality of the dinner—"catering worthy of a palace"—but one excursionist was worried by the awful cost of this to their host. "Even the hay upon which our horses fed cost $50 to $65 a ton, such is the difficulty of bringing anything over these abominable roads."

Their host, when he gave his after-dinner sales talk for the Reno Oil and Land Company, quoted figures that weren't hay. By then, the guests were in so convivial a mood they cheered everything said, and toasted Petroleum, Pithole, the People (whoever they were) and even the Press, in a giddy round of wines.

They had barely finished this repast when they were feted at a midnight champagne party "by two of the newest young millionaires here."

One of the reporters said genially, "We submit to being bored by oil millionaires with good grace."

Around 3 A.M. a Midwesterner leaped to his feet to propose another toast to Pithole, adding joyously, "God! What a hole in the ground!"

But when the rising bell clanged at 6 A.M. to begin another brisk day of touring in a worse rain than ever, such groans went up you'd have thought every guest was lying in a bottomless pit. At least half of them were too lame to get back on a horse. Others were so sodden with colds or hangovers they winced at the very thought of moving a muscle, let alone jolting up and down the miles of gullies, and fording the twisty creek back and forth. Some of their mounts, facing the prospect of repeating yesterday's horseplay, simply lay down tiredly. Host Culver, equal to any emergency (so far) collected a mass of teamsters and wagons, and the most far-gone guests were dumped in to sit or lie comatose. Some of the horseback riders revived so fast they raced each other along the road, and gaily tossed mud and jeers at the wagon-borne weaklings whom they passed at a gallop. They were now headed for the grand climax, Reno, the Cosmopolitan Oil Center of the Future.

Once there, the guests exclaimed delightedly over what a *clean,* comparatively dry and tidy place Reno was. The Cincinnati visitors were especially taken with this aspect, but the fact that it was clean and tidy because it had no great wells—none of Pithole's great boom-wealth and prodigal waste—seems not to have occurred to them. (But it must have occurred to the capitalists later, because they didn't invest the millions Culver had counted on.) Some of the newsmen babbled like local Fourth of July orators, or like schoolgirls romping through a thesaurus to turn out a theme on Our Town:

> Reno stands in a position to satisfy the lover of the beautiful in landscape in its finest and noblest features. The pencil of a *Church* alone could do justice to the majesty of these empurpled mountains, that rise in unbroken waves of color, their direct outline lost in haze, as they melt into the clouds that seem to claim them as their own. Just where the eye grows weary with its straining gaze, the broad waters of the Alleghany (running eastward past Reno) now turn toward the north, and rest for a moment, lake-like, in the shadow of the glowing hills above them. . . .

> Imagination carries us forward a few brief years, and we see its crowded ways of trade. The people hurry to and fro its busy streets. The slender spire that points its way to Heaven uplifts itself among its factories and schools. . . . [Culver had stressed the churches and schools he'd build.]

> As the sun steals downward to the forehead of that Alleghany peak which bounds our vision to the West, we hear the welcome notes of Labor's dismissing bell echoed by the river's bank beyond, telling of "something accomplished, something done." Out from the peaceful shadow settling upon the scene we wake to glance in admiration once more around us and to say farewell.

Sometimes now when I drive through the tiny hamlet that is still Reno, on the way from my hometown to Oil City—both handsome, bustling, prosperous communities—I grin a little smugly, remembering the way Culver planned to wipe rival towns off the map.

He hurried his excursion through both Oil City and Franklin that rainy October day, so that Reno—and the hour-long pep talk he made there at lunch—would stay glowing alone in the guests' minds. They arrived back in Meadville to discover that the manager of the McHenry Hotel had planned a huge ball in their honor that evening, with the prettiest ladies in Meadville as partners: "Now are heard grievous moans amongst the bachelors at the scantiness of their wardrobes, and convulsive raids are made on Meadville haberdashers for snowy kids and glossy neckties. Portmanteaus of the well-provided are seized in nervous grasp, and from cavernous depths are coaxed up the spotless vest and shining understandings. . . . Figures (in mud-spilled raiment but an hour before) leap into the arena of music and dance, transformed. . . . With the fair ladies of the place, the merry hours glide by till morning."

Considering all that the excursionists had been through, the belles of Meadville must have been fair indeed, to keep the boys on their feet till dawn. And at least one account confirms that very nicely: "The ladies were beautiful as houris and sylphs—scattered about the room like full-flushed flowers in a wild woodland."

Most of the guests who danced till dawn with these full-flushed sylphs of the woodland managed to get up the same morning and catch their special trains, bearing them back to the bulls, the bears and other mundane pursuits. Those who stayed on—mostly reporters—were escorted on carriage rides around Meadville by their ever gracious host. He pointed out such sights as the beautiful old campus of Allegheny College, and somehow, in the most modest, indirect way, they learned just which local buildings Culver had contributed to—and how much.

The day before, they had been taken to the U.S. Tax Collector in Venango County, who allowed reporters to copy from his account book the latest figures on barrels of oil taxed:

The Tax on Crude Oil amounted	in June, 1865,	to	$112,254.44
	in July	to	181,488.55
	in August	to	201,100.00
Daily production at Pithole		over	5,000 bbls.
Daily production at Oil Creek		over	5,000 bbls.

These figures, at least, were accurate and safe to quote. But what astonishes me is how gullibly and glowingly journalists from the most influential newspapers in the country repeated Culver's grandiose schemes and claims in their feature stories. And when I say *feature,* I wade in understatement. For instance, it would be safe to bet that never before or since has a promoter managed to rate *six full columns on the front page of the* New York Times, to describe an excursion-stunt and to lend prestige, directly and obliquely, to the stock about to be issued by his company.

In this front-page spread the *Times,* mentioning Culver's projected Reno-Pithole railroad, said:

> A radical and wholesome change is now at work, to revolutionize the mode of oil transportation, and reduce its cost to a tithe of the present monstrous outlay. . . . This great source of national and individual wealth will lose that uncertainty of position and instability of price so unhealthy in its action . . . just as soon as the expense of its transportation to a market is as closely ascertainable as it ought to be. [The one really radical change, Van Syckel's new pipeline, wasn't even mentioned.]

Discussing the stock company, it said grandly:

> On these twelve hundred acres [at Reno] it is proposed to build a city . . . the plan, we learn, will shortly be laid before the public. As well as we can gather from the conversation and speeches on the subject, the project is the creation of a capital of ten million dollars, stockholders being guaranteed against loss by its deposit in the Treasury of the United States, and subject at all times to withdrawal by them. A sum equal to the first year's interest on the capital [is] advanced by Mr. Culver for the immediate prosecution of the works, the development of the land, which is said to abound in oil, the laying out of streets, &c. It appears from this plan the interest on the capital *alone* is risked, as the stock is not to be sold under par.
>
> The scheme . . . seemed to us most plausible, the guarantee unexceptionable, and the avowed motives pure and praiseworthy. To develop the resources of our country, to open up its unhewn forests and their hidden wealth to our growing population and to the wandering tribes that seek its shores in daily thousands, to raise up cities along the sides of these mountain-girded waters as they sweep resistless to the ocean, making the paths of commerce easy and the labors of our fellow-man less brutal in their kind, is a truly noble work and he who leads in enterprise with such an aim and object is worthy of all praise.

I'll bet robber barons like Jay Gould and Jim Fisk whistled with envy when they read that. I copied it from Charles Vernon Culver's own scrapbook of clippings on the excursion, which must have made consoling reading later, when he was detained in jail.

For example, the *Commercial Advertiser* stressed the selfless, non-commercial spirit of the planner:

> Mr. Culver said that his sole object was to benefit as many individuals as possible. . . . He said that he would have no difficulty in getting all the stock taken by large speculators, but he wished to divide it around so that all who desired might be possessed of it.

The *Express* wanted to make sure all their readers knew just who the planner was—no ordinary promoter he:

> The head and front of it was Hon. C. V. Culver, a banker worth in common estimation from two to four million dollars. He is not over 35 years of age, and has made his fortune mainly by banking in the oil regions. . . . He is not only prosperous in his business, but munificent in his gifts and employments. Coming to this country with little or nothing, beyond thrift and enterprise, though not a manipulator in oil wells or oil stocks, he is now one of the most wealthy of the people and made so by the natural developments of the country around him. His life is an example to young men in this country. Sterling integrity, strict temperance, great industry, indominitable concentration, perseverance, and entire faith in God, country, and mankind.

The *Tribune,* in its account of the Monster Excursion, rejoiced that Culver would be a stabilizing influence:

> It is a misfortune that the Oil Regions have too long been regarded as a theater for illegitimate and abnormal speculation, partaking more of the character of a lottery than a permanent branch of mining business. The time has come when it must cease to be regarded as the pursuit of adventurers and gambling swindlers, but be governed by the same laws as all other industrial pursuits. . . .
>
> I should mention that Messrs. Culver and Grow have matured a plan which is destined to effect a gigantic revolution, both in the oil trade and in the society here, which will also prove of great pecuniary benefit to themselves and the public which is invited to become associated with them.

Well, if wholesale bankruptcy can be described as a gigantic revolution, that's what it was, all right. And no adventurers were involved, although I wouldn't go quite so far as to say the enterprise was totally lacking in swindlers. But I should explain right now that Culver had taken in a bank partner, a Mr. Penn, who was always considered completely honorable, and blameless for what happened. Ex-Speaker of the House Galusha Grow, like the carved wooden image on the prow of a ship, was not held accountable for the wreck.

The crash came March 28th, but not being so jolly and lush a story as the Monster Excursion, it only rated small paragraphs in the papers, mostly buried on financial pages. (Well, anything on a financial page is buried to me, but there must be people who read it.) The *Times* noted cautiously, under "Monetary Affairs":

> A banking firm in Nassau Street, established a year or two since from Northern Pennsylvania, and representing large interests in the Oil region, was reported in difficulty today. . . .

> We learn definitely of the failure of Messrs. Culver, Penn & Co., Bankers of this City. Their embarrassment, we understand, arose from some railroad and other heavy undertakings. It is hoped that these embarrassments will be only temporary.

The next day, the *Times* was still hoping, but not as trustingly:

> An impression appears to prevail that the creditors will receive the full amount of their claims, which are larger than at first supposed.

> The failure is attributed to the recent depression in oil trade, and the diminished marketable value of oil lands, together with the fact that the assets of the firm have been for some time locked up in the Pithole & Reno railroad, which road was constructed at the cost of the firm, but which absorbed a much larger sum of money than the estimates provided for.

Two days after the crash, under the heading "Panic Among Oil Companies" the *Times* said austerely:

> There is a flurry among the oil companies caused by the failure of several banks at Titusville, Oil City and Franklin. . . . It is reported in this city that six banks in the oil region have failed.

The banks' doors had been closed since the 28th, while frantic depositors crowded around outside. Culver was said to be "out of town on business."

The cashier of the Venango Bank in Franklin, James Austin, who was also Culver's brother-in-law, issued a statement on behalf of the Great Man:

> I will be able to pay in full with time to convert.
>
> C. V. Culver

Many people still thought he meant it. They told each other anxiously that of course it would take him a week or so to convert all his bonds into millions in cash, and pay off depositors.

As awkward timing would have it, the first enormous advertisement for Culver's Reno Oil and Land Company was appearing in our local paper that week, with a bold-face explanation of the MONEY BACK GUARANTEE, and the inspired slogan about LEGAL TENDER STOCK.

The *Spectator,* caught with its plates down, couldn't yank the ad, but simply soft-pedaled the story about the crash in the same issue. It admitted that the Oil City Bank, the Venango Bank, the Crawford National in Meadville and the Petroleum National of Titusville hadn't opened for business Wednesday morning, but it went on:

> The reputation of Mr. Culver for honor and integrity, and his well known energy as a business man leads to the general belief that his difficulties are temporary, and that he will be amply able to meet his responsibilities. . . . We sincerely hope this may be the case, and that the apprehended distress of many of our citizens will never be realized.

Ten days later The Honorable Culver called a meeting of all depositors in the Venango Bank, and gave them a heartening little talk. He also gave them each a voucher saying their money would be repaid with interest, within six months.

The *Spectator* was already getting more jittery:

> The fortunes of many of our best citizens hang trembling in the balance.

> We do not defend the course that has brought on the present disaster, but wherever he has erred, we believe he is anxious and willing to make retribution.

> When the proper time arrives, we shall refer to the details of this great disaster in a proper manner and point a moral.

Titusville citizens hadn't yet discovered that although the name plate on the bank, and the letterheads, distinctly said *National Bank,* it wasn't national at all. Another nasty surprise was that a large block of assets had been smuggled out after the doors closed; this was to come out at a trial later.

But early in April the Titusville *Herald,* like the *Spectator,* was still fairly cheerful. It even ran a little poem, "Reno Rhinoed":

> Reno! Reno! no words can tell
> What fame you have begotten
> By gulling everybody well
> That you were sound, when rotten. . . .
>
> Reno! Reno! don't leave us now
> For you we love most dearly
> And then a dry financial cow
> Would starve us sure, or nearly.
>
> Take only greenbacks for your stocks
> They're Uncle Samuel's tenders.
> Then with your base on pure gold rocks
> Throw wildcat stock to rag-vendors.

The *Weekly Register* in Oil City, the town that had refused to be Culverized, was already baring its teeth:

> The Honorable Culver was never in Congress much, and never fought for repeal of the tax [on oil]. Four-fifths of the people of the 20th District want him to resign a trust he has so unworthily filled.

The city papers were taking off their kid gloves too. The Philadelphia *News* said:

> Their (Culver Penn) failure fell like a pall on the entire country. In the oil region, it brought ruin upon thousands of hard-working men and many who a few weeks since considered themselves rich are now poor.

In Culver's home base, Franklin, the *Spectator* reflected the change in mood: "Public indignation is being manifested in unmistakable terms."

In an adjoining column, an item on animal husbandry seemed painfully apt:

> It is a cruel and injurious business to catch sheep by the wool, as much so as to pull a child by the hair. If you look under the skin after the sheep has been hauled about by the wool you would be surprised to see how much the uncomplaining animal has suffered.

Not all of our fleeced sheep in Franklin took it with a resigned Baaaaaa. At least one victim, Mr. John Duffield, a tall, determined, rock-jawed man, took stronger measures. When the cashier of the Venango Bank told him all assets were frozen, he unfroze some in a hurry. His daughter reported to a friend, "It's a secret so don't tell anybody, but Papa took his gun and went to the bank and got ten thousand dollars of his money. He told them if he didn't get it, he'd shoot."

Papa may have done just that, but he still wanted revenge, or the rest of his savings. He and two other Franklin men were the first to bring charges against Culver and the cashier of the Venango Bank. "They were arrested on April 30th, on charges of conspiracy etc., on information of John Duffield, Thomas Hoge, and P. R. Gray. Mr. Culver's bail is $20,000 . . . Mr. Austin's [the cashier] is $60,000."

Culver, out on bail, was arrested again a week later, "on a charge of trover and conversion, and after a hearing before Judge Gordon, was held to bail for his appearance in the sum of $23,000."

This time it took much longer to raise the bail, and being such a giant of industry, Culver improved the hours and weeks in prison by writing an eloquent pamphlet in his own defense, explaining his high motives, and pleading for consideration for himself and his family. This piece of Culver prose is lost, but what is left is a pamphlet written by one of his victims, answering Culver's; it's done anonymously, but gives chapter and verse of alleged misdeeds. I certainly can't vouch for the truth of any of it, but I can't resist quoting a few outraged bits:

> In his letter, he [Culver] says that he "has started many poor men in business and donated a lot to a church in Meadville, and built a boarding-house for a college." But he didn't tell you that he has got double the cost of the boarding-house in Bonds belonging to the col-

lege, and that he gave one of his creditors a lien on the boarding-house for more than it was worth; and it is to be sold at Sheriff's Sale.

He has taken near five thousand dollars from the Methodist Episcopal church at Franklin, and robbed a large portion of its members, not forgetting to take what little the preacher had saved in the last three years.

Many of the poor men that he has started in business have gone out of it with a large debt hanging over them, and forever disgraced by being implicated in the greatest swindle that has ever taken place in the United States. . . . [Boss Tweed would have been hurt at this implied slur.]

He *forgets,* or don't wish to inform the public . . . that Culver, Penn & Co. have drawn nearly seven hundred thousand dollars from the Venango Bank of Franklin which they refuse to return; about two thirds of which amount was not charged on the Books of the Bank at the proper time (but kept on a private memorandum by the cashier of the bank who was Mr. Culver's brother-in-law). Culver don't tell the public that by his own act the Bank Stock was made worthless, which was proven in court before Hon. Judge Gordon— and he found him guilty, and for want of bail he is now in prison. . . . This was for obtaining Government Bonds, and giving Bank Stock as collateral when he had rendered it worthless. . . . Some were from the rich and some from the poor, the more his friends *had,* the more he *got.* But no matter how small the amount was, he took it all. . . .

When he is likely to receive a just reward for his crimes, the cry of persecution, and sympathy, are raised for him and his family. The latter, there are *none* but pity them. But there are many others that should be thought of while sympathy is the great cry coming out of the prison. . . . Culver has brought distress and ruin on hundreds of families in this and adjoining counties. Would he soften his hard heart, and for one moment look and think of the men that he has hurried to the grave? Where is Joshua Douglass, one of his victims? Ruined not only pecuniarily, but his mind so far destroyed that he requires the constant attention of friends.

Will Mr. Culver look around and see how Mrs. Gordon and many others are to support themselves and their families? Where is the hundred thousand dollars he took from her? And made her liable for thirty thousand more, by selling to Mr. Gordon Bank Stock just when he (Gordon) was at the point of death and the stock was worthless and Culver made it so, and knew it at the time. . . .

Any one disputing the above can examine the books of the Bank, the affidavits of the book-keeper R. Irwin Jr. or any other of the Bank Directors or the Auditor General. . . . The Petroleum Bank at Titusville has been robbed of a larger amount of Bonds than the Venango Bank. Crawford County and Oil City can speak for themselves as they were all gobbled up by the same "Christian gentleman." . . .

Culver don't tell the public that they don't pay their laborers on the Reno R. R., and that he brought suit against them for quitting work, accusing them of conspiring to stop working, although Culver had stopped paying them some months before. . . .

He holds up his hands and calls God to witness that he could not secure or pay any one a thousand dollars to save him from the penitentiary; and the next breath, if it suits his purpose to reconcile his creditors better, he says; "Let me alone, have confidence in me, and I will be able to pay all my debts."

Soon after this blast appeared, Culver was out on bail again, but Mr. John Duffield, he of the shotgun withdrawal, promptly brought new charges, this time fraud and embezzlement. He accused Culver of having removed from the Attorney General's office securities deposited by the banks as collateral on notes. All that summer, until the trial, creditors kept having the financier rearrested. The president of the Petroleum Bank, Mr. Chase, got him jailed still again on June 22nd. After the trial and acquittal, in mid-July, creditors just went on suing.

In August, a Franklin man sued to recover $24,000 in U.S. Treasury Notes: "The defendant did not perform or fulfill the said agreement, but on the contrary craftily and subtly deceived the plaintiff." He got a judgment. In November John Dewar sued for one million dollars—and got a settlement of $1,106. Dr. Albert Egbert, whom we met at Petroleum Centre with the Coquette and Maple Shade wells, sued for embezzlement, and he came out of it all the worse off, because the case was dismissed and he had to pay court costs of $26.14.

One historian has said that the affair left "a stench in the nostrils of the people."

Others praised Culver's integrity, and said he was working as a surveyor and paying off all his creditors. (If a man on a surveyor's salary can pay off over six million dollars, then he is indeed a financial giant.) One writer said that Culver reorganized the Reno Oil and

Land Company, and paid off his debts that way. Since Reno never had any large wells and never became a boomtown, that would have been quite a trick too. I myself never met the creditors who allegedly got their money back, but I have met descendants of those who didn't.

The oil men who'd lost almost every cent in the bank crashes said wryly that they had helped build a railroad to the moon. Culver's dizzily curved tracks never did get to Pithole; and Pithole, like the whole oil region, reflected a country-wide panic. Inflated dollars had tumbled down to sounder values; the discovery of oil in Canada, Europe, South America and the Far East sent the price plummeting. The cities' market quotations were: "Petroleum: in less request at 26¢ and 27¢ for Crude; 39¢ and 41¢ for Refined, gallon." The federal tax of $1 a barrel took too large a bite out of what profits there were, and it was repealed that summer to help lift the depression. Exports sagged; the Irish rebellion, oddly enough, cut off one of our top foreign markets. Sales to England dropped too; our consul in London had to pay the fares home for some stranded agents of oil companies.

And stranded Pitholians were leaving their ex-Mecca in dispirited droves. The great wells had dried up and there were no important new ones. One visitor said, "They count time here by pump-strokes and the territory that ceases to produce becomes 'old' in a fortnight."

The flow of oil through the new pipelines at Pithole became a trickle, and Van Syckel lost his lines to a bank when he couldn't meet payment on notes. Whether there was anything shady about *this* bank deal or not, I don't know, but Van Syckel thought he'd been rooked and wanted to sue, as this letter to his lawyer shows. (It was a vintage year for suits; lawyers must have been the only ones who made money then):

> Sir:
> Enclosed please find the names of the Directors of the First National Bank, Titusville. Those men was also stockholders. . . . Our Transaction commenced in the Spring while Briggs was President. We must go for Fletcher, Abbott, Briggs, Watson, Brewer and Angier as those men have been more or less mixed up in the pipe swindell. . . .
>
> Yours Truly,
> S. Van Syckel

Pithole's spot was secure in oil history, as the birthplace of the first important pipeline—and the most brilliant spontaneous-combustion town ever struck. Instead of crumbling away, the city that had shot up in a bright, hot blaze of glory burned out in a series of devastating fires, mostly in 1866 and '67. Horace Greeley came to Titusville and lectured for $78 at a benefit to raise money for Pitholians who'd lost everything in the fires. The $60,000 Bonta House, where he'd stayed on his visit to Pithole, tried to auction itself off at $10 a chance, but there weren't enough takers. Ida Tarbell's father finally bought the Bonta for $600 for the lumber, carted it to Titusville, and built a house on East Main Street, so that Ida could go to the high school in town.

Several of the other buildings that had been spared by fire were hauled off in pieces to the next boomtown, Pleasantville, and put together again. I'm pleased that the Chase House and Murphy's Theatre got a new lease on life there, but they must have felt lonely sometimes, because Pleasantville was "as chaste as a Quaker meeting." French Kate and Ben Hogan never tried to set up shop there, but they opened gymnasiums in almost every other Pennsylvania oil town. At Parker's Landing, a sizzling boom spot several years later, a wave of reform closed Hogan's place and he took to the river. He outfitted a boat, the *Floating Palace,* with his girl gymnasts and gambling tables, and anchored just beyond the reach of the law. In three years, he made $210,000. One popular feature—customers were encouraged to slip out of their hot clothes and bathe in their skins with the *Palace* females, splashing playfully beside the boat. Bully Ben still liked wholesome sports.

His chronicler of Pithole days, the wild-blooming Crocus, moved over to the *Herald* after the *Record* folded, but Titusville itself was so hard hit by the panic and Culver debacle that the editor announced he might have to suspend publication. When the generous-hearted proprietor of the American Hotel, Major Mills, heard this, he hurried right over and invited editor Henry Bloss to move to the hotel and bring most of his staff. The Major would provide roof and board till the depression was over. He said to Bloss, "My God, Henry, if the *Herald* stopped, this town would go plum dash to destruction."

TWELVE

——◆◆◆——

Spies and robbers

THE *Herald* was plum dash feeling its oats a year later, in the up-
turn that brought the crowds rushing back to new wells:

"What is the definition of America?" it asked friskily.

"A place that supplies cash and clean clothes to the residents of
Oil Creek."

The biggest boom that year was sparked in the oddest way yet.
A rabid-eyed spiritualist, James Abrams—known to his many de-
tractors as Crazy James—was riding from Pithole to Titusville with
three friends, on a blowy November day in 1867, when just below the
little crossroads settlement of Pleasantville, he suddenly bounded
from the buggy and leaped over a fence into a field on the Porter farm.
Here he proceeded to run around like one possessed, which is exactly
what he was, or so he said when he came out of his trance. His
friends reported that he turned a series of cartwheels down the field,
his long, bony legs waving like a scarecrow's stilts, while they stood
stupefied, watching. Crazy James explained later, "I was violently
influenced and controlled by a power outside myself. Becoming entirely unconscious, I was moved some distance across the field and
made to stop upon a certain location, where my controlling influences
said to those present, pointing towards the earth, 'Here is an immense
amount of petroleum!' "

His spirit control also told him to stick a penny in the earth at that
spot, as a token payment on an option, which shows the spirit was a
pretty shrewd operator.

Unfortunately, the bankers and oil men who'd been caught in the

Culver crash were wary of accepting spirits as security on a loan. And Farmer Porter asked more substance than ectoplasm for a lease on his land. It took Crazy James three months to raise the money. What really rocked the natives, and made them tap their foreheads significantly, was that he trustingly built huge tanks and kept the driller going down, down, down—below eight hundred feet. He called the well the Harmonial, after his spirit doctrine, but one irreverent kibitzer called it the Bottomless Witch.

When the Harmonial flowed, it started a great new leasing binge just as oil prices went up: from $1.55 in January to $4.72 in June. By midsummer, daily production at Pleasantville hit over 2,000 barrels. Titusville, six miles away, profited even more than the provincial little boom spot, because most of the crowds made the Queen City their headquarters and rushed off each morning, then came back to comfortable hotels like the Crittenden at night. One visitor reported, "Yesterday thirty-two stage loads of passengers went from Titusville [to Pleasantville] between the hours of seven A.M. and three P.M."

Pleasantville's pretty little white houses looked like Virtue keeping her skirts clean while the greasy shacks pushed their way in, but Vice never even soiled her hem. The town council ruled that only one store might sell liquor; there were no saloons or brothels. A jail built hurriedly to accommodate rowdy transients got only one prisoner during the entire boom. Sinners never cottoned to Pleasantville, or vice versa, and who can blame either side?

One of the few natives who forgot himself was a Pleasantville farmer who made a fortune on leases and began drinking and carrying on like a junior model of Coal Oil Johnny. He had several wells on his land—and he had three small children. Probably at his wife's insistence, he made over one well to his offspring, with a wooden sign nailed to the derrick, crudely lettered: "The Childrens Well." And every cent of royalties from that one well went into a bank account he couldn't touch, to be kept for the children.

Another millionaire farmer, down near Petroleum Centre, had lost such a fortune in the Culver crash that he wouldn't trust banks much at all. At least he refused to put all his nest eggs in one bank—or even in several—but kept a great pile of cash at home, and this brought on the most spectacular masked robbery of the oil regions, as much talked about all over the country as the Brink holdup of our own era.

The mean thing is that the victim, farmer John Benninghoff, got a much worse mauling in the press than the man who'd been largely responsible for his nervously hoarding at home, Charles Vernon Culver. Benninghoff was described as a stingy, dirty, illiterate German. Actually, he was a sixty-seven-year-old farmer of German-English descent, "well-posted for those times," who had worked like a mule to till 240 acres and earn enough to support twelve children. It wasn't until early 1865, when producers took to the highlands to drill, that his hillside acres a mile above Petroleum Centre were leased. The Huidekoper and De Kalb oil companies were two of the firms that swelled his income—and their own. His royalties averaged $6,000 a day, although they had dropped to a mere $1,000 during the depression. Whatever he'd lost in banks then, he made up for in a hurry. By early 1867, the *Herald* reported that Benninghoff had a million in cash:

> Recently he was complaining to a friend that his agent had granted six leases on his corn patch, and what he should do for corn the next summer he knew not. "I must break up a new patch of ground, and for a man of my years it's too bad." This gentleman called on him a few days after this, finding him holding the plough, breaking up his new corn patch. He refused to lease more than one-fifth of his property, or have his woods cut down.

A man who cares more about his crops and his trees than he does about leases isn't the miser he was painted as, but it's true that Old Benninghoff pinched pennies rather hard. For instance, he made his wife and the one son still living at home economize even on kerosene for the stove. And he bought a rusty second-hand lock-and-key safe to hold his money.

A son who lived near Meadville got so worried about the dangers of robbery that he sent down a trustworthy (he thought) hired man of his own, to be a guard for his father. This guard was improbably named Geiger, and keep your eye on Geiger, because he'll lead us straight to the holdup plot.

On the night of January 17th, 1868, Geiger and old Mr. Benninghoff were sitting around the stove in the kitchen, with hired man Cornelius Ethridge, plump, gentle little Mrs. Benninghoff, and a pretty visiting niece, a Miss Heise, who was having Auntie help her piece together a patchwork quilt. It was seven-thirty in the evening, and son Joseph was at church. (One robber explained at the trial that Geiger said they should come either on Thursday, when Joseph was always safely out of the way at prayer meeting, or on Saturday when he called on his girl. The holdup men put their faith in prayer-meeting night.)

When a knock came at the kitchen door, Geiger, who had strict orders never to open to strangers after dark, leaped to unbolt the door. Four men walked in, "all of them masked with handkerchiefs, cloths or comforters. The men drew pistols and presenting them at the heads or breasts of the family, threatened them with immediate death if they should make the least noise."

Geiger and the hired man never let out a peep, just sat down meekly. But old Mr. Benninghoff was so furious—and so upset by Geiger's suspicious behavior—that he yelled and fought. "The ruffians then struck him in the face and stamped on various parts of his body, and then half dragged, half carried him to an adjoining bedroom. . . . They tied his arms and legs and threw him on the bed and . . . rifled his pockets and took from one of them . . . a key to one of the safes."

While the intruders were busy subduing the old farmer, his gentle little wife risked her own life trying to save him. She managed to get a pistol out of a table drawer and slip it to Geiger, who simply put the gun in his pocket. Geiger explained later, "I thought she was just giving the gun to me for safekeeping so the robbers wouldn't steal it."

The masked men relieved him of this awkward weapon and trussed him up with the hired man; they tied Mrs. Benninghoff and her niece to beds in another room. Then, without asking any questions about "Where's the money?" they went upstairs to Benninghoff's rusty old safe, used his key, and took out $200,000 in greenbacks and $60,000 in bonds. This more-than-a-quarter-million loot was neatly bundled up by the yeggs in two of Mrs. Benninghoff's pillowcases. Next they tried to open a second safe, but that was one Joseph had bought, a good sturdy iron hulk with a combination lock, and only Joseph knew the combination. The four bandits now decided to wait till the young man came home and make him open it. They unbound the niece, and made her serve them homemade pie and milk. A sociable hour went by, while they ate and drank. One of the men complimented Mrs. Benninghoff on her light hand with pastry. Another said to the niece gallantly, "You're quite a pretty girl. I might come back and marry you."

By nine o'clock, they got tired of waiting for Joseph, so they took Geiger out to the barn and had him harness a horse to a cutter. Then they retied the guard to a kitchen chair—for the looks of the thing— and drove off.

The niece had already wriggled out of her ropes and was untying her aunt and uncle when Joseph arrived. He didn't get a chance to finish his anxious questions about whether his parents were hurt; Papa bellowed, "Quick—go report the robbery," and off Joseph went to Petroleum Centre.

The next day the Benninghoff's horse and cutter were found a mile and a half from the farm. It was obvious from the marks in the snow that the robbers had had a sleigh waiting there for their getaway. But getaway to where?

Geiger must have convinced the police, temporarily, that he was an innocent bystander, because the *Herald's* first accounts of the holdup made no mention of his being a suspect, but did say that the second safe had contained more money than the one looted. This brought a screech from the family:

January 21, 1868

Mr. Editor—Sir:

. . . I see a note in your paper the other day stating that the other safe contained a larger amount than that taken, which is not correct, and hereafter you will do me a favor not to advertise for robbers until I tell you to do so.

Yours etc.
Joseph Benninghoff

The *Herald* replied:

> We cheerfully publish the foregoing letter by way of correcting
> the mistatement referred to. Mr. Joseph Benninghoff was at prayer
> meeting when his father was robbed, laying up treasures in Heaven—
> where thieves do not break through, nor steal. But Joseph, being a
> son of the old man, appears to take the misfortune to heart as seri-
> ously as though the spondulicks had been his own. . . .
>
> We have never had any intention of advertising for robbers and are
> glad to know there is less money in Mr. Benninghoff's other safe.
> We would advise him to throw away his safe altogether, and cord
> up his greenbacks in the vaults of the Second National Bank. There
> is where we keep our heavy surplus and we have never lost $210,000
> since we opened a bank account.

Other papers, especially big city ones, were even more merciless
in their roasting of the Benninghoffs. The *Tribune* said the old farmer
had seven million dollars tucked away around the house, and counted
it in relays. One writer told gravely how Mrs. Benninghoff, during
spring house cleaning, always laid a million or so in greenbacks out-
doors on the grass in the sun, to rid them of mildew, while her husband sat beside her holding a loaded shotgun.

Joseph, stung by the ridicule, got his father to offer a reward of
$25,000 for information leading to the arrest of the criminals, and
hired a private detective from Pittsburgh who must have been the
silliest, reward-greediest bloodhound ever unleashed. His first sniffing
turned up the fact that three prominent Titusville men—Major Mills
and pipeline owners Henry Harley and Dan Cady—had gone off for
a sleigh ride to Petroleum Centre the night of the robbery, *and they
had been gone exactly long enough to burgle the Benninghoffs.* Incredibly, the detective got Harley and Cady arrested, but probably
even the greenest deputy refused to arrest the popular Major Mills.
All of Titusville was in an uproar. Harley and Cady were promptly
released, and each sued the Benninghoffs for $50,000—"for arrest
and defamation of character."

The detective's next idiot-play was to wire the police in Missouri to
arrest another prominent Titusvillian—attorney Ira Briggs—*who had*

left town just after the holdup and gone west. Briggs was yanked all
the way back home for a hearing. That mix-up was quickly straight-
ened out, but Briggs' fellow lawyers in Crawford and Venango
counties were so indignant they published a statement signed by all of
them, saying what they thought of the attorney's integrity and the
way he'd been mistreated.

The first sensible break in the case came when a rum-pot named
George Miller, who lived in the village of Saegertown above Meadville, began spending money like a drunken thief. Police grilled him
till he confessed and named the others involved, then they let him
go free, temporarily, so as not to alarm bigger game.

It turned out that the master mind of the holdup, who had already vanished with most of the boodle, was James Saeger. He was
a handsome young man of a respectable family—they had founded
Saegertown—who had already gambled away one inheritance. He
and Lewis Waelde, an uncle of Geiger's, had heard Geiger describe
the Benninghoff cache, and decided to get it.

A minor accomplice, Jacob Shoppart, was the first man actually arrested. Not knowing that it was George Miller who had informed on
him, he sat down trustingly in jail right after his arrest, and wrote
Miller a friendly tip to scram before the police caught him too:

> Pittsburg, July 11
>
> Friend George:
>   I seat myself to inform you of My bad luck. I have ben arrested
> and am in jale here in Pittsburg. . . . God dam L. Waelde's Sole. I
> wrote him twist for money. . . as I knew I would be arrested if I
> did not get it . . . but never got even a scratch of a pen from the
> dam mean Son of a Bitche. . . . George, they [the police] know
> all about it, and they even told me things that you and James Sager
> and myself talked when we were alone or thought we was alone,
> and where you and me got our money. . . .
>   You will be arrested in a few days as they told me they were
> going to arrest you before long but they wants get James Sager
> first if possible and I think you had better leave but you must be
> sharp . . . or they nab you in getting away. . . .
>   Well, I must close burn this just as soon as ever you get this don't
> delay a moment and let me know what you are going to do.
>   J. K. Shoppart

If he had known what Miller had already done—squeal—he might have regretted passing up an invitation to murder the blabmouth. This came out in Shoppart's testimony at the trial in Franklin:

> "In October, 1867, George Miller came into the shop where I was working in Saegertown and proposed to me to go into a conspiracy to rob John Benninghoff of Venango County. He said another man would speak to me about it the next morning. I said I wanted time to consider.
>
> "The next morning James Saeger . . . took me into a field half a mile from Saegertown and I took the oath not to divulge any of the secrets of the conspirators. George Miller's name was signed at the bottom of the written oath. A short time after I was sworn in I met Saeger, Lewis Waelde and George Geiger at Fogle's saloon. . . . Saeger told Geiger he need not fear me, that I was one of them. . . .
>
> "Our plan was to get expert robbers from the city. James Saeger went to Philadelphia for this purpose. . . . The day before the robbery was committed Saeger proposed to me to kill George Miller. He said that Miller had told the plot to me before the others had consented that I should be asked to go into it, and if he would tell one he would tell others. He said we would get a flask of whiskey and take him down along the creek and then two of the Philadelphia chaps would come up and knock him down and put him under the ice. I told him I would not consent to killing Miller. . . .
>
> "After the robbery Saeger gave me two packages of money, one for Miller and the other for myself."

Each package contained $1,300.

Neither the tongue-wagging Miller nor Shoppart had gone on the actual holdup, and I can't understand why they were enlisted in the first place, unless for comedy relief. Waelde drove the sleigh and waited near the farm. But it doesn't make sense to think that the masked men who went into the Benninghoffs' with Saeger were professional burglars. Real safecrackers—even if they were Philadelphians—wouldn't have sat down to eat pie and wait for Joseph to get home from prayer meeting to open up the other safe.

The best guess has always been that the others were Saegertown or Meadville pals—but never identified.

At 4 A.M. the night of the holdup, the men all met at the Iron

Clad Saloon in Meadville, to divide up the loot and arrange iron-clad alibis. Waelde got $45,000, and he vamoosed to Ohio and bought a brewery there. By the time the police caught up with him, he had invested every penny in the new business, and old farmer Benninghoff, a teetotaler who shuddered at the very word beer, had a choice of taking over the brewery or taking a total loss. Much as it hurt, he took the brewery.

At Waelde's trial, the prisoner asked the sheriff if he might step to the door of the courtroom and get some fresh air. He breathed deep —and took off. The sheriff found him the next day in Meadville, and brought him back to be sentenced to five and a half years. Shoppart got the same. Miller cried so lushly and babbled so sorrowfully about his sins that the judge only sentenced him to eighteen months. Everybody thought Geiger was guilty, and the other men's testimony said so, but for some weird reason he was acquitted "for lack of evidence."

James Saeger, who had got away with at least $150,000, wasn't heard of till 1874. One day a cattleman from Texas, who had brought up his herd on the Texas-Colorado trail, swaggered into a Denver bar with a party of friends. The bartender, an ex-Meadville man, Gus Peiflee, recognized him as his old acquaintance from the Iron Clad Saloon: James Saeger. Gus remembered the big reward the Benninghoffs had offered, and rushed to a telegraph office. Three days later Joseph Benninghoff and Titusville Chief of Police Rouse arrived in Denver, panting on the trail. Their informant, the bartender, led them to Saeger all right; the hunt was over, but we get a mixed bag of endings. The more dramatic version has it that a hundred of Saeger's cowboys were in Denver with him, and threatened to shoot any man who tried to lay hands on their boss.

Another account is that Saeger said he'd spent the money, and the Benningoffs were so sick and tired of the whole long mess they decided not to take him back to stand trial and perhaps be acquitted. A third story is that Saeger turned over $50,000 and in exchange the Benninghoffs agreed to drop charges. One thing sure is that Saeger lived to an overripe age in Texas as a wealthy cattle king, and he was reputed to go straight there—but of course Texas had no oil millionaires for him to rob.

At the time of the holdup, Venango County still produced five-sixths of all the oil in this country, with small quantities in West Virginia and Ohio. A Philadelphia paper mentioned condescendingly that "a small pond of oil has been found in Texas"—but nobody cared about ponds while Pennsylvania had spouters.

The boom shifted to other mushroom towns in Venango—Red-Hot, Shamburg, Cash-up—then downriver to the Lower Regions—Clarion, Armstrong and Butler counties—curving next up the Allegheny to Warren and Bradford. I wish I could follow the crowds, but there isn't room in this book, so I'll stick pretty much to my home county, with one exception. We're about to take off after a rip-roaring red-headed young Irishman Pat Boyle, as he rides on his oil-scouting escapades.

If I make scouting sound too much like a game of Cowboy and Indian with a dash of the Scarlet Pimpernel, well, that's how it strikes me. But to the men involved, it was a serious, often dangerous job, a new occupation tailored to the skulduggery rivalries of big business. By 1871, there were Oil Exchanges at Titusville, Oil City and Franklin, and powerful companies or syndicates were replacing lone speculators. Prices were manipulated up or down; rumors were manufactured to confuse rivals and make a fast killing on the market. A company about to bring in a big well would fence it off from observation, set up armed guards to discourage snoopers, and not even let word leak out of how far the drilling had gone. Sometimes they'd even rig a juicy strike to look dry for the first few days. Every big gusher meant an oversupply that lowered the price of oil; by fooling other companies into thinking a well was a dry hole, or a duster was a spouter, the owners would make a profit on the market—buying or unloading—before their rivals got wise.

By 1880, all the big companies had scouts to sniff out news, spread red herrings, and by hook or crook grab scoops for their employers. As an ex-driller, Pat Boyle knew wells inside-out, and he knew a scoop from a hole in the ground; already he'd been a roving reporter for the *Herald*, the Oil City *Derrick,* and *Petroleum World.* Once he'd covered a hanging of a murderer in Smethport, Pennsylvania, for the *Herald,* and sweet-talked the murderer's lawyer into letting him see a long statement which the killer had left to be opened after his death. Pat explained sunnily that he just wanted to get an idea ahead of what the document looked like, but he got such a good idea of its sensational contents that he made off with the only copy, and caught the last train to Titusville. The next day, the *Herald* ran columns and columns of exclusive quotes from the confession, and the fuming reporters from big-city papers had to eat crow—raw.

In the next years, Pat Boyle applied this technique to scouting for the Union Oil Company, on strikes at Cherry Grove, Thorn Creek and Macksburg. He and his beautiful black horse Daniel Webster became a kind of Flying Irishman legend. At the Grandin well No. 4, Boyle forged an order purporting to come from the owner, generously urging the driller and toolie to take a few hours off. He sent this in by messenger. After the workmen left, puzzled but pleased, Boyle stationed a guard of his own outside, with orders not to let anyone in. Then he settled down to test-drilling the well himself. Meanwhile, the owner arrived, eager to find out if they'd struck oil— and the guard refused to let him past. The poor owner roared and yelled and carried on something awful, but the guard kept saying doggedly, "I'm hired by Pat Boyle and Pat says don't let no one in without identification."

Pat discovered the well was dry—before the owner even knew it— and tactfully left by the back way, sneaking through the brush till he located Daniel Webster tied to a tree. Then he and Daniel were off to flash the word to Union Oil.

The night he sneaked past guards to do some test-drilling on a well across the creek, he bribed the ferryman handsomely not to make any more trips until morning, so that no other scouts, or nosy owner, could catch up with him. If there wasn't time to drill—and most scouts weren't expert enough to do it, anyway—they often sank fishing line to measure the depth of a well, or snitched samples of sand to examine for traces of grease.

Pat often teamed with the small, dark, wiry Jim Tennent, scout for oil man Captain Jones of Bradford, and Tennent has described the time they heard that the superintendent of a well going down had arranged to use a tin whistle to signal the owner across the ravine. Pat promptly hired an old sharpshooter, Scarface Charlie, to hide in a tree near the well, and explained the situation simply: "If you see

Andy Gratlan raise a whistle to his mouth, shoot it out of his hand."

Tennent said he was almost sorry when they managed to steal the whistle before the signal was ever given; he wanted to see Scarface Charlie perform as per Pat's instructions.

Next, Pat got the idea that he and Tennent should use some such signaling device themselves, but nothing so common as whistles. He found two old hunting horns, and he and Tennent took these and stood on opposite sides of the ravine, bellowing like maddened moose. The plan was for Pat to signal from a spot near the well to Tennent stationed at the pipeline's branch telegraph office, and Tennent would wire both Union Oil and Captain Jones. Word of these practice sessions reached every scout who wasn't stone deaf; several of them bought horns too, and added their toots to the din, jamming communications.

They probably needed to let off steam anyway, because on their tricky midnight prowls to spy out wells, if a twig snapped, bang went a guard's gun. Tennent lost the tip of his ear that way, to a bullet.

Often scouts didn't get out of their boots for a week at a stretch, hiding in the woods with their field glasses trained on a derrick, and eating cold beans out of a can. Pat once managed to install a field telephone in a hemlock tree, and this was considered pretty fancy. To prevent rivals' tips going out, he sometimes attached new copper wires to telegraph wires, then fastened these to a spike in the earth and grounded the message.

Another trick was to bribe a telegraph operator to show a copy of a wire being sent. To foil this, all the companies used codes, and changed them every few months. Each code book was numbered; when it was given to an employee, he was responsible for that copy and Heaven help him if, say, No. 23 Book was mysteriously missing when it was time to lock the codes in the safe overnight.

The codes were as ingenious—and at times as devil-may-care—as the scouts who tried to steal them. I give a few cherished samples from a code used by John McKinney, a top oil producer in Titusville:

Abdomen	—	1
Amatory	—	65
Babble	—	Advance funds
Babe	—	Accept draft
Bang	—	Can arrange money matters

Bastard	—	Funds will be sent
Calomel	—	Buy quietly to cover
Carrion	—	Must make plump offer
Carve	—	Other parties are offering to buy
Caress	—	If you cannot buy at our figures, telegraph
Dagger	—	Advise selling short
Diaper	—	Oil for Sale
Flag	—	Likely to advance any moment
Guitar	—	Withdraw from market
Lap	—	April or May
Mankind	—	Erie Railroad
Manure	—	Franklin
Mars	—	Henry Harley
Maternal	—	S. D. Karns
Mermaid	—	Phillips Brothers
Mimic	—	John D. Rockefeller
Mince	—	William Rockefeller
Minos	—	Joseph Seep
Monster	—	J. J. Vandergrift
Naked	—	Are there any judgements entered on the docket against _____?
Noise	—	Reported weak
Occult	—	Have written fully by mail
Panic	—	Everything running nicely
Parsnip	—	Is flowing
Peevish	—	Struck salt water which interferes
Pelvis	—	The sand is poor
Pirate	—	What royalty do they want?
Raid	—	Cannot explain until I see you
Regal	—	No friend of ours
Restive	—	Well running over!

One telegram in a later McKinney code reads:

FEEL FERMENT FLESHY FESTOON

but the reader may fuddle this out for himself.

A telegraph operator named Badger, an old pal of Boyle's and
Tennent's, let them look at one coded wire concerning the Patterson
well, for a stiff bribe of $25. Badger figured it wouldn't hurt much,
because they couldn't crack the code. What he didn't know was that
their colleague, oil scout Si Hughes, had already wangled a code book

of that company's (Anchor Oil), and the three pooled their resources for a neat bit of detection.

Another time, they brazenly bribed the driller himself, and
watched through field glasses while he signaled progress by the way
he carried his bit; on the right shoulder meant *Now drilling in slate
below red sand*.

The superintendent of the most famous mystery well of all—No.
646 at Cherry Grove near Warren—was so determined to prevent a
leak that he hand-picked the workmen and made them take an oath
of secrecy before a justice of the peace:

> Such information as they may hereafter obtain as employees of the
> future developments of the well shall be held secret and inviolable.
> That they will not by either act, word, deed or other manner convey
> to any other person excepting George Dimick, Superintendent of
> said Company, any intelligence of the depth, nature, or character of
> said well. . . . That they will not give to any other person any
> sample of sand—and will use all reasonable efforts to prevent any
> and all other persons from obtaining information.

The workers took this oath so seriously, or were threatened with
such penalties if they broke it, that even Pat Boyle's blarney and
bribes and combustious ideas got him nowhere. He and Tennent were
scooped on that well by Si Hughes. Si wriggled under the barbed-
wire fence at night and hid under the derrick for the crucial forty-
eight hours, without food, buried to the neck in mud. He got out the
first flash on the strike, and earned a fat bonus from his employer.

Si, like Tennent and Boyle, scorned the crudities practiced by some
younger scouts, such as spiking drinks with laudanum to conk out colleagues while the trickster sped off to send his wire first. One scout
used to get a head start to town by tossing lighted firecrackers behind him as he rode. The explosions scared all the other scouts'
horses into bolting and the cracker-thrower got there fustest, but he
wasn't too popular, somehow.

Pat had one amateur rumor-monger who never knew how he was
used as a transmission belt. If Union Oil was keeping a dry hole
dark, for instance, Pat would wire a gossipy tank builder, Tom
McGrow:

WANT YOU TO LOOK UP FOR ME RUSH TWO 1200 BBL. TANKS. WILL
BE THERE IN MORNING. DO NOT LET THIS INFORMATION BECOME
KNOWN

PAT BOYLE

Within a half-hour, McGrow would be happily confiding all over
town that Union Oil had a gusher and needed tanks fast.

Boyle himself was the flabbergasted butt of the funniest trick of all.
In 1884, all the top scouts—except Pat—were gathered in Marietta,
Ohio, for news of the first strikes in the nearby Macksburg field. In
fact, they'd been waiting there for so many weeks they were bored
stiff even with poker—and itchy for mischief. One of the men who had
taken a brief trip to Pittsburgh spotted Pat at the Newcomerstown
junction waiting for the train to Marietta; Union Oil had decided,
belatedly, to send him along. The man wired Jim Tennent in Ohio:

PAT BOYLE IS HERE, DRESSED TO KILL. HE IS GOING TO PARALYZE YOU
BOYS AND YOU OUGHT TO MEET HIM WITH A BAND. PLAY HIM FOR
GOVERNOR PATTISON. HE WILL BE ON EVENING TRAIN

TIM MULLEN

The oil scouts were charmed with this notion, and went rushing off
to put it into action. Jim Tennent wrote a handbill and had five hundred printed up that afternoon and distributed by small boys all over
town:

Governor Pattison, of Pennsylvania, will arrive at 4 P.M. on the
C. & M. He will be met by an escort with a band. A parade will
follow down Main Street to the river front and up to the National
Hotel. We desire to have all oil men turn out to greet His Honor,
regardless of political belief. All come and show him that we appreciate the honor of his visit.
(Signed)

By Order of the Committee

While townspeople and oil men were reading this with respectful
interest, the scouts were hiring a drum corps.

By the time the train pulled into the sleepy little Marietta depot
in the late afternoon, the streets were lined with citizens eager to do
neighborly honor to the Governor of the next-door state. Pat stepped

off the train, and as promised in the wire, he was definitely dressed to kill, in a nobby white linen duster almost to his ankles, and a tall white plug hat.

The drum corps struck up a thumping welcome. Tennent led a jolly "Three Cheers for Governor Pattison," and Boyle looked around expectantly for the visiting celebrity. The oil scout who'd been chosen as master of ceremonies because he had the most dignified bay window—portly Jim Chambers—went up to Boyle, pumped his hand, and said loudly and heartily, "Governor, this is an honor. Let me assist you." He grabbed Boyle's bag with one hand, and held on to the astonished victim with the other.

Pat, facing the drum corps and the cheering throngs, gulped and finally grinned weakly. "All right," he muttered. "This one is on me, boys. I'll see you through."

The major-domo motioned His Honor to the head of the procession and he swung the drum corps into line just behind Pat, with a dozen scouts and several civic-minded oil men marching next, followed by fifty or more whooping small boys. The crowds lining the sidewalks and leaning out the windows cheered and hoorayed. Women waved handkerchiefs; men waved their hats. All the citizens felt it was darned decent of Pennsylvania's Governor to come pay a visit to such a tiny Ohio town, and they were determined to show their appreciation.

Pat, on his part, was equally gracious. He kept raising his tall white plug hat to the ladies, and smiling and bowing. As Tennent reported happily later, "I don't think Governor Pattison himself would have made any better impression."

When the parade reached the door of the National Hotel, the proprietor was standing on the front steps, galvanized by this unexpected honor. Several dozen of the enthusiastic citizens who had watched the parade and were now quite in the spirit of the occasion, wanted to come inside and "shake the Governor's hand."

At this point, Pat began to look mutinous, and Jim Chambers made a hurried little speech, explaining that His Honor was somewhat tired, and would retire to his room for a brief rest, but would be delighted to receive them after dinner. Then His Honor made a little speech, explaining nicely that some oil men had asked him to carry a bag full of nitroglycerin all the way to Marietta, and this had been a bit of a strain, so would they excuse him? The crowd was sympathetic; several even murmured indignantly, What a thing for oil men to do—make the Governor of Pennsylvania lug nitro around—why, he might have been blown to smithereens. They cheered him once more, for his bravery.

The proprietor then led Boyle to the finest suite in the hotel, with the oil scouts trailing along. His Honor didn't appear after dinner, but he sent down word to the citizens who had shown up again that he hoped they'd go into the bar and have a drink on him. They gratefully obliged. When Pat saw the size of his bar bill the next day, he debated how to word this item on his expense account to Union Oil. *Toasts to the Governor? Spreading Good Will Between States?* After thoughtful reflection, he entered the bar bill as "Sundries."

It was the grand finale of his scouting assignments. The next year he became publisher of the Oil City *Derrick*. By then, the *Derrick* was ardently on the side of Mr. Rockefeller's Standard Oil, and Boyle was in the thick of the name-calling, waving his pen like a shillelagh.

THIRTEEN

Swallow without chewing

WHEN twenty-one-year-old John D. Rockefeller took his first look at Oil Creek, he's supposed to have gone back to Cleveland and reported that it was "chaos and disorder, waste and incompetence, competition at its worst."

If that's really all he saw—and I don't believe it for a minute—then an oil man who summed up young John D. as "that bloodless Baptist book-keeper" was just about as accurate. It's true that Rockefeller had a mind as precise as a watchspring, and he totted up his plans as neatly as a bookkeeper striking a monthly balance. But the plans themselves—and the way he carried them out—had a Hannibal daring and drive, and a second-sight eye on the future. One of his liveliest Oil Creek opponents, who later switched causes in midstream, explained that Rockefeller could always see farther ahead than the rest of them: "And then he sees around the corner!"

In the early 1860's, Rockefeller's foresight took a good look around the corner, and decided that the refining end of the oil business was the place to be. He and his partner in the produce commission house, Maurice Clark, invested first in a small refinery started by Samuel Andrews, a candlemaker who had already worked with lard oil. This was so successful that they expanded the firm with Maurice's two brothers, as Andrews, Clark and Company. But two more Clarks upset the applecart; Jim Clark, especially, sneered and swore at Rockefeller's "Sunday-School-superintendent" discipline and fussiness for details. To have to itemize his expense account as the firm's salesman for a stern-eyed twenty-three-year-old partner was too galling. In turn, Rockefeller detested Jim Clark as a loud-mouth tricky speculator, and got free as soon as he could.

In February of 1865, the Cleveland *Leader* ran an interesting little announcement:

> COPARTNERSHIP NOTICE—the undersigned, having purchased the entire interest of Andrews, Clark & Co. in the "Excelsior Oil Works," and all stock of barrels, oil, etc., will continue the business of the late firm under the name of Rockefeller & Andrews.
>
> John D. Rockefeller
> Samuel Andrews

Two weeks later, a notice inserted by the old firm said:

"J. D. Rockefeller retiring."

He was almost twenty-six, and he said later he dated that separation as the beginning of his success, although sometimes he lay awake at night thinking, "You have a good property now. But suppose the oil fields gave out!"

In his own meticulous, controlled way, he took as many chances as a wildcat producer; during the depression of 1866, while the Culver bank crash was reverberating along Oil Creek, he opened a second Cleveland refinery, the Standard Works. The next year, he opened a New York office to handle export, with his brother William in charge.

William Rockefeller was a cheerful, kind, broad-shouldered, wide-cheeked man, as unaffectedly friendly as a country squire, and far more popular than John in our neck of the woods. When William came to Oil City on buying trips, he'd sit around and swap stories or horsy talk; he loved fast horses, and the new oil kings had some beauties. They were never at a loss for words with William, any more than the small-towners he'd gone to school with; every year he went back to Owego, in upper New York, for a visit with old friends and a woodchuck dinner.

John seemed rigid in comparison, expanding only like a steel tape measure. He was thinner than William—narrower is probably more apt—with pale clear skin, reddish-sandy hair and mustache, well-set searching blue eyes, tight nostrils, thin-chiseled lips. The main recollection oil producers had of him was whipping out a little memorandum pad "and reducing everything to figures." To the men who sat on a mud throne, kings of a primitive, lush, outspilling new empire, Rockefeller's passion for business economy, not just pinching pennies but peeling them, was disgusting. They might have understood better if they'd known how many times in his poverty-shadowed childhood his Puritanical mother had told him, "Willful waste makes woeful want."

Yet oddly enough, he was the one in the firm who had an uncanny talent for borrowing vast sums of money for expansion. When William in New York got a telegram in code from John saying only "Amelia," it meant "I got the money! Everything is lovely and the goose hangs high."

It was lovely indeed; Henry Flagler, whom John had first known in the grain business, came into the firm as his right-hand man, and by 1868 Rockefeller, Andrews and Flagler had the largest refinery in the world. Its size enabled Flagler to get a freight rebate of around fifteen cents a barrel on the forty-two-cents carrying charge on crude oil from Venango County to Cleveland. There was nothing unusual about the practice then; several other Cleveland firms got rebates, and Sam Downer, the Corry refiner, said boomingly to Flagler, "I'm opposed to the whole system of rebates and drawbacks—without I'm in it!"

In an era when railroad magnates behaved like robber barons, carving up spoils with the Tweed ring, Rockefeller's practices in the 1860's had no unusually strong odor. In fact, speculators were up to far more destructive tricks with the oil business. In 1868, a group of European bankers financed a ring to get control of the whole vast oil export trade. With the conniving of American speculators, they began inflating the price of crude like a balloon, but new wells flowed so lavishly that they couldn't keep it up.

The most mammoth oil corner of all hit the industry just when Jay Gould and Jim Fisk were trying to corner gold. A group of Pittsburgh refiners teamed with the Pennsylvania Railroad * to raise a joint kitty

---

* Actually, it was a subsidiary of the Pennsylvania, the Allegheny Valley Railroad; passengers on its rickety twisting tracks called it the Valley of the Shadow line.

of one million dollars to buy up enormous quantities of crude. The ring went about this so deviously that dozens of producers and agents signed contracts promising delivery, without smelling a rat. Nice to relate, the syndicate got squeezed in its own tight corner, caught with a half-million barrels they had to sell short. Not that it was good for anybody concerned. The Titusville *Herald* said bitterly:

> The conspirators are architects of their own or of others' ruin. And yet they are all honorable men, and some of them perhaps raised the communion cup to their lips, and bowed to the prayer, so that they might be enabled to do unto others as they would that others should do unto them.

A new series of bullish schemes, mainly by producers, to send up the price of crude made the going disastrously rough on small refiners. Their main product was still kerosene, but by 1870 they had to sell it for just half the price they'd got in 1865. Too many new firms had bobbed up and now the weaker ones crawled along a suicidally narrow, overcrowded ledge: the shrinking margin of profit. A Titusville man summed up their plight in a mournfully angry letter to the Pittsburgh *Gazette:*

> Refined is so low that refiners cannot run their works. Many have suspended because they cannot pay the price for crude and sell it at the price that refined has been so long. Taking present prices as a basis, refineries cannot make even cost of their stock. . . . Are they willing that the shippers shall make their 33 per cent, and they make their percentages in losses, as many refiners have been doing for the last year?

To add to the din of complaints, both New York and Pittsburgh refiners were howling that because of railroads playing favorites, Cleveland was getting the lion's share of the business and they were getting a starved carcass.

Next, Cleveland set up a counter yelp. The Pennsylvania Railroad had just acquired lines across New Jersey, and had offered Eastern refiners the highest rebates yet. The Pennsylvania's swashbuckling vice-president, Tom Scott, had decided to shove both Cleveland and Pittsburgh aside and build up a fast new freight service directly from Oil Creek to Philadelphia and New York.

The Cleveland *Leader,* pointing out that their city had Mr. Rockefeller's newly incorporated Standard Oil of Ohio, said:

> Fortunately for us, the Erie [Railroad] managers have a keen eye on Mr. Scott and we may rely upon them to so adapt their oil rates to the market that Cleveland refiner interests will not suffer.

Rockefeller still wasn't suffering, but he genuinely disliked the cut-throat competition between cities, and thought the oil industry as a whole couldn't survive without some agreement for mutual control. What he lovingly called "Our plan" was to consolidate all refineries to whittle down waste and end hot and cold skirmishes. Naturally, Standard Oil, being the biggest, wouldn't get lost in the shuffle; it would lead the giant, efficient parade. As a first step he raised capital, mostly from local bankers, to form a merger with other Cleveland refiners. After that, he intended to tackle the firms in other cities, persuade the railroads to end their rate wars, and get the industry to try some self-discipline and end overproducion. Compared to the plan he got involved in, his was a sweet-smelling rose—or beanstalk.

He was staying at the St. Nicholas Hotel in New York, in November of 1871, when Peter Watson of Vanderbilt's Lake Shore railroad brought him a scheme swaddled in the benign sounding title, the South Improvement Company.

It had been thought up by all three major lines to the oil fields—Vanderbilt's New York Central, Tom Scott's Pennsylvania, and Jay Gould's Erie, with their three subsidiary lines—and it was as ruthless and ruinous to nonmembers as anything ever devised by rogues. The gist of it: all the railroads would raise oil-freight rates anywhere from 100 per cent to 250 per cent. Refiners who belonged to the conspiracy would get enormous rebates on everything they shipped, and also *on every barrel their competitors shipped.* The railroads would divide their own share of the spoils evenly.

Rockefeller always insisted afterward that he didn't like the plan and much preferred his own, but that he first had to go along with this scheme because it had the powerful backing of all the oil-carrying railroads. And once he'd said yes, the head of Standard Oil wasn't the man to sit on the sidelines and dabble his toes. He got in it up to his neck, as one of the directors of the new company, and it was perhaps the worst mistake he ever made in his life.

Things still looked fairly simple when he wrote his wife from New York in January of 1872, "We have fully agreed with Mr. Vanderbilt to come into the So. I. Co. as also Mr. Bostwick [a New York refiner], some progress every day but these men (Gould, Harley & others) are *selfish* and cant ask enough, and it is very trying."

It was to be worse than that—more like hell-on-wheels—when the railroading scheme got into the open, but as yet, it was a secret guarded like the gold reserve. Thirteen refiners were already signed up, including Rockefeller. They in turn called in a select group of other refiners to invite them to join, and promised not only the lures of the rebates, but a guaranteed market for all their oil. Before even explaining the details of the plan, they made each man approached sign this pledge:

> I, _____, do faithfully promise upon my honour and faith as a gentleman that I will keep secret all transactions which I may have with the corporation known as the South Improvement Company; that, should I fail to complete any bargains with the said company, all the preliminary conversations shall be kept strictly private; and finally, that I will not disclose the price for which I dispose of my product, or any other facts which may in any way bring to light the internal workings or organization of the company. All this I do freely promise.

> Signed _____

> Witnessed by _____

One of the refiners Rockefeller especially wanted as a member was twenty-four-year-old John Archbold. And because Archbold was to become one of his most obstreperous foes in the battle shaping up, and later was the man Rockefeller chose to succeed himself as head of Standard Oil, it's time to take a look at that ingenuous face, and the dynamo behind it.

John Archbold, the son of a circuit preacher, came to Titusville as a downy lad of fifteen in the early days of oil. He got a job as shipping clerk to William Abbott, the refiner who was also a producer and pipeline operator. The boy was so bright and likable that Abbott soon treated him like my-son-John, and trained him in every facet of the business. In 1866, the Oil Creek line put on a branch called the Farmers' Train that chugged slowly down the seventeen miles from Titusville to Oil City each day, with stops at all the big wells along the way. So many oil men took this three-hour trip that the railroad added a special car for them, and it became an informal oil exchange, a kind of traveling extension of the group that met at the American Hotel. Each day the train left Titusville at 7:30 A.M., and Abbott with his eager, glowing young protégé was often aboard, in the cracker-barrel club car where men sat around the box stove doing business.

Most producers now kept their oil stored with the pipelines, and were given receipt slips for each 1,000 barrels. These certificates made handy currency to use in deals. Agents and refiners bought certificate oil "On the spot," which meant rush; or "Regular" (delivery in ten days); or "Future." Almost all the agreements were verbal, and most oil men's word of honor was as solid as the Mint, although with prices fluctuating so wildly, honor was sometimes a painfully expensive virtue. While they talked out their deals on the train, the boyish John Archbold sat soaking up experience.

It was said later that he'd had so little schooling he had to invent his own system of mathematics, but the practical training he got was better than multiplication tables. At nineteen, he was a partner in Abbott's firm. When that shakily financed business failed, Archbold borrowed $800 from a dump worker and bought into the refinery of Porter and Moreland. By nature, he was an irrepressible Johnny-jump-up, spilling over with gaiety. He captained the local baseball team, could play a nonstop night game of poker, and was one of the founders of the Titusville Literary Association. He did business with the same whirlwind zest; he built up the firm into the largest in town, and championed the producers' battle to keep the price of crude high. When oil slumped again in 1871, Archbold's brash rallying cry was "Four dollars a barrel." Rockefeller, on one of his many trips to Oil Creek, signed the register at the American Hotel, and looked in surprise at what was written on the line above, bold and black:

JOHN D. ARCHBOLD—$4 A BARREL

I think the impulsive Johnny may have written it there partly as the attention-getting gesture of a young man in love; he was smitten with proprietor Major Mills' charming teen-age daughter, whom he later married.

The slogan wasn't Rockefeller's idea of good sense; he was already convinced crude must sell for less, but he was so amused and impressed by the gesture—and Archbold's business record—that he made a point of inviting him to join the South Improvement Company. Archbold turned this down indignantly, and told the schemers that if they thought oil men would submit to this, they had a surprise coming.

Another young refiner who threw the offer back into the face of the SIC was Henry Rogers, and like Archbold, he later became a bright star of Standard Oil. Rogers was a suave ex-New Englander, thirty-two years old, brilliant, magnetic, and witty, but while Johnny Archbold radiated the gaiety and clarity and driving heat of sun, Rogers was the polish and shine and grace—and the tricky bend and thrust—of a dueler's sword. Rockefeller had already spotted him as a coming champ, and was rather hurt at his contemptuous refusal to join the South Improvement Company.

Both Rogers and Archbold, having sworn on their honor as gentlemen to keep their mouths shut even though they'd turned down the SIC offer, kept their word, temporarily. But they or some of the other No-men approached must have managed to drop a few hints. Several newspapers heard rumors and ran up storm signals, although they weren't quite sure yet what was brewing. The Cleveland *Plain Dealer* was closest. On February 21st, it gave warning about "a gigantic little game" of monopolies and railroads.

It's always gratifying when the secret plotting of up-to-no-good conspirators cracks wide-open because of human frailty. All the SIC members were shrewd enough to know they needed more members and more preparation before they put the scheme into operation. The railroads had sent out copies of the new rate rises to their freight agents, with orders to hold them in strict secrecy until they got orders to roll. But a Lake Shore agent got word that his son was dying and was so distraught that when he left the office he forgot to instruct his assistant to hold off on the rate rises. This aide innocently put through the increases right away, jumping freight costs, for example, from eighty-seven cents a barrel to $2.14. An Eastern firm wired their Oil Creek buyer that the new rate was prohibitive, ending irately, "What is the matter?"

By the next day oil men were rushing around asking each other, What *was* the matter? The crowds overflowed into the streets, piecing together the rumors in voices that rumbled with anger. John Archbold, now that the black cat was out of the bag, felt released from the secrecy pledge and told them all he knew. Up and down the Creek the anger rose "like a torpedo filling." When three thousand enraged men met two nights later, in Parshall's Opera House in Titusville, many of them carried banners: "Down with the Conspirators! —Don't Give up the Ship!" John Archbold got up to speak, and described how he'd been approached, and the way he'd told the SIC off. He looked barely old enough to shave, but his bonny youth and bonnier indignation made listeners cheer all the more.

Not much except noise was generated at that meeting, but at least the men knew now what faces this many-headed hydra wore, and they were unmistakably united to fight it. A few days later, they met in Oil City at Love's Opera House, still just as mad, but ready to get down to business. They reactivated an old Oil Creek association under a new name: Petroleum Producers' Union, with a board of directors headed by Captain William Hasson of Oil City, whose family had owned most of the town when it was still Cornplanter. Fellow directors included Henry Beers, co-owner of the famous freak-rhythm * Yankee well, and Captain Jacob Vandergrift who had devised the first oil-tanker barges down the Allegheny River to Pittsburgh. Vandergrift was another of the men Rockefeller and the SIC had hankered after who had turned them down.

John Archbold, who'd been elected secretary, made another fight talk for union "against the common enemy." A producer got up and said he'd finally figured out why it was called the South Improvement

---

* The Yankee flowed seven minutes, stopped for twenty minutes, and never varied from this stop-and-go schedule. The only one more freakish was the Sunday well—it wouldn't flow on weekdays at all.

Company—because it planned to enslave even white men. The handsomest and strongest speaker that night was young producer Lewis Emery, and he turned out to be the most stickatitive oil-man opponent Rockefeller ever had. Emery kept on battling Standard Oil, with courage and brains and cool-headed independence, all his life. That evening he gave the buzzing mob of men their first clear battle plans. Every producer should cut his production down by one-third; no new wells would be drilled for thirty days. Union members would agree not to sell crude oil to any agent of the South Improvement Company or ship it on any SIC railroad. Emery's resolution passed with a roar of approval. There'd be no trafficking with the enemy.

To keep their memory fresh on just who the enemy was, the editor of the new Oil City *Derrick,* Coleman Bishop, ran a black list under the masthead day after day, naming the president of the SIC and seven directors, including Rockefeller.

Bishop had come down from Chautauqua Lake, where as editor of a Jamestown paper he'd already built up an awesome reputation for speaking his mind in print. Once the naval hero who had captained the *Monitor* when it sank the *Merrimac,* Commander Cushing, stomped into Bishop's second-floor office yelling that he'd come to horsewhip the blankety-blank editor and throw him out the window. Bishop said happily, "Try it." He then threw the truculent Commander downstairs, and his whip after him.

The Commander must never have caught up with him, because when Bishop got to Oil City, he was still in fine fighting trim. He bought out the weekly *Times* in partnership with two other men, and planned a daily of the same name. At least his partners thought that's what they were doing, but Bishop had a wee surprise up his sleeve, confided only to the foreman. Early on the first morning of publication, in September of 1871, sleepy citizens heard raucous yells on the streets: "Here's your derrick. Come get your derrick!" In an oil town, people tumbled out of their houses fast to investigate. They found newsboys hawking Bishop's surprise baby, a paper with the now-famous masthead of a derrick spouting newspapers over the top.

Even that first issue gave a hint of what the *Derrick* would later become under Pat Boyle. A long report on Petroleum markets vied on the front page with news of the Franco-Prussian war and New York's plans to welcome visiting Grand Duke Alexis. From then on, no foreign wars and no dukes, not even domestic scandal, ever got as much coverage as oil in the *Derrick*. Bishop hired John McLaurin, whom I've already mentioned as the rollicking best of all oil writers, to be a roving correspondent from Venango down to Parker and later up to Bradford. For variety, Mark Twain's brother, Orion Clemens, wrote special features. McLaurin said that Orion was the exact opposite of Twain: "His forte was the pathetic. He could write up the death of an insect or a reptile so feelingly that sensitive folks would shed gallons of tears over the harrowing details."

The trouble was that Orion wanted to spend weeks on each of these tearful prose gems, and his editor, probably sniffling a bit too, had to let Clemens go. It's probably just as well he was gone before the SIC battle started, because that was a fray for seasoned newspapermen, and Bishop was seasoned—with wit and red pepper. Each day he thought up a new name for the monster, the SIC, to run as a caption under the black list in the *Derrick*: "Behold the Anaconda in All Its Hideous Deformity" was one, but it never caught on like "Octopus."

For the third mass meeting held in Franklin, a local artist did a mammoth charcoal cartoon showing SIC President Peter Watson being tossed by a bull while he tried frantically to grab its tail and his scared fellow schemers scuttled to safety. Sketched around this bull-fight scene were the Region men hollering jubilantly, "No oil for the Ring!" When this rowdy masterpiece was unrolled like a chart and hung behind the speaker's chair, the audience's cheers fairly lifted the roof. "After the fun subsided, the meeting proceeded to business."

The Independents were so full of fighting spirit that a bit of the energy was bound to run a-gley. The SIC's president, Watson, owned storage tanks in Franklin, and somehow all the oil was let out and run into the ground. Watson cried over spilt oil, but he cried even louder over his honor being impugned. Producers had misunderstood his intentions, he said; he and the SIC directors had *meant* to include them all in this do-good scheme, but somehow they just hadn't got around to mentioning it. A broad-minded member of the

Producers' Union invited Watson to come and present his side before a meeting, but he nervously refused to appear in that overcharged atmosphere.

He'd have been crazy if he had. Feeling was running so hot and high that workmen with the barest connection to SIC were in danger. For instance, member-refiner Bostwick had a plant at Titusville that became a target for angry oil men. When they tried to get in to wreck some stills and raise general hell, most of the employees ran off in a hurry. Only two were lion-hearted enough to face the mob: Joe Seep, a bald, pink-faced, sweet-natured German who was Bostwick's oil buyer—and the rough-tongued, fast-moving County of Clare Irishman Dan O'Day, head of the firm's transportation. They stood guard for weeks, and even slept at the plant, to hold off marauders.

Tempers were triggered so edgily that the two men were brought before a special meeting of the Titusville Oil Exchange, to answer charges of aiding and abetting the enemy. When both Seep and O'Day said honestly they knew nothing whatsoever about SIC and didn't even know Bostwick had joined it, their accusers leaped up and closed in on them, yelling and shaking their fists. In that touch-and-go moment, Seep remembered later, "Little John Archbold, his boyish face aglow, rose out of that meeting of angry, bearded, husky men and in his manly voice protested against the proceedings. He said we shouldn't be held responsible for the views or doings of our employers."

Archbold's listeners calmed down, and returned to their seats rather sheepishly. As the tense weeks went on, most of the Region men admitted that Seep and O'Day showed a courage they had to admire. (Mr. Rockefeller admired it even more; he was already planning how to reward them.)

The fighters on the Independents' side were just as stout-hearted. Small well owners who couldn't afford the loss of revenue still held resolutely to the stoppage pledge, and refused the higher-than-market prices offered for their oil by SIC agents. (Ida Tarbell's father turned down a fat offer for an entire year's output.) Millionaire producers took their turn on the nightly patrol of all wells, hiking or on horseback, to make sure no bootleg drilling went on, and no furtive shipments. The night the Independents heard that a renegade member was shipping out 5,000 barrels to Standard, men surged to the tank cars and made an implacable human blockade. The attorney for their Union, Roger Sherman, the young lawyer who had started out at Pithole, was working around the clock on the legal front. He drew up a petition to the State for a free pipeline bill, and sparked the committee that went down to Washington to ask Congress to investigate this interference with free trade.

The young Franklin lawyer, "radical" Sam Dodd, went to Harrisburg to speak in the State Legislature, with white-hot words and ice-clear logic, against the rebate system, and to demand that the charter of the SIC be repealed. Actually, the Legislature had no business issuing such a loosely worded, sky's-the-limit charter in the first place, to the Pennsylvania Railroad's Tom Scott. Several members of the SIC explained aggrievedly that if Tom just hadn't happened to have that old charter lying around handy, they would have gotten a new one in the name of the American Co-operative Association.

If the definition of *co-operative* that year was the greatest good for the smallest number, then the alternate name would have been dandy. Even in so rough-and-ready an era of plunder, the country as a whole was shocked by the SIC, and a good part of the press hollered "Robbery." The *Sun* called it "one of the most villainous schemes ever known." The *Tribune* said, "Under the thin guise of assisting in the development of oil refining in Pittsburgh and Cleveland, this corporation has simply laid its hand upon the throat of the oil traffic with a demand to 'stand and deliver.' "

To the great honor of Oil Creek, almost no one delivered—not then. For forty lean, tense, proud days, the embargo went on. The SIC member railroads got none of their freight. The monopoly refiners got not one drop of their oil.

The heads of the railroads were the first to cry Uncle. By the end of March, a committee of twelve men from the Producers Union went east to give their terms for ending the blockade. It gratified their pride that the powerful Tom Scott came humbly to their hotel, to say the Pennsylvania line was finished with SIC. The president of the New York Central, the bluff Commodore Vanderbilt, said it was his son William who had made the SIC deal; he explained to the oil men, "I *told* Billy not to have anything to do with that scheme."

At the final meeting of the Producers' committee with all the railroad heads, Rockefeller and Peter Watson tried to get in, but the oil men refused even to talk to them. A *Times* reporter saw the two tycoons cooling their heels in the corridor, and said they went away "looking pretty blue."

Mr. Rockefeller didn't look blue for long. Although the SIC charter had been repealed, Standard was stronger than ever by the time the Oil War was over. It had absorbed twenty out of twenty-six Cleveland refineries, and this had only whetted Rockefeller's appetite.

Early in May, he and Henry Flagler, with three Pittsburgh refiners—all ex-SIC members—arrived in Titusville as a peace-it-should-be-wonderful delegation. They were all dressed as elegantly as if they'd come for a wedding, and in fact it was a new form of matrimony, not a shotgun match, they had in mind. Their plan was a voluntary alliance of all refiners—no coercion, just friendly cooperative control for the good of the industry.

The *Derrick* screeched like a siren, warning its readers: *"Timeo Danaos et dona ferentes!* Liberal translation: Mind your eye when the Cleveland refiners get generous."

Just the same, even the Independents admitted something drastic did have to be done, to control ruinous overproduction. And the new plan sounded so sensible that even several of the strongest ex-foes fell into step as friends. The hold-outs, Lewis Emery, Captain Hasson and others, called them bitter names: deserters, ringsters. But the unity was broken; oil men were tired of stoppage for high principles; they wanted sales at high prices, and that's what the new association promised. By the end of that summer, four-fifths of the firms in the United States belonged to the National Refiners Association, with Rockefeller as president.

He didn't want the best men just as allies, he wanted them working for Standard, and he got a prize bag in those next years, with John Archbold and Henry Rogers heading the converts. The Producers' Union attorney, Roger Sherman, became a lawyer for Standard, but after five years he swung back to what was left of the Independents and their union. When Sam Dodd of Franklin joined Standard as head counsel and wrote the first trust, even ex-colleagues who felt sorrowfully that he'd betrayed a cause admitted he would never have done it for money or power. One old friend said, "I guess it was just too interesting a problem in corporation law for Dodd to resist."

Quite a few producers and refiners on Oil Creek sold out to Standard, thankfully or greedily. Others only came to it when they'd been harassed and obstructed or pressured to the breaking point. On the surface at least, most of these mergers seemed affably, impersonally Big Business, but I think the most poignant line of the whole long March of Progress was the cry of one producer: "The Standard would swallow us without chewing."

There seems to be no question that Standard had the best labor policy, and perhaps the fairest system of rewards for service, of any vast outfit of that day. When it took over the Bostwick refinery, Rockefeller immediately showed his deep gratitude to Joe Seep and Dan O'Day for the way they'd stood up loyally and risked their necks for their firm during the stoppage war. Joe Seep became head buyer for Standard and remained that for almost forty years, and even Independents who cursed his employer adored and trusted him. (On his seventieth birthday, when he was still actively on the job, Standard sent him three hundred rosebuds, and oil men of every shade and conviction joined in flowery but almost tearfully sincere tributes to their beloved Joe, "the man who's never made an enemy.") He and O'Day had been close friends ever since they'd turned the plant into a two-man fortress held against the mobs. They even had an amiable rivalry over which one would have more children. Joe Seep won—with eleven. The two men used to trade keepsakes like small boys. On one convivial evening, each solemnly cut the buttons off his shirt and handed them to the other. Their wives said that was carrying the keepsake business too far.

Dan O'Day was in charge of building a pipeline system for Standard and drove the job through with such vim that he soon had a line to the Clarion field, and then to Bradford. By the end of 1876, Standard had grafted onto its own network a dozen other small lines and called the over-all system the American Transfer Company. Next, Mr. Rockefeller aimed his cool blue gaze at Captain Vandergrift's line, and when he heard through his own private pipeline to banking circles that the Captain was short of money, he moved with his usual speed. Standard Oil paid about $230,000 for a third interest in the line. They also had Captain Vandergrift to head it, a defection that shook the Oil Creek Independents, because he had been one of their sturdiest pioneers. His pipeline, plus Standard's American Transfer Company, covered four hundred miles, and had a tank capacity of 1,400,000 barrels.

For the late nineteenth century, these operations were so Gargantuan that you wouldn't have thought they'd lend themselves to tall stories, but the most famous storyteller of the oil fields was no respecter of size. Anything Standard could do, Gib Morgan could improve on in the telling. He was a tall, grizzled man with an outsize hat cocked jauntily over one blue eye, and a blue flannel shirt to match. During the Civil War, his stories had made him the pet of his regiment, the Venango Grays. As a driller and roustabout afterward, and a man who gravitated to a saloon as naturally as the tide to the moon, Gib was a wandering minstrel with derricks for castles. Old-time listeners have tried to describe the special flavor of his voice, and the way he built up suspense. Perhaps Gib and his stories can't be yanked out of their smoke-hazed liquid context and put flat and neat on paper, but I'll try one or two, and you needn't stop me if you've heard them. If you're an oil man, you've heard them, all right.

Gib liked to tell about the time he built a pipeline clear from Oil Creek to New Jersey tidewater, for the Scarcely Able Oil Company. His crew on this job numbered in the thousands, and his cooking and feeding arrangements were somewhat unusual, but nicely geared to the traditional appetites of pipeliners. The pancake batter was mixed in a 100-barrel tank. The griddles were fifty feet square, and they were greased by three active colored boys who strapped sides of bacon on their feet and skated hither and yon. The heat on the iron griddles was pretty fierce, so the boys had to be spelled right often.

Just after the pipeline was finished, Gib said, his helper Big Toolie received the shocking news that his wife, who lived in New Jersey, was about to elope with a coal man—the worst disgrace an oil man could face. How to get Big Toolie there from Oil Creek in time to halt this horrendous betrayal? Gib solved it in a hurry: he would send Big Toolie right through the new pipeline. He gave the traveler a box lunch to take along: a gallon of rum and two dozen wild-turkey sandwiches. Then he wished him Godspeed and piped him through. But Gib had forgotten to warn Big Toolie about the *Y* in the line where one arm branched to New York, so Big Toolie arrived in two pieces. He was only half a man, and that still should have been enough to beat a coal rival, but he couldn't seem to pull himself together in time.

Some of the stories inspired by Standard weren't as genial as Gib's. Rockefeller heard echoes of the continued hostility, and he was disturbed at the way the Oil Creek press stayed stoutly on the side of the Independents, with the *Herald* and the *Derrick* in the lead. At some point—and it may have been as early as 1876—Standard quietly acquired, through an agent, an interest in the *Derrick*. The paper's founder, Bishop, had been frozen out earlier because his partners found him too free-swinging a crusader to have around. There was a rumor that in retaliation for his hammer-bill attacks on the old SIC, and his blasting of rebates and monopolies, the railroads had threatened to remove their shops from Oil City if he didn't shut up. Bishop wasn't a man to be muzzled. He eventually became editor of the humorous weekly *Judge*. The *Derrick* went rapidly downhill in the next years, and there was a time when it burbled so much praise of Standard that one Independent called it the *Emetic*.

When Pat Boyle came riding to the rescue in 1885, the *Derrick* was a limp little four-page sheet that had lost all its spirit and all but a few local readers. Boyle, as the new owner and editor, promptly subheaded it "The Organ of Oil"—and built it up to be just that. He put in daily reports from out-of-state fields and opened branch offices wherever big strikes flowed. The *Derrick* collated pipeline storage figures, described improved methods of production, and ran market quotations from all foreign and domestic exchanges. All that and trade gossip too. Every oil man—millionaire or pumper, monopolist or lone-wolf producer—had to read it to know what was going on.

There are rambunctious newsmen who seldom fight for the principle of the thing, but for the sake of a good rousing fight. Pat Boyle was soon ardently in the thick of the battle on behalf of Standard Oil, throwing invectives like stink bombs at independent-minded critics in and out of Venango. He referred to a rival editor, for instance,

as "that addlepated, monkey-eyed, monkey-browed monogram of sarcasm and spider-shanked, pigeon-witted public scold, Major Bilge-
water Bickham and his back-biting black-mailing, patent medicine
directory, the Journal."

Even in a name-calling era, this was considered a bit thick.

But as even Ida Tarbell has said, any writer on oil must turn
gratefully to the *Derrick* files for the best statistical records.

Of the people who were around in the first oil rush, Miss Tarbell
is the only one I ever met, when she was in her bustling eighties, and
I in my brooding twenties. It was rather a command appearance:
she wanted to see me because we had both gone to Allegheny College
and we were both from the oil region, and I was a beginner writer
who'd had a few pieces in a magazine. She said gaily that day, "I
hope you noticed I made *The New Yorker* myself this year. My
family bet me I couldn't sell them a piece and I bet I could. And I
did!"

I was of the admiring opinion, and still am, that Ida Tarbell could
do anything she set her brilliant mind to. She was certainly the best
foe Rockefeller ever had. He once said crossly to a colleague, "That
Miss Tarbarrel!"

In the early 1900's, her famous series for *McClure's* on Standard
Oil helped spark a new congressional investigation, and the ruling
that this trust violated the Sherman Act. When the Court ordered
Standard to divest itself of subsidiaries, thirty-odd companies splin-
tered off, almost exactly a half-century after Rockefeller had put his
carefully counted savings into the Excelsior Oil Works.

Now that I've looked at a few million words on the subject, it
seems to me things weren't as bogey-man versus brave, happy, prosperous independent brotherhood as Miss Tarbell believed, although
by instinct and upbringing I too am on the side of the independents.
But the oil industry in the early 1870's was a too-fast-grown giant
that hadn't learned to co-ordinate. It was being tossed up and gored
by bulls, mauled and bashed by the bears; it devoured too greedily
and spent too recklessly, and brawled too wastefully. Rockefeller
helped give it stability, direction, coherence, and the strength to survive against foreign giants. And if at times the process carried un-
dertones of "He made the trains run on time," many oil men who

were in a position to know felt that far more good than harm resulted. Other oil men thought the monopoly was a monstrous evil, and they too were in a position to know—hugged by an octopus.

Pro-Standard men said it was used as a punching bag for anybody with a grievance. John McLaurin, who as a roving correspondent talked to thousands of oil men, wrote indignantly:

> If a man in Oildom drilled a dry-hole, backed the wrong horse, lost at poker, dropped money speculating, stubbed his toe, ran an unprofitable refinery, missed a train or couldn't maintain champagne-style on a lager-beer income, it was the fashion for him to pose as the victim of a gang of conspirators and curse the Standard. . . . This trick is as old as the race. Adam started it in Eden, Eve tried to ring in the serpent and their posterity take good care not to let the game get rusty from disuse! . . .
>
> The Standard, regardless of malevolent assaults and villainous distortions of facts, goes right on with its business of furnishing the world with the best light in the universe.
>
> Russian competition, the extent and danger of which most people do not begin to appreciate [this was in the 1890's] was met and overcome by sheer tenacity and superior generalship. . . . Deprived of the invincible bulwark the Standard offered, the oil-producers . . . would have been utterly helpless. The Muscovite bear would have gobbled the trade of Europe and Asia, driving American oil from the foreign markets. . . .
>
> Instead of ranking with the busiest, happiest and most prosperous quarters of the universe, as they are today, the oil-regions . . . would have been irretrievably ruined, dragging down thousands of the brightest, manliest, cleverest fellows on God's footstool.

But to put the shoe on the other footstool, Mr. Rockefeller would have been in a sorry mess without all those "brightest, manliest, cleverest fellows," the oil men. Starting from scratch, they improvised the whole marvelously ingenious business of getting oil out of the ground. Some of them lost their last dime down a hole, but very few lost their spunk, or a daring that strode through the mud and confusion with seven-league boots.

Certainly it would be twisting the facts into a pretzel to picture the lusty, still-roaring Oil Region of the 1870's as conquered territory or a company town. In fact, although Mr. Rockefeller did much more good with his money, other new millionaires were having much more fun with theirs, and some of the quick-change acts were enough to glaze your eyeballs. One observer said tartly, of an up-from-the-mud millionaire: "He washed his face and the disguise was perfect."

F O U R T E E N

Pure gold rig

People liked to quote Mrs. Means' jovial, "While you're a-gittin, git plenty, I say," to describe how the first oil princes waded in with both feet and grabbed their green-gold fortunes. But for a lot of them, it was even more a case of "While you're a-spendin, spend plenty."

Western Pennsylvania was still the magic Oildorado, but now a mud throne wasn't enough. There had to be palaces for the kings, and royal trappings—or what passed for royal trappings in a town that had been a primitive village ten years before. Titusville got its first fancy mansion in 1870, the start of Millionaire Row on East Main Street. Jonah Watson had been the first oil millionaire on the creek, and it was only fitting, people felt, that he should build the first mansard-roof palace and emerge as the Grandest Tiger in the Jungle, with rare orchids and other exotic tropical plants "jamming the $50,000 conservatory."

I've already mentioned that he had twelve gardeners tending the grounds, but it must have been a bit hard to see the flowers for the furbelows. All the beds were laid out in mammoth designs: the national flag in red, white and blue, with no smidgen of Kelly green grass allowed to mess up the patriotic hues. There were also galaxies: huge yellow stars of chrysanthemums; and floral designs of shields, like a family coat of arms. In the center of the fish pond, which was wider than the great wooden fretworked mansion, there was an island with another garden on it. You crossed to it by a stone bridge, or if you were a dainty female or midget, you rode in a tiny white boat with silver oarlocks.

The mansion's dining hall was suitable for serving a wild boar's head on a silver platter, and it contained what is still my favorite décor of any oil-spouted household: two carved wooden moose heads topping the huge marble-slabbed sideboard. Fox hunting had just become fashionable up north, and big-game hunting had always been a sport of kings. But Jonah Watson didn't want to hunt tigers or moose—he wanted to hunt more oil—and yet a man who builds the town's first mansion must obviously do the manly, fashionable thing. So his hunting trophy was wooden, and a very sensible idea too, vermin-proof and easy to dust. Admittedly, it's the sort of thing a wife might think up, but I don't think Jonah's wife should be given credit for this, because she was more entangled with spiritualism than ever, and if her spirits levitated, they never rose as high as moose antlers. Maybe the star-design flower beds in the garden were her doing, because astrology was going great guns, competing with crystal balls and trances, but the wooden stag at bay was, I wager respectfully, all Jonah's.

It was the gardens that delighted the townspeople. For ten hectic years they'd been surrounded by tree stumps and oily mire; now the earth that had grown only derricks and shanties was blossoming with color and elegance. "Choice flowers are counted by the acre," one visitor to Jonah's exulted. Marveling over the exquisitely weeded floral designs, a reporter rejoiced: "The aesthetic is in danger of being neglected in the turmoil and bustle of our busy town, and everything like this tends to revive it."

If aesthetics was in danger of being neglected before, it now got such a workout it was in danger of dropping dead from overexertion. The race toward Beauty was on. Oil man George Anderson, a restless bounding-about man with quirky eyebrows and lively glands, soon had a garden that made Jonah's look like a stamp album. Near the Grapery, a fountain the size of a small ballroom had stone urns all around the rim, filled with even more exotic blooms than those jamming Jonah's conservatory. There were marble swans hissing jets of water, and stone lions' heads spouting right back at them. Even a plain common garden variety of fountain had never before been seen in Titusville—just watering troughs for horses—so this was Versailles, only better. The *pièce de résistance* was an outsize statue of Hebe, the goddess of plenty, pouring water from a pitcher. Why nobody thought to have her pour claret lemonade I don't know, but I guess Hebe's waterworks were complicated enough, because a plumber had to come *all the way from Philadelphia* to attach her pipes and keep her flowing. At the time, George Anderson's wells were flowing $5,000 a day in royalties, so he must have felt he had the goddess of plenty right in his lap, and pouring forevermore. He had himself insured for $315,000, which was reputed to be the largest life insurance policy in the country.

But there's no life insurance for wells, and George's died out much sooner than he did. He tried to recoup by drilling at Bradford, and then by wilder and wilder speculating, but his goddess Hebe had stopped pouring. Or rather, she poured for the next oil man who took over the estate after the sheriff's hammer struck—millionaire Emerson. George Anderson got a clerk job with the New York insurance company that had once written his vast policy, and eventually went out to Mexico and died there. An acquaintance mourned: "No gentle wife or child or valued friend was there to smooth the pillow of the dying man, to cool the fevered brow, to catch the last whisper, to close the glassy eyes and fold the rigid hands above the lifeless breast. Wealthy beyond the dreams of avarice, the confidant of presidents and statesmen, a social favorite, the owner of a home beautiful as Claude Melnotte pictured to Pauline, he drained the cup of sorrow and misfortune."

There was no hint of misfortune in 1871, when George Anderson and twenty other top producers were whisked off in a private car by pipeliner Henry Harley to spend a week in New York as his guests. Harley, ever since he'd hired Pinkerton men to trap the teamsters sabotaging his pipeline, had been gamboling in clover. He was a sleekly plump man, well dressed in a plushy way, studded with huge diamond rings and stickpins, "a high-roller of the brightest stripe." Jay Gould and Jim Fisk, the buccaneers who controlled the Erie Railroad, owned stock in Harley's pipeline; this was a year before the railroads dreamed up the nightmare South Improvement conspiracy, and relations were still so friendly that Jim Fisk himself turned out to welcome the producers from Oil Creek and help Harley show them the town.

When they went to the races at Jerome Park, several of them rode in Jim Fisk's six-in-hand carriage, with two more horses than even Astor and Belmont had, white and black, with gold-plated harnesses, two Negro coachmen in dazzling white livery and two paleface footmen in pitch-black. When the Oil Creek visitors went to the opera, Harley and several chosen favorites went with Jim Fisk in his closed carriage which was modestly upholstered in gold cloth. If Fisk took them to see his notorious, beautiful mistress Josie Mansfield, who had a bosom and hips that outclassed even French Kate's, the producers somehow neglected to tell their wives that, when they got back to Oil Creek. But Josie Mansfield or no, they had been so plied with high living, and so overwhelmed by their host's hospitality, that they decided to show their appreciation by giving Harley a testimonial banquet at the Parshall House, Titusville's splendid new brick edifice. There were tables laid for seventy-five guests, with centerpieces of great macaroon mounds like igloos, with roses stuck up in the middle. The wines and the menu, it was reported, impressed "even Harley who is accustomed to recherché déjeuners of the metropolis." They ate, among other things:

Green Turtle Soup

Boiled Kennebec salmon with Lobster Sauce

Sweetbreads larded with Spinach

Saddle of South Down mutton

Green peach pie with French kisses and Spanish kisses.

The climax came with the green peach pie, when the producer-hosts presented Henry Harley with a bowl they'd had made up for him at a cost of $3,700. It was sterling silver, weighing thirteen and a half pounds, gold-lined, with pure gold rigs for handles. The outside was beautifully engraved with a series of scenes depicting every minutest operation in the drilling of a well. The driller held a temper screw that was accurate to the last thread. The bowl's ladle was shaped like a barrel, and the handle was sections of gold pipe adorned with gold and silver stopcocks.

This token—and the whole affair—was a wham-bang success and nobody begrudged a penny of it. Oil men as a whole were the most open-palmed easy-come, easy-go givers, and that's what makes their neglect of poor Drake so puzzling. After he'd lost everything in the oil brokerage venture in New York, Drake had written the druggist in Titusville:

> My old Friend Wilson
>
> If you have any of the milk of human kindness left in your bosom for me or my family send me some money. I am in want of it sadly and am sick
>
> Yours Fraternally
> E. L. Drake

Six months later he wrote again:

> Friend Wilson
>
> For God sake send me some money I am in want of some have been sick most of the time since I was out there and need money to pay board for my family, direct to me at no 59 Liberty St New York as before.

Every now and then, in the fast-pitched next years, some oil man would say, "We ought to raise a fund for Drake. I hear he's in a bad way," and his listeners would agree cheerfully and nothing got done. Their consciences must have given a sharp jerk when in 1869 the *Herald* ran Drake's obituary, copied from a New England paper, saying he'd died in an almshouse. It was weeks before anyone learned that the obituary had got the wrong man. Edwin Drake was still alive and kicking, but kicking feebly. A friend had loaned him and his wife and four children a seaside cottage in New Jersey near Long Branch, named in that gruesomely sprightly manner of resort real estate, Highlands-of-Never-Sink. The dank, foggy cold there had made Drake's spinal neuralgia worse than ever; his wife was supporting them by sewing, and they lived mostly on potatoes and salt. Things got so desperate she scraped together the fare for Drake to go over to New York to look for work for himself or his twelve-year-old son. He had already been turned away at the Customs House

and was walking along the wharves by the warehouses when an old
Titusville friend, Zeb Martin, an oil buyer, saw him limping along.
It shocked Zeb to see Drake wearing the same long black coat he'd
worn ten years before; both he and the coat looked worn to a frazzled
thread. Zeb took the exhausted, gaunt man into a restaurant for a
good dinner, gave him a twenty-dollar bill, and promised to spread
the word when he got back home.

Jonah Watson and Drake's old friend, storekeeper Reuel Fletcher,
headed the list of Titusville men who rallied and called a meeting in
Corinthian Hall, where the vigilante committee had sat in judgment
on arson suspects a few years before. The men who listened that December night, clothed in their warm alpaca and broadcloth, and
their smug prosperity, might well have sat in judgment on themselves when a letter was read describing a visit to Drake's miserable
seaside refuge. The nameless friend who had gone there wrote:

> I found them . . . without any of the comforts of life, and living
> on the bare floor. . . . I am sure the picture of Colonel Drake's
> home would open the heart of any one who has a soul to do good.
> In speaking to the Colonel about there being snow enough in
> Titusville for sleighing, he exclaimed with tears in his eyes, "Thank
> God we have not had much cold weather here. What should we do
> without fuel and my children's shoes worn out, and comparatively
> nothing in the locker, and I a cripple, if we had a very cold winter?"

Several of the listeners at the meeting protested that if Drake had
stayed in Titusville they would never have let him suffer such want.
If only they'd *known*. And now that they knew, why, the whole Region would join them in raising money. They'd raise enough, they
said, to buy a house and bring Drake and his family back to Titusville
to live out his days in comfort. There were emotional speeches about
how much they owed him—"the man who had laid the foundation
of so many splendid fortunes and had pioneered the way to the
grand spectacle of industrial activity witnessed in all this region."

And for a day or so, there was a surge of enthusiasm; the committee collected about $3,000 in pledges overnight, and some cash.
Fletcher sent $200 of this right on to Drake. But from then on their
campaign raised more arguments than money: Was Drake really the

pioneer, the discoverer of oil? Hadn't he been just an employee of an oil company who did what he was told? So why did he deserve contributions?

The *Herald* answered these carpers furiously:

> Colonel Drake was voted a visionary and a fool. The company neither paid the well's debts nor advanced for expenses,* and Colonel Drake "played it alone." And the well was only finished by the individual credit of Col. Drake, and loans and endorsements from well known citizens of Titusville . . . After oil was struck, when the well was a success, the New Haven company sent on their representatives to settle but not before . . . Colonel Drake was the first to conceive the idea, and to execute the work of oil development.

But still the oil men argued; in the next year, they donated, altogether, $4,833.53—about what they'd spent on the banquet and silver bowl with gold-rigged handles for the bluff Henry Harley. One-fourth of the money had been forwarded in driblets, and the balance was sent to Drake's wife because people said Drake himself never could handle money—why, he'd been known to tip a stable boy twenty-five cents.

A year later, the State of Pennsylvania voted an annuity of $1,500, "to the said E. L. Drake or to his widow in the event of the death of the said Drake."

That "angel of mercy," Mrs. Drake, wrote the *Herald's* editor, Henry Bloss, early in 1880, from Bethlehem, Pennsylvania:

> He has not walked in seven years. . . . We are surrounded by the kindest people living; they are warmhearted sympathizers and have left nothing undone for Mr. Drake's comfort. As long as he was able to be put into a carriage he had one at his command. . . . He is a patient sufferer, taking it as coming from the Lord, who knoweth what is best. He is always bright and cheerful. . . . As he has so many sleepless nights, he has taken an interest in all the new developments of the age. In Titusville we both cherish a deep interest. We hear nothing of it the past few years, but ever remember the exceeding kindness of the good people during our stay in their midst, and of their pecuniary help in our distress a few years since. I trust not one contributor will ever see the need of it as we did at that time. It is very gratifying to me to hear of the Herald's movement

---

* They had advanced $5,000 for expenses and salary, over a period of fifteen months, before deciding they'd squandered enough.

in regard to a suitable monument. Nothing would give me and my children greater pleasure than that his name should be perpetuated in that region. . . .

> Very respectfully,
> Mrs. E. L. Drake

The obituary that appeared that same year was true at last.

Drake's body was moved to Titusville twenty-two years later, to lie under a $100,000 monument donated by Standard Oil's Henry Rogers. The sculptor Niehaus did the bronze statue of a driller, and Pat Boyle, the *Derrick's* editor, wrote the inscription carved on the high-backed granite benches flanking the figure:

> . . . Called by circumstances
> to the solution of a great mining problem,
> he triumphantly vindicated American skill
> and near this spot
> laid the foundation of an industry.

> . . . He sought for himself
> nor wealth nor social distinction,
> content to let others follow where he led,
> at the threshold of his fame he retired,
> to end his days in quieter pursuits.

> His highest ambition
> the successful accomplishment of his task,
> his noble victory the conquest of the rock
> bequeathing to posterity
> the fruits of his labor and industry . . .

But it was an obscure local writer with a true sense of history, Edwin Bell, who carefully and quietly assembled, for over fifty years, the basis of what is now the real memorial to Drake: the collection of early petroliana, unique in all the world, housed in the Drake Museum * outside Titusville.

---

* Dozens of oil men helped make the museum possible. The American Petroleum Institute financed the building and deeded it to the State of Pennsylvania, as an historical park which now covers 229 acres. There's an exact replica of Drake's well, and the collection itself includes his letters, thousands of Mather photographs, oil-sand samples, early hand-forged tools, a spike from the crazy Culver railroad-to-the-moon, and the hotel register Horace Greeley signed at Pithole. If I list any more, you'll think this is a plug—and so it is.

Perhaps the neglect of Drake-alive stemmed partly from the oil pioneers' almost superstitious code, "Accept your luck and no squawking." The idea of a man who'd hit bottom and stayed there, not even trying to sink one more well, was as irritating as the sight of a beggar at a great noisy feast. If you were a real oil man, you behaved as if the next strike was just around the corner. One producer said scornfully, "God has no use for the man a dry hole knocks out."

There was a popular notion that the other side of the coin was, "God helps those who go after gushers, so long as He gets His cut." Religion ran neck-and-neck with race horses as a worthy object to spend money on, that decade of the Sumptuous Seventies. Sometimes the church contributions must have been given as a kind of fire insurance; people who'd catapulted from Spartan living to having money to burn wanted to make very sure they themselves didn't burn in the Hereafter. They were as nervously preoccupied with God as their descendants would be with Freud.

In Franklin, one of the most talked-about new oil kings poured money into building up the Baptist church, and for over forty years he taught a Bible class of three hundred men, the most famous in the state next to John Wanamaker's in Philadelphia. He did this with one hand, and with the other he fed sugar to his race horses that were collecting trophies at all the major tracks in the country. This was General * Charles Miller, the head of Franklin's rolling-in-wealth Galena Refinery, which furnished rich black lubricating oils for 90 per cent of all the railroads in this country, Canada and Mexico. He and his partner Joseph Sibley launched an era of grand gestures, in private and public relations, that at times must have put even Barnum's nose out of joint. The Oil Region had already been hailed as "the only circus that's even bigger inside the canvas than on the posters." Miller and Sibley held up our end of the show something elegant.

As a thirteen-year-old, Charles Miller had worked in a country store for $35 a year and board. Eight years later he owned the store, which is slightly ahead of Horatio Alger schedule. He was a strong-beaked young man, like a bald-headed eagle, with an almost blazingly

---

* A title from the National Guard.

direct gaze, when he came to Franklin and opened a small store in 1866. Like everybody else, he wanted to get into oil, but he never went lease-gobbling up the creek. Like Rockefeller, he had decided on refining, and soon he took out a patent on a high-pressure lubricant and founded the Galena.

His seven-years-younger brother-in-law, the blond, free-swinging, debonair Joe Sibley, had been clerking in Miller's clothing store, and now he too patented lubricants: valve and signal oils. Mr. Rockefeller, on his visits to Franklin, watched these goings-on approvingly, and by 1878 Standard Oil had bought an interest and reorganized the young men's firm as Galena Oil Works, Limited. (Standard also took over the much larger Eclipse Refinery, just outside town.) Charles Miller was still president of the Galena, and the refinery still manufactured mostly railway oils, under the terse names: Coach, Engine, Car, Machinery, Lubrication.

There was loud rejoicing at the plant when Vanderbilt's New York Central broke the world speed record held by England, rolling up sixty-four and a third miles an hour because it used our good grease. But Miller and Sibley, not content with having Vanderbilt's and other railways their faithful customers, set up a rather astonishing program for keeping them happy. The Galena heads presented Shetland ponies raised on the Miller-Sibley stock farm to engineers who had children —and who oiled their wheels right. They installed a mammoth humidor room at the plant, stocked with fine cigars for customers. Franklin's one modest tobacco shop was kept by Mose Bacharach, a narrow hole-in-the-wall, the entrance guarded by a fierce wooden Indian brandishing an upraised tomahawk. But Mose soon got rich supplying the Galena with tobacco, and the wooden Indian was hauled away and chopped up for firewood.

For years, the Galena sent a local merchant to Europe each fall to pick up worthy Christmas bibelots for railroad magnates. General Miller chugged around the country constantly in his private Pullman, the Franklin, and one admirer said, "Wherever he may be, in New Orleans or San Francisco, conferring with a Vanderbilt or the humblest manager of an obscure road, he is always the same genial, generous examplar of belief in the universal fatherhood of God and the brotherhood of man."

He and Sibley donated the colossal pipe organ to the Baptist church, and snared a well-known Chicago minister by paying most of his salary themselves. But the silver-tongued high-living Sibley wasn't quite the Sunday School type his partner was; General Miller often dumbfounded tycoons by breaking off a business conference to rush halfway across the continent in his private car in time to get home for Bible class. He hardly ever missed a Sunday. He also founded a free night school for local boys who, like himself, had had to go to work when they finished grade school. He had done his own homework brilliantly; his library in the great house on a hill overlooking Franklin contained thousands of leather-bound volumes, but with cut pages, well fingered. Bouguereau-like cupids flew their rosy dimpled buttocks over the bedroom ceilings, and Madame Pompadour would have loved the bathrooms.

Once General Miller asked a dinner guest who'd admired the beautiful china, "Do you know who ate off that plate?"

The guest ran hurriedly over in his mind some of the General's distinguished acquaintances. "Mr. Rockefeller?"

"Rockefeller's a bread-and-milk man," the General said, more in pity than anger. He himself had been born in Alsace, and although he'd come to this country as a child, he still had a Frenchman's palate. "Guess again."

His guest tried other likely visitors: Carnegie, McCormick, assorted railroad tycoons, governors and statesmen. Each time the host shook his head impatiently.

Finally the guest gave up.

"Napoleon ate off that plate," the General said.

And he probably had.

Joe Sibley's first mansion was down on the river bank below French Creek, very near blacksmith Evans' "Dad's-struck-ile" well. It moldered there when I was a child, a top-heavy monstrosity, like something an architect had perpetrated in the throes of indigestion. By then, it was Mrs. Sousa's boarding house, and her meals were no cause for indigestion, but one newcomer sat glowering through dinner each night while the old-timers regaled him with tales of Franklin's past glories, when Miller and Sibley and our other oil princes were top of the heap. The newcomer suffered these gassers in silence for weeks, till finally one night he snapped: "If you people could suck as hard as you blow, the whole Atlantic Ocean would be flowing up French Creek."

Probably one of their brags was about Michael Angelo being brought bawling to Franklin: a prize calf that Miller and Sibley had bought for $12,500. Stock breeders from all over the country—and from South America and Europe—came to see their thousand-acre stock farm, Riveridge, a mile or so outside the town. Sibley had finally built a baronial stone castle there, with terraced vineyards sloping down to the Allegheny River just as if it were the Mediterranean. The grapes grown were measly, not worth trampling on in bare feet, but the effect was very Continental. In the wooded part of the estate, deer and antelope and elk cavorted, and peacocks waddled on the lawn. The stables were relatively modest because Miller and Sibley kept most of their horses at another farm near Meadville, in a stable with two hundred stalls.

At Riveridge, it was the Angora goats and the Jerseys that were noted, and breeding stock like Michael Angelo, almost worth its weight in diamonds.

By then, Franklin had diamonds home-grown, or at least millionaires no longer had to entrain to Pittsburgh or New York to buy trinkets for their wives, mistresses or Sunday School teachers. A New York jeweler, Feldman, moved up to the Oil Region to be where the greenbacks grew thickest, and the carriages beat a path to his door. Liberty Street, where he had his store, got its first paving stones about that time, but Franklinites complained they were "fearfully rough."

Jeweler Feldman designed a spoon especially for the town's new Nursery Club, engraved with a derrick, and the inscription, "Franklin, the Nursery of Great Men."

A Pittsburgh woman invited to come up for a luncheon at the Club was rather surprised to walk into the dining room and find all the chairs entwined in American Beauty roses. Even the legs.

The ladies got *their* first club after Joe Sibley went to Congress. Mrs. Sibley came back from the Capitol and told her Franklin friends about a daring new project there: a literary club for females only. She said with a gay toss of her Carvallo bonnet, "I am sure you ladies in Franklin are just as smart as Washington ladies." They were sure, too, and rightly so. They formed a literary club—the Wednesday Club—that very day, and were the second group in the whole country to join the National Federation of Women's Clubs.

When Joe Sibley ran for re-election to Congress against oil tycoon Lewis Emery of Warren and Bradford, the betting outdid the gambling whirls at Petroleum Centre. Oil men in town were laying their wads on Sibley and taking every bet the Bradfordites offered on their boy Emery. The day before the election, Frankliners decided to stop being pikers with twiddly bets of five hundred or a thousand apiece. They put down a final $100,000—and I don't want to stir up any trouble with Bradford, but the way I heard the story is that their boys *paled* when they covered that last bet. They probably waxed even more waxen as the returns came in. The Galena had two telegraph wires set up in the plant, and six hundred guests gathered for a gala Election Night hope-fest. When the Galena's man Sibley won, Franklin let loose with a jubilee to wake the dead: tin horns blew, bands played, bonfires burned till dawn. I guess they were kind of quiet that night in Bradford. But at the rate wells were spouting there, a few hundred grand in lost bets shouldn't have worried them long.

There were all kinds of fascinating ways to lose money, but Jesse Heydrick, a cousin of Franklin's best-known lawyer, had the freshest approach of all. He and his brothers sold their great Wolverine well at Henry's Bend on French Creek, and the skylarking Jesse went off with his share of the proceeds, about $300,000, to play the market in New York. Not a peep was heard out of him for over a year; he might have dropped from the earth. Then he came home stony broke, as chipper as ever, and explained he hadn't lost one cent to the Wall Street sharpers as rumored. Not at all. He said that right after his arrival there, while he was strolling along a wharf, he had been shanghaied by robbers and borne off to Latin America. He had some dandy stories to tell, of his adventures with Cuban bandits. Then he settled down to make survey maps, some of the best ever done of the oil fields.

He could have lost the $300,000 almost as fast, but with less fun, in his own town's oil exchange. Oil City's was now so big-time that as many as ten million barrels a day were traded there. In fact, the whole town was humping to catch up to Titusville and Franklin. It called itself the Hub, which was fair enough, because it was still the main transportation and shipping center of the Region. And now it was even becoming a fit place to live in, with handsome new houses perched on Cottage Hill on the east side of Oil Creek, "stuck up like pictures on a wall," removed from the muck below.

The town's first mayor, William Williams, had been an outrider on a wagon train in the gold rush. He'd started back by boat from California, ran out of money in Panama, and had to walk across the entire isthmus in the rainy season, but he said even *that* wasn't as mucky as Oil City. Anyway, he started the trend to gracious living when he became mayor in 1871. He had all the lumber for his new house pre-cut in Pittsburgh, and brought up nice and dry.

Oil City got such impressive new churches that when Henry Ward Beecher came there to preach, he said unctuously, "If I were not pastor of the Plymouth Church in Brooklyn, then I would be pastor of a church in Oil City." His listeners were awfully flattered, but later on when the scandals about him started popping like corn in a popper, they were just as glad they hadn't got him. Let Brooklyn keep him, was the shocked consensus, but even Brooklyn found him a handful.

Beecher was quite a lion with the ladies of the parish on his visit, and much more sociable than President Ulysses Grant when *he* came. Grant wasn't much of a ladies' man and he couldn't speak for sour apples, although he did bend down and kiss the little daughter of the proprietor of Oil City's Duncan House. This child put court plaster over the hallowed spot, and was passionately envied by her little un-kissed friends.

The President made pretty much the same speech in Oil City that he made in Titusville, Petroleum Centre, Rouseville and Franklin. (Even a taciturn ex-general has to say something, and say it often, when he's up for re-election.)

> Fellow citizens—I feel very grateful to you for this kind reception. This is my first visit to the oil regions. I am aware that this section of the country furnished its full share of men and means for the suppression of the rebellion, and your efforts in the discovery and

production of petroleum, aided materially in supplying the sinews of war, as a medium of foreign exchange, taking the place of cotton. You are aware this is a much longer speech than I usually make. I again return you my thanks.

The most popular and democratic guest of all was the big, handsome Emperor of Brazil. He came to Oil City in 1875 to visit Andrew Cone, who had been the U. S. consul in Brazil, and his friend Captain Vandergrift, and he stayed in the Vandergrifts' fine new mansion on Colbert Avenue. Don Pedro was as crazy about the Oil Region as its inhabitants were about him: he wanted to see everything. When they were torpedoing a well (down at Foxburg) he watched as eagerly as a small boy while the shooters filled the torpedoes. Then they big-heartedly let the Emperor drop the go-devil, and when the explosion went bang-bang and oil shot into the air, the Emperor clapped his hands gleefully.

He also wanted to see the great Imperial Refinery and oil-tool works outside Oil City, and when he drove there with Captain Vandergrift, crowds lined his route and he kept standing up in the carriage and doffing his broad-brimmed white hat while he bowed.

The Imperial Works was a branch of Oilwell, a company started by a nineteen-year-old that became the largest supplier of oil tools all over the world. One of the employees sent from Oilwell to help the Russians drill at Baku was A. E. Culbertson. He married a Russian girl, and their son Ely Culbertson was never much in the oil business but played a pretty fair game of bridge.

Oilwell kept growing so fast it absorbed other plants like a giant flycatcher; one of the manufacturers who sold out, a Mr. Inglis, was so pleased at the price he got that he promptly called in his sixty-five workers and gave each one a credit slip entitling him to "the best suit of clothes obtainable." A friend thought that was overdoing the largesse, and Inglis said happily, "Oh, no, they deserve it."

With Oil City spreading itself fast and fancily, the sporting residents made sure they kept room for a good race track, probably in what is now Hasson Park. Miller and Sibley had built the best kite track in the country at Meadville, and another track at Franklin, and their race horses played the neighborhood circuit when they weren't running for high purses at Jerome Park and other chic eastern tracks. After their trotting stallion St. Bel, bought from Senator Leland Stanford for $10,000, became a national champion, they turned down an offer to sell him at $75,000.

At the peak of the gambling fever in Petroleum Centre, oil men even held horse races in winter on the ice-covered creek. What gave the betting a special fillip was that nobody ever knew when a horse might fall through. No thoroughbreds like St. Bel were used to break the ice, but commoner beasts provided bloody sport.

Titusville had to have a track now too, naturally. Oil men formed the Driving Park Association and built a half-mile track just west of town, where the June Races were a social event of the Seventies. Spectator costumes were as fancy as the Royal Enclosure at Ascot; if they didn't knock your eye out, the point of a parasol would. Reuel Fletcher, who had loaned Drake his first horse, had a beautiful fast-stepping mare, Lillie, and owned a piece of Jonah Watson's $5,000 filly, Acuff.

There was still a kind of rollicking innocence of enjoyment. All the new toys—the race horses, the statues, the sapphire-blue velvet divans, the china dinner service for fifty with hand-painted sand pumps and rigs—hadn't had time to get broken or tarnished or tiresome. One observer, borrowing the cadences of "Where the Lotus Grows," described this fraternal idyll, this Happy Land:

> Gain is surest, beer is purest
> Word once plighted goes.
> Babes are sweetest, ankles neatest
> Nags are fleetest, joys completest
> Where the oil-well flows.

The Arts were approached with burbling pleasure and a "Look-what-we've-got" satisfaction. Everybody trooped to the Parshall Opera House to see *Rip Van Winkle* and *Camille* and *East Lynne*. The management stuck chairs in the aisles for the eager overflow. The night Clara Louise Kellogg sang there, the *Herald* reported:

> Long before the curtain rose the scene within was one of great animation and brilliancy. The solid men of Titusville, the petroleum aristocracy, the learned professions, the beauty and chivalry of the whole oil region filled the auditorium to do homage to the fair

cantatrice. There was a great deal of fashionable display in dress, hats, shawls, opera cloaks, diamonds, silks, laces, and the fair sex levelled their glasses from point to point with kindling admiration, wholly devoid of a particle of envy or the spirit of criticism.

Obviously a man's-eye view of the fair creatures, but women hadn't yet taken over society reporting. And perhaps no woman would have done quite such fond justice to the singer's figure:

> Miss Kellogg was dressed in great elegance and simplicity, wearing a pink silk, with long trail, the overskirt gathered into a pannier behind. The artiste possesses a form of remarkable symmetry, the poise of the head and columnar neck, the bust that sculptors love to copy and that belongs to Nature's singers, with a finely-rounded arm, whiter than snow and smooth as monumental alabaster. . . .
> She can sound passions as well as sport with lighter sentiments, storming and weeping in tragic vales or heights, as well as dallying with rosebuds amid the twitter of birds in a summer garden.

Townspeople savored new words, like *acoustics,* and chattered proudly about how their fifteen-hundred-seat opera house compared with Milan's. It had one feature they seem to have taken for granted that impresses me mightily: through some carpentering and engineering magic, a great platform rolled out to cover all the seats, "when the hall is required for a ball or festival."

Worth's bustle was in full bloom by now, and nowhere more flouncily than on the behinds of oil queens treading the varsovienne, the lancers and schottische. One much-admired gown of Worth's was of ivory satin, hand-embroidered all over with cherub faces framed in medallions, even on the yards-long train where cherubs are apt to get stepped on.

Tassels swung all over town, from bosoms and hips, from gold brocade draperies, chair tidies and magenta silk candle shades. Young oil matrons had their tintypes taken in pairs, with fichus stuffed about their necks like tissue paper, skirt overdrapes arranged in glued layers, and their heads bent coquettishly close together, as if about to break into close harmony.

Under the new finery, both sexes wore the fashionable new perforated buckskin undergarments, an exclusive item at Carter's store, advertised as "The Great Preserver of Health, a Sure Cure for Rheumatism." And not cheap either. "Gents' Shirts or Drawers, $6; Ladies' Drawers, $5, and a perforated buckskin Victorine for $2."

Everything was getting more expensive; Arbuckle coffee was sixteen cents a pound. But McEowen's wholesale grocery in Titusville did a million dollars a year in business. In the great upper storeroom, the finest jasmine-scented teas and costly nerve-cut tobaccos were heaped against hogsheads of herring and mackerel, and tins of pâté de foie gras. But even McEowen's storeroom couldn't supply enough Lucullan delicacies for the most elaborate event ever staged so far in Oildorado: the wedding of Miss Sadie Farrel in the fall of 1871.

Sadie was the daughter of James Farrel, who had been cheated out of his yoke of oxen and spent $200—a sinful waste of money— to go to court and get title to the cheater's property. Now that his oil royalties from that stony soil had cascaded into millions, no one called it a sinful waste to spend a wad that would choke an elephant on the wedding. Nothing was too good for Sadie, "a natural beauty of the brunette order," who went down the aisle of the First Presbyterian Church in a breath-taking gown of stand-alone white silk with insets of point lace, set off by her simple real pearls.

I myself think the bridegroom must have been even more breath-stopping. This was William Sterrett, the son of another new oil king; he "appeared to the best advantage in a blue dress coat with gold buttons, white silk vest and necktie, white gloves and lavender pantaloons."

His mother had given the lucky young couple a huge Bible bound in Turkish morocco with elaborate gold trimmings and a parlor stand to hold it, inlaid with mother-of-pearl and covered with gold incrustations. Refiner William Abbott's wedding gift to them was a sterling silver berry set of fifteen pieces, gold-lined. There were several solid silver tea sets. More modest remembrances included solid-gold napkin rings, antique bronze vases the size of burial urns, and chased-silver card cases, call bells and nut picks. A thoughtful personal touch was struck by a Mr. Tuttle: "An elegant oil painting executed by himself, and representing the bride and two lady friends reclining beneath a shady tree and surrounded by croquet and other summer implements of pastime."

As for the reception at the Parshall House, it "far exceeded the most extravagant expectations of all present and formed a scene of nuptial gaiety that is seldom witnessed in older and more favored cities."

The Queen City of Oildom really outdid itself that night. "Three hundred guests surrendered to Terpsichore and his enchanting amusement . . . to the irresistible strains of gay waltzes, galops, and polkas, rendered by the band which was from Buffalo and the best to be found in Western New York."

At half-past ten, the galops abandoned, the three hundred guests glided into the dining hall, where the walls were covered with garlands of smilax and mottoes wishing the lavender-pantalooned bridegroom and his lady such felicities as, "May your life be as bright as it seems tonight."

If their married life lived up to that night, it was going some. The banquet alone would have put Epicurus to shame: "All present were accommodated at the same time with seats, and ample justice done to the bill of fare which will challenge comparison with the best efforts of the metropolitan caterers. The many courses of delicacies were served in the proper rotation, and with methodical precision that gave the most perfect satisfaction to all at the festal board." One of the most spectacular dishes, served up in a great heap like John the Baptist's head on a tray, was: A Pyramid of Buffalo Tongues. No wonder buffaloes became extinct.

But the oil men would never become extinct. As some went bust and moved out of Millionaire Row, others took their places in an endless tragicomic game of Musical Chairs. Jonah Watson's house and jungle conservatory was put up for auction in 1876, after he'd drilled a few hundred dry holes too many. His wife had wandered off to California to a more congenial cult of spiritualists than Oil Creek provided. Jonah, an oil man to the last, went on drilling; he had an obsession that wells could be sunk deeper and deeper, and people were pulled between pity and ridicule when he even drilled one thirty-five hundred feet down. (Some of the newest wells are so deep they make that seem like a gopher hole. Jonah was digging beyond his time, always a thankless occupation.) Proud and independent, he went back and revived some of the old wells around the Drake, and got out enough oil to subsist on until he died, "a brave, hardy, indefatigable oil pioneer."

Pipeliner Henry Harley overextended himself in one florid scheme too many, and had to sell or pawn everything, even the $3,700 silver bowl given him by Oil Creek producers. He finally went to jail for fraud. His wife, a charming and cultured woman, insisted on living in jail with him, and received their many callers there with real aplomb. Henry's diamonds were long since gone but he'd had them copied in paste, so he still gave off dazzling rays—and most of his old bonhomie.

Ex-schoolteacher John Fertig, who had taught "quiet," was one of the millionaires who hung on to what he had. Even the puff biographies of that era, which usually read like patent-medicine testimonials, refer in pussy-foot prose to his "frugal, not prodigal nature." While his friends were buying race horses, John wrote a lawyer in town:

> I have concluded to accept your proposition of $175 for my dapple gray riding horse. When shall I deliver him—tonight?
>
> John Fertig

He was mayor three times, with a good thrifty eye on the town budget. Gas lights and wood paving blocks they got, but no gold bricks.

Ex-shoemaker William Barnsdall, who had kicked down the second well on the Creek, was another thrifty mayor, and invested his own money solidly in a business block.

The merry John Archbold went off to dwell in the high unholy upper echelons of Standard in New York, and his mansion in Titusville was taken over by merchant Perforated-Buckskin-Undergarments Carter after he launched a lush new career in oil. Carter's son went east to Andover and Yale, and comes down to us tintyped: posed by a two-wheeler as tall as his shoulder, his bowler tipped on the back of his head and one hand on his hip, truly world-weary nonchalance; and his pants too tight to walk in.

John McKinney, he of the secret code that made "Mince" of a "Rockefeller," operated with his brother James in all the new oil fields in the state before he sold out his holdings to Standard. James took over a mansion which had turrets, battlements, everything but a moat and drawbridge, and he loved the whole show. A friend said beamingly, "He keeps fast horses, handles the ribbons skillfully, can guide a big enterprise or an untamed bicycle deftly, and is companionable and utterly devoid of affectation."

One of the McKinney partners in a well near Butler was John Galey. And Galey went on to team with the ex-Pithole town clerk James Guffey, whose most ringing pronouncement was, "Never take any man's dust in oil or politics."

You may possibly have heard of Guffey and Galey in what we Pennsylvanians think of as their years in exile, after they were called down to Texas to show the natives how to make do, and provided a nice little show near Beaumont, at a cow pasture called Spindletop. The Texans think Spindletop was the greatest, but you know how Texans talk—through their ten-gallon hats. I'll bet they even try to make out that Guffey and Galey were Texans born, bred and bragged.

But the grand-daddy of all the great oil days to come was conceived with guts and laughter and curses and prayers in the mud along Oil Creek. And here's to the bold, bright shades of the men who did it.

FIFTEEN

---◄•►---

Postscript in the present

WESTERN PENNSYLVANIA no longer attracts the wickedest men in the world, but we still have oil in tidy, respectable amounts, and an industry that is modestly prosperous without any vulgar display of air-conditioned, diamond-back Cadillacs. Our state has the third largest refinery capacity in the U. S.: 645,000 barrels a day in 1957, if you throw in Pittsburgh and Philadelphia. Home-grown crude accounted for around 22,500 barrels a day: about 7 per cent from Venango County wells, and over three-quarters from the Bradford fields. The rest of the crude for our refineries is piped in, mostly from the west.

The only derricks left are a few blackened skeletons. Modern drilling rigs are small, and as neat and inconspicuous as our present-day millionaires. Wildcatters are scarcer too. But 328 wells were completed in 1957. Of these, 48 yielded oil (at an average depth of 829 feet), 61 were dry, 210 were gas, and 9 were drilled for underground gas storage. There were 627 secondary recovery wells drilled the same year, a method of forcing up the yield of one oil well by encircling it with four or five that pump water or repressure with gas. One interesting experiment, first tried during World War II, is horizontal drilling. A shaft was sunk 429 feet deep, opening into a work chamber, and from there two wells were drilled sideways through the sand about 2,500 feet. These two horizontal wells are equal to two hundred vertical holes, and are still producing after sixteen years. Recent scientific estimates, rather astonishingly, give 126,490,000 barrels as the amount of crude still in the ground in our state. But with the price of crude low,* smallish wells don't pay off, and companies are concentrating more on petroleum specialty products such as insecticides and paving asphalts. Petrochemicals have bolstered our refineries too. Just the same, western Pennsylvania lubricants, from the oil "black as a stack of ebony cats," still rate sky-high for export.

In the summer of 1958, an oil man spotted greasy seepage in a long-abandoned well at Pithole. When the well was redrilled, lively black oil spurted seven feet into the air, a baby gusher but an astonishing and gala sight in western Pennsylvania these days. It has subsided into a purring 2-barrel-a-day producer, but its leaping debut was a happy omen for Oil's centennial, celebrated in 1959.

The exuberant ex-boomtown of Pithole is beginning to rise from the dead too. The current owner has whacked away the underbrush and marked the once-famous sites of everything from the Chase House and French Kate's to Murphy's Theatre where the oil men tossed a five-hundred-dollar bill as a mash note to Lady Macbeth.

Venango County oil men no longer toss Large Filthy Lucre to deserving young actresses, at least not so you could notice it. We leave all that child's play to a few Heap-Big-Hats who supply joke fodder now, just as Coal Oil Johnny once did. They'll eventually outgrow the shenanigans, or fall down a dry hole and vanish. Meanwhile, all over the world, there are oil men who go right on following their profession with the dedicated verve of petroleum pioneers a hundred years ago. Much more has been written about early gold prospectors, but they never had the same impact on the rushing forces of history, and were pretty flash-in-the-pan compared to oil hunters. The gold-rush days yielded a lot of yellow stuff that's now stuck away in Fort Knox and other burial vaults. But the oil rush changed the pace of the world and greased the wheels into the machine age. It lit up the future, fueled wars and speeded peace, and is still flowing strong. And western Pennsylvania is still proud to call itself oil country.

---

* Although Pennsylvania crude still fetches a higher price than any other in the world.

BIBLIOGRAPHY

Asbury, Herbert. *The Golden Flood*. Alfred A. Knopf, 1942.

Boatright, Mody. *Gib Morgan, Minstrel of the Oil Fields*. Texas Folk Lore Society, 1945.

Bishop, Jim. *The Day Lincoln Was Shot*. Harper & Brothers, 1955.

Botsford, Harry. *The Valley of Oil*. Hastings House, 1946.

Bristow, Arch. *Old Time Tales of Warren County*. Tribune Publishing Co., 1932.

Brown, George. *Old Times in Oildom*. Derrick Publishing Co., 1911.

Derrick Handbook of Petroleum. Derrick Publishing Co., 1898.

Eaton, S. M. J. *History of Venango County*. J. A. Caldwell, 1879.

Eyssen, Marguerite. *Go-Devil*. Doubleday & Co., 1947.

Fleischer, Nat. *The Flaming Ben Hogan*. Press of C. J. O'Brien, 1941.

Floherty, John. *Flowing Gold*. J. B. Lippincott Co., 1945.

Gale, Thomas. *The Wonder of the Nineteenth Century: Rock Oil in Pennsylvania and Elsewhere*. Sloan & Griffith, 1860.

Giddens, Paul. *Birth of the Oil Industry*. Macmillan Co., 1938.

———. *Early Days of Oil: A Pictorial History*. Princeton University Press, 1948.

———. *Pennsylvania Petroleum*. Pennsylvania Historical & Museum Commission, 1947.

Henry, James Dodd. *History and Romance of the Petroleum Industry*. London: Bradbury, Agnew & Co., 1914.

Henry, J. T. *Early and Later History of Petroleum*. J. & B. Rodgers, 1873.

Leonard, Charles (Crocus). *The History of Pithole*. Pithole *Record*, 1867.

McLaurin, John. *Sketches in Crude Oil*. McFarland Co., 1896.

Millard, Joseph. *The Wickedest Man*. Fawcett Publications, 1954.

Miller, Ernest. *Oil Mania*. Dorrance, 1941.

———. *John Wilkes Booth, Oilman*. Exposition Press, 1947.

Miller, James (ed.). *Derrick and Drill*. Privately printed, 1865.

Miller, Max. *Speak to the Earth*. Appleton-Century-Crofts, 1955.

Nevins, Allan. *John D. Rockefeller*. 2 vols. Charles Scribner's Sons, 1940.

Pennsylvania Songs and Legends. University of Pennsylvania Press, 1949.

Porter, Corneila. *Fabulous Valley*. G. P. Putnam's Sons, 1956.

Reynolds, John E. *In French Creek Valley*. Tribune Publishing Co., 1938.

Riesenman, Joseph, Jr. *History of Western Pennsylvania*. 3 vols. Lewis Historical Publishing Co., 1943.

Ross, Victor. *The Evolution of the Oil Industry*. Doubleday, Page & Co., 1920.

Ruggles, Eleanor. *Prince of Players*. W. W. Norton, 1953.

Seep, Joseph. *This Is My Birthday* (Compilation of speeches on Seep's seventieth birthday). Privately printed.

Smiley, Alfred. *A Few Scraps, Oily and Otherwise*. Derrick Publishing Co., 1907.

Smith, Theodore Clarke. *The Life and Letters of James A. Garfield*. Vol. II. Yale University Press, 1925.

Steele, John Washington. *Coal Oil Johnny, His Book*. Hill Publishing Co., 1902.

Tait, Samuel. *Wildcatters: An Informal History of Oil Hunting in America*. Princeton University Press, 1946.

Tarbell, Ida M. *History of the Standard Oil Co*. McClure, Phillips & Co., 1904.

Taylor, Frank (with Earl Welty). *Black Bonanza*. Whittlesey House, 1950.

Tennent, J. C. *The Oil Scouts*. Derrick Publishing Co., 1915.

Trainer, George Francis. *Ben Hogan: The Wickedest Man in the World*. Privately printed, 1878. ·

Way, Capt. Frederick. *The Allegheny*. ("Rivers of America Series.") Rinehart, 1942.

Wright, William. *The Oil Regions of Pennsylvania*. Harper & Brothers, 1865.

SPECIAL SOURCES

Roger Sherman letters in Yale University Library.

Lamb letters, producers' secret code, Pithole city directory and other memorabilia from James Stevenson collection now in Drake Museum. Raymond papers in the Drake Museum, also Townsend and Brewer papers, letters, hotel registers, menus, playbills, etc.

Old clippings on S. C. T. Dodd, loaned by John Budke; also legal documents on land owned by John Wilkes Booth.

Clippings on Milton Egbert and Petroleum Centre, loaned by Mrs. R. L. Browne.

Venango County Courthouse Records.

Anniversary issues of Titusville *Herald*, Franklin *News Herald*, Oil City *Derrick* and *Oil and Gas Journal*. Earliest issues of the *Herald*, Venango *Spectator* and Pithole *Record*. Also New York and Philadelphia papers; Pennsylvania State Archives; articles in *Harper's* and *Atlantic* in 1860's.

Charles Vernon Culver's scrapbook, loaned by Charles Suhr.

ABOUT THE AUTHOR

HILDEGARDE DOLSON was weaned on juicy stories about the early oil boom, growing up as she did in Franklin, Pennsylvania, twenty miles from the first oil well ever drilled, in 1859. "Like most children, I didn't give a hoot about Olden Times," she says. "All I could think of was learning the Charleston and going to live in Greenwich Village." She landed in New York in the depression of the Thirties, wrote advertising copy for Macy's, Saks Fifth Avenue and other stores, and has been a free-lance writer for many years. Her pieces have appeared in *The New Yorker, Ladies Home Journal* and other magazines. For occupational therapy, she gardens on the balcony of her apartment, and paints sub-primitives of the school that might be described as Womb Boom. She also writes song lyrics, not for therapy, but as a recurrent form of moon-madness.

Her first book for Random House was *We Shook the Family Tree.* Others are *Sorry to Be So Cheerful, A Growing Wonder, The Husband Who Ran Away,* and *The Form Divine.* In her newest, *The Great Oildorado,* Miss Dolson locks horns with history for the first time, and gives it a happy shake-up.